The Economics of Belonging

A Radical Plan to Win Back the Left Behind and Achieve Prosperity for All

Martin Sandbu

PRINCETON UNIVERSITY PRESS

PRINCETON AND OXFORD

Requests for permission to reproduce material from this work
should be sent to permissions@press.princeton.edu

Published by Princeton University Press
41 William Street, Princeton, New Jersey 08540
6 Oxford Street, Woodstock, Oxfordshire OX20 1TR

press.princeton.edu

ISBN 978-0-691-20452-9
ISBN (e-book) 978-0-691-20453-6

British Library Cataloging-in-Publication Data is available

Editorial: Sarah Caro and Josh Drake
Production Editorial: Mark Bellis
Jacket Design: Karl Spurzem
Production: Erin Suydam
Publicity: James Schneider and Kate Farquhar-Thomson
Copyeditor: Ashley Moore

The writing of this book was made possible by the generous award of
a Journalist Fellowship from the Friends Provident Foundation

This book has been composed in Adobe Text and Gotham

Printed on acid-free paper. ∞

Printed in the United States of America

10 9 8 7 6 5 4 3 2 1

For Theo

CONTENTS

Acknowledgments   ix

PART I. WHAT WENT WRONG?

1 The End of Belonging   3

2 Who Are the Left Behind?   17

3 Culture versus Economics   37

4 Half a Century of Policy Mistakes   50

5 Scapegoating Globalisation   71

PART II. WHAT IS TO BE DONE?

6 Economics, Jobs, and the Art of Car Maintenance   95

7 Economic Policies for Empowerment   111

8 Macroeconomic Policy for the Left Behind   131

9 A Smarter Financial System   148

10 A Tax Policy for the Left Behind   168

11 Whose GDP?   188

PART III. THE WAY FORWARD

12 Globalisation with a Human Face   211

13 Beyond Left and Right   229

Notes   241

Index   273

ACKNOWLEDGMENTS

Like many others, I have spent the last few years digesting the two political shocks of 2016—the Brexit vote and the Trump victory and what deeper phenomena they may represent—and trying to turn the state of consternation in which they left me into something constructive. In my case, the result is the book you hold in your hand.

There are many tributaries to the river that a finished book aspires to be. For this one, three have been particularly important.

First, I have been fortunate to spend those years at the *Financial Times* (*FT*), an intellectual environment that is at once welcoming and demanding while at the same time securely rooted in long-held liberal values. There is no better vantage point for trying to make sense of our chaotic world. So I extend my thanks first to the former and current editors, Lionel Barber and Roula Khalaf, for giving me the opportunity to formulate my own reactions, interpretations, and proposals for our current economic and political turmoil. My *FT* writing, especially the Free Lunch column and newsletter where my team leader Andrew Jack let me roam freely, has been the nurturing incubator for the arguments that have grown into this book. Those arguments are the better for the many exchanges I have had with *FT* colleagues about these issues, even—especially—when they disagreed with me. I want to mention in particular Sarah O'Connor, David Gardner, Tim Harford, and Martin Wolf, all of whom generously read early chapter drafts, as well as the many other colleagues with whom I have discussed economics and populism, including Chris Giles, Delphine Strauss, Valentina Romei, Gavyn Jackson, Simon Kuper, Ed Luce, and Gideon Rachman.

Second, the writing of this book would not have happened without the generous award of a Journalist Fellowship from the Friends Provident Foundation. The foundation's call for submissions prompted me to organise my vague thoughts of a book into a proper plan, and its support did not end with the grant that allowed me to take time off from the *FT* to write. The foundation also arranged for in-depth feedback from Alison Benjamin and Tony Dolphin on successive chapter drafts, as well as a workshop on the first full manuscript with Alison and Tony, Danielle Walker, and Nicola Putnam. Thanks to all of them and to all the foundation's staff and associates.

Third, Princeton University Press has for a second time been an excellent companion in the painful work of getting a book from conception to finished product. Thanks to my editor, Sarah Caro, for spotting early on the potential for a book in a column and believing in it when many others did not. Her perfect balance of encouragement and pushback has made the book much better. Thanks also to all her colleagues whose professionalism has helped me over the many hurdles in the process.

Beyond those three groups, there are too many others to be able to mention them all. Catherine Fieschi provided a forum where some of my early ideas were consolidated. Mark Blyth, Erik Jones, Anand Menon, Ernesto Semán, Tormod Stangeland, and Giles Wilkes all read drafts. Among the many people who have over the years given me ideas, information, inspiration, knowledge, feedback, or encouragement are Dimitra

Alexopoulou, David Autor, Richard Baldwin, Torsten Bell, Jared Bernstein, Michael Goldfarb, Heather Grabbe, Jason Furman, Arancha Gonzalez, Sandra Kanthal, Joris Luyendijk, Philippe Martin, Branko Milanovic, Karl Ove Moene, Yascha Mounk, Christian Odendahl, Jan Piotrowski, Dani Rodrik, John Springford, Simon Tilford, Kevin O'Rourke, Betsey Stevenson, Arvind Subramanian, Adam Tooze, Karen Helene Ulltveit-Moe, Anne Case, Diane Coyle, Angus Deaton, Swati Dhingra, Ben Friedman, Marcel Fratzscher, David McWilliams, Halvor Mehlum, Adrian Wood, and many, many more. I thank them all and apologise for the many names I have surely left out.

First and last comes family. My wife, Ana, has shown admirable tolerance when my attention has been monopolised by the writing. (The cats less so, but they are encouraging in their own way.) And I dedicate this book to my son, Theo, in the hope that it contributes a little to ensuring that my contemporaries do not rob him and his generation of their birthright to an open and liberal society.

Martin Sandbu
London, February 2020

PART I

What Went Wrong?

1

The End of Belonging

Spring had not yet arrived in Washington, DC, on Saturday, 4 March 1933, but the air was nonetheless filled with a sense of revival and new growth. A huge crowd had turned out to witness the swearing in of Franklin Delano Roosevelt, who had been elected US president in a landslide against the backdrop of a collapsing economy, extreme unemployment, and debilitating deflation. Roosevelt did not disappoint those who looked to him for hope. Declaring his inauguration a "day of national consecration," he announced in words still remembered today that "the only thing we have to fear is fear itself."

Across the Atlantic, the objects of fear were all too real. The very next day, while Roosevelt busied himself in the White House making good on his promise of "action—and action now," Germany held a parliamentary election amid a campaign of violence and intimidation. Just five weeks earlier, Adolf Hitler had been appointed chancellor of a coalition with conservatives. Now he was using all the powers at his disposal, as well as the frenzied atmosphere following an arson attack on the parliament building, to arrest, abduct, and terrorise his political opponents. His Nazi Party swept to victory, dominating the new legislature, which would grant him dictatorial power. That same Sunday in March extinguished the last sliver of hope for Germany, just as hope was being reignited in America.

It is one of history's quirks that two of the West's biggest powers had their fates sealed and their courses set on diametrically opposite trajectories on the very same weekend almost nine decades ago. But what does it mean for us today? There is much talk of learning the lessons of the 1930s, and so we should. The rise of illiberal nationalist movements across the West today carries loud echoes of the interwar years. The poet William Butler Yeats wrote in 1919,

> Things fall apart; the centre cannot hold
> Mere anarchy is loosed upon the world.
> The blood-dimmed tide is loosed, and everywhere
> The ceremony of innocence is drowned;
> The best lack all conviction, while the worst
> Are full of passionate intensity.

Yeats's "The Second Coming" is unsettling because his anguish perfectly captures the unmoored politics of the West today, a century later. Now as then, the political centre has come under siege as a result of both economic breakdown and the experience of violence (in the form of military misadventures, terrorism, or both). Now, as then, the insurgent extremes are "full of passionate intensity." It feels as if the twentieth century has come full circle, and we know that last time the direst warnings were vindicated. But as that fateful March weekend shows, there is another lesson we should remember from the 1930s, which is that we are not powerless in the face of ill portents: we can turn things around for the better. This is a book about how it can be done.

For three generations after the Second World War, a particular ideal of how society should be governed anchored the most successful and prosperous countries on earth and inspired many more to emulate them. For a short, triumphal moment after the fall of communism in 1989, it even looked like a model every nation was eventually destined to adopt, and the world would be a better place for it. It is this social order that is facing its biggest challenge since 1945.

"Liberal democracy" is a common name for it. That is not incorrect, but it is incomplete, for it is an order held up by *three* pillars, of which liberal democracy is only one. This first pillar is a set of political principles centred on individual rights, equality before the law, and competition for political power organised through regular free elections, all scrutinised by free media and enforced by independent institutions. The second pillar is a social market economy where both "social" and "market" matter: a capitalist system, but one where competition is governed by rules in the common interest and whose growing prosperity is broadly shared. The third pillar is openness to the outside world in both political and economic terms—a commitment to gradually lower borders of all kinds between nation-states and their citizens and to realise the benefits of this social order jointly.

A broader term is simply "the Western social order." For this way of life was created by the West, the democratic capitalist countries in which the model was consolidated after 1945, and rooted in the Western Enlightenment. At the same time, the values that underpin it are universal and not confined to the

West at all. While it originated in Europe and North America, the Western model spread far beyond those regions, encompassing, for example, countries like Japan and the "Asian tigers" that followed its path of economic development. And there are important variations within "the West" defined in this broad sense. It is a long stretch from the US system of relative laissez-faire, even in the immediate postwar decades, to the Nordic mixed economies. But they are all recognisably of the same family. With their liberal democracies, regulated market economies, and embrace of globalisation, Scandinavian countries were indisputably on the Western side of the Cold War dividing line with the communist bloc.

As the Cold War showed, the Western social order has always been contested from the outside. While the Soviet Union's demise removed communism as an ideological rival, today China's authoritarian state capitalism consciously presents itself as an alternative to the Western model of social organisation—and not without success, even though China's own spectacular rise owes a lot to the country's having created limited copies of the Western model's second and third pillars.[1] But national leaders who might once have aimed to join the ranks of the rich liberal democracies have understandably had second thoughts about the West as a model after the disaster of the global (but in origin Western) financial crisis of 2008.

A social order can survive without being the uncontested winner on the international stage. Losing the support of one's own people, however, is an existential threat. That is what happened in 2016. Fringe antisystem forces had been on the rise for years, but two political earthquakes that year marked the first time since 1945 that such forces won decisive electoral victories in any major Western country. And not just any country, but the two powers that had done the most to set up the postwar order in the first place. The British referendum to leave the European Union showed a major European nation turning its back on the European project, which had gone further than any other part of the world in realising the West's borderless, rules-based ideal. Then Americans elected Donald Trump as their president—an authoritarian who hides neither his racist-tinged nationalism nor his contempt for democratic principles and the rule of law—and thereby repudiated a world order the United States had shaped and led in its own image. Through these choices, voters at the core of the Western system showed that they no longer feel they belong to it. This end of belonging was a colossal fall from grace for the Western model, and one that has energised illiberal antisystem movements on the extreme fringes of politics in almost every Western country and beyond.

These forces have a straightforward take on two of the Western model's three pillars: they reject political and social liberalism as well as globalisation as ends to be pursued. That is what has led to the comparison with the 1930s and raised fears that democratic and open societies could again descend into fascism at home and close themselves off from the integrated global economy abroad. Admittedly, some supporters of Brexit and Trump style themselves as liberal globalists—they claim to want more or better trade deals than the established elites have achieved. In practice, however, what both groups have used their power for is to increase trade frictions, raise barriers to economic exchange across borders, and challenge the global rules—even the notion that there should be global rules—that make commerce between countries easier.

The attitude to the remaining pillar—the postwar social market economy—is more complicated. Ultimately it is also the most consequential, for, as I will argue, the other two pillars of the Western order will stand or fall depending on whether it can deliver on its economic promise.

The Western-style social market democracy that thrived in the postwar decades was an unwritten but firm social contract. One of its vital elements was economic solidarity: a promise that everyone would share in the fruits of growth. Common to most of those rallying behind illiberal or nationalist forces is their sense that the economy has changed for the worse in general, and for people like them in particular. The reason why the slogans about restoring past greatness—"Make America Great Again" and "Take Back Control"—have such appeal is that the economic and social order of the postwar decades is remembered not as something to be rejected but as something to be restored.

Behind the illiberalism and nationalism, therefore, there is a prior *economic* claim. This claim is that the economic opportunities on which previous generations thrived have dried up, and those that still exist have been closed off and reserved for an elite to which "normal people" don't belong. Those turning against the Western order are those who feel left behind in it, but not just that: they feel left behind *by their own*—betrayed by the elites who constructed the system and were entrusted with making it deliver.

I call this "the end of belonging" because the notion of belonging captures the psychological and sociological, and in the last instance political, fallout from economic change. The sort of economy common to all Western countries in the decades after 1945 was one in which members of virtually every social group could aspire to an attractive place for themselves. Jobs were plentiful and offered increasingly adequate incomes and, just as importantly, status and dignity (which was gradually extended to previously marginalised people). Most people could come of age expecting that a willingness to work and get along would be rewarded with material comfort and security, as well as with social respect. Incomes were growing closer together, both between social classes and between geographic regions, which narrowed differences in how life was lived. The populations of Western countries could justifiably see their national economy—and, by extension, their national society—as one where they all belonged, and belonged together.

In the first part of the book, I tell the story of how this togetherness unraveled because of technological changes and domestic economic policy choices, rather than because of economic openness. While much is made—including by friends of the liberal political order—of "hyperglobalisation" and such "shocks" as the rise of China, I will argue that globalisation is too often used as a scapegoat. But before we get into the *causes* of the economic changes the Western world has undergone in the last four to five decades, we should contemplate their most important *consequence*. This is that the Western social order no longer fulfils its promise of an economy that offers a (good) place for everyone. And just as such an economy used to sustain a psychological, sociological, and political togetherness, so the end of economic belonging has undermined those types of cohesion.

Large numbers of people in the West who could previously expect decent earnings in secure jobs are instead confronted with, at best, precarious employment that pays them too little to provide for themselves, let alone for a family, without serious economic stress. Economic insecurity has made a large group of people dependent on others, risking exploitation and abuse. And it is becoming increasingly clear that this particularly afflicts certain places and regions, destroying the communities that call them home. When, at the same time, the economy provides other groups with more prosperity and richer opportunities than ever before, it is natural for those who are excluded from them to feel aggrieved, and to see the economy and the rules that govern it as rigged for the benefit of others. An economy—and a politics—that benefits some people and places while locking others out of prosperity is what the end of belonging means.

In this sense there is both truth and logic to the populist onslaught on Western institutions and the mainstream parties that built them. The truth is that a large group of people have indeed been economically left out or left behind; as I show in the pages that follow, Western economies have turned into something that many people legitimately feel they no longer belong to. The logic is that the end of *economic* belonging is used to reject the postwar Western order in its entirety. The populist antisystem offer is this: since the system and its elites failed you in upholding the economic part of the bargain, you should now throw them and their whole social contract out— including its social and political liberalism and its openness to the wider world.

That logic is flawed insofar as the proposed solution will not solve the problem. But rather than dismissing it altogether, the argument of this book is that we should turn the logic on its head. Since the Western order is under threat from the erosion of one of its pillars—an economy to which everyone belongs— rebuilding that pillar in a way fit for today's social and techno- logical conditions holds the promise of restoring support for the Western model as a whole. What we need, in short, is a new economics of belonging. That is the right lesson to draw from that March weekend in 1933.

Back then it was far from obvious that the United States would escape the scourge of fascism. Another interwar literary work that feels hauntingly relevant today is Sinclair Lewis's fictional account of a fascist takeover in the United States. *It Can't Happen Here* is a chilling narrative of how the breezy presumption of the novel's title is proved wrong.

And why not? After all, the social and economic conditions were not all that dissimilar on the two sides of the Atlantic. Americans had suffered unemployment and deflation as bad as the Germans had from the start of the Great Depression in 1929. While the US First World War experience was less traumatic than Germany's, millions of Americans had been mobilised to fight in Europe, and hundreds of thousands were killed or wounded. And in the United States, xenophobia also followed conflict, with immigration radically curtailed by the end of the 1920s.

In reality, of course, it didn't "happen here." The United States avoided fascism in the 1930s, and Roosevelt went on to be reelected several times. Why did Lewis's dystopia not come to pass? Roosevelt and his contemporaries had to contend with a situation resembling in many ways that faced by the West's leaders in 2008: a deep financial crisis, a shadow of recent wars or terrorist violence, and electorates stunned by unemployment and shrunken incomes. What distinguished his leadership, however, was a degree of economic radicalism his successors never came close to emulating.

Roosevelt's New Deal was the epitome of crisis turned into opportunity. Within months of taking office in 1933, the new president had taken one previously unthinkable measure after another. He broke the dollar's link with gold to stop deflation in its tracks and stimulate the economy. He shut down the banking system nationwide, then equipped it with government-backed deposit insurance before reopening it. He launched large public works programmes. He radically tightened the regulation of Wall Street and introduced a minimum wage. Social security, trade liberalisation, and housing policy reform followed soon after. Even today, any one of those measures would be radical. To adopt all of them together, in a society with no history or other democratic examples of the government taking a large role in the peacetime economy, was revolutionary.

Today's economic challenges resemble those faced by Roosevelt in scale and sometimes in nature as well. There are, of course, important differences given how much the world has changed since then. The nature of technological disruption is different. The threat of global climate change is unprecedented. Today's decision makers are challenged in their choice of policy options by slowing productivity growth and population ageing in a way that Roosevelt and his contemporaries were not. So the point is not to go back to all the policies that worked for him but rather to take away one crucial insight behind his success and apply it to our times. His were largely *economic* policies, yet they were successful in staving off a *political* threat—the attack on liberal democratic capitalism. Economic radicalism came to the rescue of political moderation in New Deal America. In western Europe, too, there were Roosevelt-like attempts at changing the economic system in the 1930s, and after 1945 fundamental economic reforms in many European countries won democracy a lasting political victory over the extremism that had been defeated militarily. In all cases, the architects of these reforms consciously pursued economic policies as the best weapon against political dangers. And the thrust of the reforms was to include everyone in national prosperity—to create what I call economies of belonging.

The New Deal was exceptional in its hyperactivity. But large-scale efforts to recast economic systems are not a historically uncommon response to crises. At the start of the twentieth century in the United States, endemic financial instability and increasingly concentrated wealth led to a permanent income tax, the creation of a central bank, and the attack of an earlier Roosevelt (Theodore) on the power of the big corporate monopolies known as trusts. The Second World War forged a consensus in all Western countries around some variant of a social democratic mixed economy, with the unquestioned dominance of the state during the war years paving the way for transformations that might have required literal revolutions only decades before.

The contrast with our own times is stark. Western politicians have responded with nothing like Roosevelt's boldness to the two biggest economic disruptions since the war: the peak and subsequent decline of industrial employment starting in the 1970s, and the global financial crisis of 2008. In the next four chapters, I will explain in more detail how these economic tectonic shifts triggered the political earthquakes that have shaken the Western order, and how policy makers have mishandled the response. In the second half of the book, I outline a new economic radicalism—a concrete programme for building an economy of belonging—that can restore the wavering support for the West's open liberal system in our day as it did once before.

The idea that a programme of economic reform can overcome the backlash against the Western order is far from a consensus view. So before starting out, it is worth clarifying how it differs from two other positions that are more commonly heard in this debate.

One concerns the role of globalisation in eroding the economy of belonging in Western countries. It is not just illiberal populists who criticise globalisation; many who swear by rights-based liberal politics consider it threatened by international economic integration. They say globalisation has gone too far. In this book I argue that this is a dangerous mistake.

I will show (in chapter 5) that the lowering of economic borders between countries has not been a major factor in the weakening of domestic social contracts. That weakening started earlier and was worsened by avoidable *domestic* policy mistakes (set out in chapter 4), and, given those mistakes, it would have happened even if globalisation had been less intense. Most importantly, globalisation does not tie the hands of national governments, in whose gift it remains to restore an economy of belonging through better policy choices without pulling back from the international economy. I show how I think this can be done in part 2 of the book (chapters 6–11). If anything, wherever a domestic economics of belonging is pursued with dedication, more economic openness will reinforce that pursuit rather than threaten it (see chapter 12).

The other common position is about the importance of economics itself. Not everyone accepts the primacy of economics in the backlash against the postwar Western order. Some instead take the political pillar as fundamental and attribute the populist surge to irreconcilable splits over identity and values between cosmopolitan liberals and national or nativist communitarians. There is a lot of resistance to the idea that economic change can explain how citizens of mature democracies have come to support xenophobes and authoritarians—and conversely, to the idea that an economics of belonging can restore support for the liberal order.

Resistance to the economic argument does not come only from those who deplore illiberal attitudes. There is a strand of opinion arguing that xenophobia is a perhaps regrettable but entirely natural reaction when elites dismiss ordinary people's preference for their own kind and their dislike of cultural change. For proponents of this view, the solution is to sympathise more with complaints that immigration has been too high, that the cultural changes spearheaded by urban elites have harmed the social fabric of the "common people." We owe it to our countrymen, they argue, to be less accommodating towards foreigners, towards companies trading across borders, and towards global rules—for cultural even more than for economic reasons.

Both arguments lead to the same conclusion. If political divisions boil down to disagreements over culture and identity that are impervious to economic change, the inevitable outcome can only be a culture war in which irreconcilable value differences must simply be fought out until one side wins. The debate over whether culture or economics is the ultimate cause of today's divided politics is clearly crucial to the argument of this book, which is premised on the view that since economic change is the root cause, better economics can improve our politics. So I devote chapter 3 to addressing that debate in detail and refuting the view that cultural and ideological conflict is irreducible. That is *not* to say culture and values are irrelevant; it is obvious that the electoral insurgency against the liberal order and globalisation is expressed in terms of a political culture war as much as if not more than economic interests. But the key question as to what we ought to *do* about it is whether economics can explain that cultural conflict or whether disagreements over values are fundamental. If the former, a new economic radicalism to restore belonging will help. If the latter, such a reform programme is destined to disappoint.

For now, let me just make a simple appeal to intellectual pragmatism to convince sceptics why they should treat economics as both a root cause of antiliberalism and the key to disarming it. Even if voters opposed to the open Western liberal order—the millions of Americans, French, or Germans who support Donald Trump, Marine Le Pen, or the Alternative for

Germany—are motivated by cultural identity or authoritarian and illiberal attitudes, the question remains why identity and attitudes of this sort have become so much more politically powerful in the last decade. Have voters become more nativist and illiberal—and if so, why did this happen? Or is it that such attitudes have always been present to the same extent but their influence on how people vote has increased—and if so, why did *that* happen? Answering these questions convincingly is impossible without the economic story this book tells.

The United States offers a stark illustration. A decisive number of American voters swung from supporting Barack Obama in 2008 and 2012 to voting for Donald Trump in 2016. Those two leaders could not be more different. However strongly identity and values matter, it is hard to see how they explain how anyone could switch their allegiance from one to the other. Yet enough former Obama voters in the key battleground states did precisely this—in particular white, working-class voters—to make it fair to say that it was they who brought Trump over the threshold to the White House.

The economic trajectory of these groups helps us see why they did. So let us begin by understanding that economic trajectory as the first step towards changing their economic future and that of other groups who are being left behind.

2

Who Are the Left Behind?

In the land where oil jobs were once a guaranteed road to security for blue-collar workers, Eustasio Velazquez's career has been upended by technology.

For 10 years, he laid cables for service companies doing seismic testing in the search for the next big gusher. Then, powerful computer hardware and software replaced cables with wireless data collection, and he lost his job.

—*NEW YORK TIMES*, MIDLAND, TEXAS[1]

Education is not something the working-class people of Tilbury have traditionally gone for. You didn't need O-levels to heave sacks of malt and bales of tea in Tilbury Docks, an outpost of the Port of London in the Thames estuary which was, until the 1980s, the biggest employer. The dockers' wives were too busy raising children to have a career. Then came shipping containers and dock mechanisation. By the mid-1980s almost a fifth of the town's men were on the dole, sending Tilbury into a downward spiral from which it has yet to emerge.

—*ECONOMIST*, TILBURY, UK[2]

In 2016, rage boiled over in the West. Support for illiberal, anti-system movements had been building in country after country since the financial crisis, until finally the politics of two countries at the heart of the Western order—the United States and the United Kingdom—were irreversibly ruptured by the victories of Brexit and Donald Trump. But the fuses of that rage had been lit long before, including in places far beyond the Anglo-American economies. Those angry yells to "take our country back" did not come from people who had lost their country overnight.

Their narrative is one of a lengthy usurpation. It says that what was rightfully theirs—well-paid employment, the social status it provided, and the communities structured around it—has been taken away from them. Gone are the plentiful factory jobs that once received able-bodied men straight from school, and which made what Americans call the blue-collar aristocracy. Gone, too, are jobs in mining, trucking, and construction, as well as the dock work and "roughnecking" jobs on oil rigs that once sustained places like Tilbury and Midland.

Who took them away? In some tellings, it was foreign competitors and "the great sucking sound" of offshoring to low-wage countries in Asia or eastern Europe. Alternatively, they were stolen by "others" at home: women, minorities, immigrants, all those who used to be at the margins of the labour market. Or it was the fault of self-serving elites so far removed from real people's lives that they seemed as alien as the foreign forces to whom they had sold the country out.

Whoever is blamed, the idea of usurpation is central to this message, which fringe political figures have been promoting for decades (and indeed regularly throughout the West's modern history). But it took an elephant to make the usurpation story go mainstream.

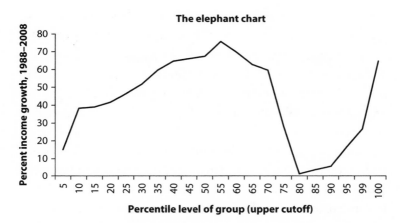

FIGURE 2.1. Income growth, 1988–2008, for each 5 per cent global income group and top 1 per cent.

Source: Christoph Lakner and Branko Milanovic, "Global Income Distribution: From the Fall of the Berlin Wall to the Great Recession," *World Bank Economic Review* 30, no. 2 (July 2016): 203–232, https://elibrary.worldbank.org/doi/abs/10.1093/wber/lhv039.

This elephant first appeared a few years after the global financial crisis, in a statistical graphic developed by economists Christoph Lakner and Branko Milanovic (Figure 2.1). Summarising hundreds of surveys of living standards around the world, the "elephant chart" depicts how each segment of the global income distribution—from the world's very poorest to the global top 1 per cent—has fared over the last few decades. The elephant-shaped curve reflects how unevenly the benefits from global growth were distributed in the two decades after globalisation first began to take off in the mid-1980s, tracing how much each group's income rose, fell, or stagnated.

The back hump and the raised trunk show the large income gains enjoyed by the global middle—the hundreds of millions lifted out of poverty and into the middle class in emerging economies, above all China—and by the world's very richest. The lowered tail reflects sluggish incomes for the poorest. But the politically most explosive part of the graph is the low base of the trunk. It shows that those around the eightieth to ninetieth percentile of the world income distribution—roughly, the bottom half of the old industrialised West—saw the fruits of globalisation pass them by.[3]

Three main facts lay behind this stagnation. One was a steep increase in income inequality in Western countries in the 1980s. This was not reversed in the decades that followed, and in some places it got worse. A second phenomenon (and part of the reason for the first) was that midrange labour incomes fell behind the growth in labour productivity.[4] In other words, the gains from higher productivity disproportionately flowed to the owners of capital or to the very high paid.[5] And third, labour productivity growth itself slowed down sharply. The total amount by which living standards could increase every year, even ignoring any distributional changes, was meagre compared with the postwar decades.

These disappointing developments had been noted for some time, but the elephant chart juxtaposed them starkly with how much better other groups had fared, and with how much the *global* distribution of income had changed in just one generation. This one simple image thrust into the spotlight the latent angst about the distributive effects of globalisation that the political mainstream had preferred to ignore or repress. When the silence was finally broken, the elephant chart went viral. It was covered in the *Financial Times* and the *Economist*. It was used in presentations by leading policy makers and technocrats. The World Bank, the World Trade Organisation, and the International Monetary Fund published an unusual joint report on how to make trade openness work for everyone.[6] One could no longer ignore the intense suspicion that was about to over-whelm Western politics—that globalisation had been good for China and other emerging countries, but not for the average person in the West.

But too often, the frenzied debate about globalisation that erupted has failed to make a crucial distinction. It is one thing to say that during the great globalising era, a large group in the West failed to see much benefit to them, which is what the elephant chart shows. It is quite another thing to say that globalisation was the *cause* of this, and that the gains to poor-country workers and the global super-rich came *at the expense* of the West's lower-middle classes. The usurpation story makes the second, more sweeping claim. On its own, however, the elephant chart only documents the first, narrower claim. But in the age of populism, the two are often run together.

The difference matters enormously when thinking about what we ought to do. It is only if the base of the elephant's trunk is so deep *because* the hump is so high that the former can be lifted up again by pushing the latter back down. That is the tantalising promise held out by antiglobalisation move-ments (including those that do not oppose liberal democracy). But should we really believe that if the West had refrained from letting poor countries benefit from connecting with its markets—that is to say, if the West had globalised less—it could have "reserved" more growth for itself as a result, and that any of the alleged additional growth would have particularly ben-efitted those now left behind? In this and the following chap-ters, I explain that the answer is no. It was not "others" who unraveled the social contract of Western countries; that was the result of technological forces at work everywhere, and of domestic policy mistakes that varied in nature and degree from one country to another.

FIGURE 2.2. US manufacturing employment (seasonally adjusted monthly figures).
Source: US Bureau of Labor Statistics, via https://fred.stlouisfed.org/graph/?g=pP4Y.

The kernel of truth at the heart of these betrayal stories, how-ever, is that factory jobs (and the related jobs I mentioned) have indeed been disappearing in the West. Figure 2.2 has been called the one picture that best explains why US voters are angry.[7] It shows that the number of American factory jobs has been on a decades-long slide from its peak at the end of the 1970s. Similar patterns hold in other established industrial economies. The blue-collar aristocracy fell on hard times long ago.

What is to blame for its demise? The stories of Tilbury and Midland—whose workers have suffered as much as those of the factory towns—show the flaw in the usurpation story. It would be absurd to argue that greater trade brought down a port city whose shipping volumes have continued to grow, or that foreigners stole the jobs that Texan rig workers could otherwise have done. In both cases, if there was a job thief, it was technology.

More precisely, it was the human ingenuity that keeps finding ever-better ways of producing more with less. Sometimes, as in Midland's oil fields, this happens by investing in more machines or other technology to automate or speed up tasks previously done by humans. Sometimes it happens by finding smarter ways of using existing capital and workforces—such as packing shipments into metal containers rather than the previous unstandardised assortment of sacks, crates, and boxes.[8] In either case, the result is to make it possible to produce more with fewer workers. (Note that more investment does not have to mean "more" in financial terms, since technology has become steadily cheaper. Just think of how much less you pay for the computing power in the smartphone in your pocket compared with the cost of the vastly inferior mainframe computers of the 1970s.)

In the factory economy, too, it wasn't foreigners who put blue-collar workers out of business. If globalisation did not kill US industry, who did? The answer is no one, for US industry never died. Look at Figure 2.3, which shows the volume of industrial goods produced in the United States. The fall in employment is not mirrored by any fall in output. Despite what many people think, American factories produce as much physical stuff as they ever have. If the factory employment chart is a one-picture explanation of political anger, we need this second picture to understand why aiming that anger at foreigners is wrong.

Some retort that the figures showing continued industrial volume growth are chimerical because they are driven by hard-to-measure (because of their rapid rate of change) computer electronics. This is not quite true—America's noncomputing

US factory output

FIGURE 2.3. US manufacturing output (seasonally adjusted monthly figures).
Source: Board of Governors of the Federal Reserve System, via https://fred.stlouisfed
.org/series/IPMAN.

durable goods manufacturing has also held steady—but in any case, look more closely at the most complex industrial sectors and it is clear that much of "real" US manufacturing operates at historically high output levels. The United States produces more cars and trucks than ever. Consumer goods output is near boom-time record highs. The same is true for medical equipment, aerospace and aircraft, service industry machinery, and measuring and control instruments.[9] *Some* types of industry—typically the simpler, lower-value-added kind, such as textiles—have seen output fall. But across the board, factory output was on a steady rise for decades after the peak in factory employment, punctuated by dips in recessions and a particularly deep setback in 2008–9. Production has now recovered to precrisis levels or above.

This contrast between rising or constant industrial *output* and disappearing industrial *jobs* is also not a US-only phenomenon.

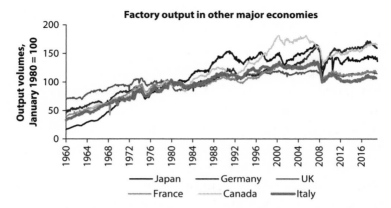

FIGURE 2.4. Manufacturing output volumes; total industry output volumes for Italy (seasonally adjusted monthly figures).
Source: OECD, via https://fred.stlouisfed.org/graph/?g=pP5N.

All rich countries—we used to call them "the industrialised world" because there was so little industry anywhere else— continue to churn out manufactured goods. But like the United States, they need ever-fewer workers to do so. Figure 2.4 shows this pattern for the other members of the G7, the world's seven once-biggest industrial economies. We could look at smaller Western countries, too, and find the same pattern. Everywhere, output grew at least until 2000 and remained largely constant if not still growing until the crisis; it has been recovering since, except where there has been a double recession. Yet everywhere, employment peaked in the 1970s and has been on a long slide ever since.

Nobody stole the factory jobs; it was productivity growth in manufacturing that got rid of them. But this raises two questions. First, what about the radical reshaping of global manufacturing with the rise of China and other emerging economies? I address this at length in chapter 5, where I show that their effect on Western job opportunities is at most a small fraction

of the impact of technology—and that, if anything, less globalisation would have intensified the technological developments. Second, how can productivity have killed jobs when—as
I mentioned at the start of the chapter—productivity growth
has slowed to the point of stagnation across the Western world?
The answer is that greater productivity in manufacturing and
closely related sectors has not been matched by the service sector. So even if fewer hands are needed in factories, the labour
released into the service sector has often not been put to more
efficient use but rather lingered in low-productivity, low-wage
service jobs. To anticipate the argument in the second part of
the book (see especially chapters 6 and 7), an economics of
belonging should pursue productivity growth in manufacturing *and* services, and harness it to create better jobs across the
board.

The productivity story about why the good jobs are gone
goes against the conventional wisdom that allows populist
politicians to play up the usurpation story, stoke the anger that
sustains their support, and direct it at external enemies so as
to legitimate their own authoritarianism. But in one sense it
does not matter whether the usurpation story is true or false;
what matters for political success is that the rhetoric is widely
believed. And it is widely believed for a reason. Even though
the usurpation never took place, it helps to make sense of a
loss that really did.

That loss is the dark side of something very good. After all,
creating more riches with less toil—the definition of greater
labour productivity—is an eternal human dream, a dream that
has spurred innumerable inventions. It is the only thing that can
make us all richer in the long run. In fact, it already has. The rise
in productivity since the Industrial Revolution is why simply
staying fed and clothed—a challenge that has demanded most

of humanity's attention for most of its history—has largely disappeared as an economic problem in the West.

But that achievement came with a lot of trauma. The birth of industrial society in the late eighteenth century meant masses of people were no longer needed to work the land but had to adjust to the factory jobs that now were at the core of economic activity. Since the 1970s, the West has gone through a transformation just as deep as that earlier shift from agriculture to industry, with the source of economic value moving from manufacturing to services.

In the old industrial economy, people built physical things. But we no longer need many workers to fulfil our needs for physical products, just as we no longer need many people to grow enough food to feed us. Instead, the new economy puts people to work most productively by using their knowledge to produce immaterial goods and services, to produce physical goods more efficiently, or to invent new ways of doing things—a software algorithm or a fashion design, an entertainment show or a piece of art, an academic research project or a business analysis, a set of corporate accounts or a transport logistics plan.

But when a society switches to new, more productive ways of doing things, and entirely new activities emerge that require new skills and abilities, the old ways are abandoned. And the danger is that those who thrived on the old ways are abandoned along with them. That is what has happened in the West. Here are four ways how.

1. *The plight of the uneducated.* What does it mean to say we live in a knowledge economy? It means that information, know-how, and cognitive skills are the central source of economic value. That is obviously true for the research and innovation

that makes other activities more productive. But such skills are also vital for managing and coordinating the immense complexity of an advanced economy. A typical car, for example, can have thirty thousand parts; the companies that produce them employ hundreds of thousands of employees in many countries, plus outside suppliers. And because new technology can improve the efficiency of virtually every aspect of production, almost all jobs must adopt it or be left by the wayside.

Increasing technological complexity requires something of us in return. It is cognitively demanding and rewards those with the right skills. Managing a complex society relies on a huge network of professionals who together weave a web of rules, expectations, and communication that makes all the different parts of the economy fit together: accountants, logistical experts, lawyers, and regulators are just some of them. Traditional production industries are also increasingly turning into cognitively complex activities. Factories and mines need workers who can operate robots and steer production processes, not replicate machines on an assembly line or excavate minerals by hand. In the Midland oilfields, "computers now direct drill bits that were once directed manually. The wireless technology taking hold across the oil patch allows a handful of geoscientists and engineers to monitor the drilling and completion of multiple wells at a time—onshore or miles out to sea—and supervise immediate fixes when something goes wrong, all without leaving their desks. It is a world where rigs walk on their own legs and sensors on wells alert headquarters to a leak or loss of pressure, reducing the need for a technician to check."[10]

The flip side of the increasing reward to such skill—as well as to the social skills that help manage knowledge-intensive work and workers—is the diminishing use for manual or routine effort that uses little knowledge or initiative, or for business practices that rely on it. The central economic fact about our societies in the last half century is that the areas where a person's mechanical effort alone can make a useful contribution are shrinking fast. As a result, routine labour is less and less in demand—at least at a wage commensurate with what was once the case. If the world today offers much less than it once did to routine workers with only basic schooling or training, it is because they are less useful to the modern economy.

2. *The triumph of cities.* Until a generation ago, prosperity spread across the land both in the United States and across Western Europe. Poorer areas grew faster than richer ones, so the countryside and small-town periphery were catching up with the big central cities economically. But around 1980 this changed on both sides of the Atlantic. Since then, the richer cities have pulled away from a small-town and rural hinterland where incomes have increasingly fallen behind and economic opportunities have become more limited (I discuss this at greater length in chapter 11).

Deindustrialisation is again a big part of the reason for this. The big shift from manufacturing to services favours some kinds of places over others.[11] The industrial economy is shaped by the scale economies of the factory, which once allowed high-value economic activity to centre on midsize towns. Industrial production that keeps its technological edge still can. But knowledge-based services thrive in the concentration of people and activities found in the big cities, whose bubbling human diversity and greater potential for serendipitous interaction make them the richest cauldrons of ideas. So one result of the postindustrial economic transformation is that the biggest cities draw in people and capital—and, above all, today's most valuable skills and talent—because that is where the leading economic sectors can be at their most productive. As a consequence, the most lucrative economic activities tend to cluster in cities.

Technological developments have also favoured already-thriving places by strengthening the market forces that produce inequality. The new communication and information technologies that have arrived like whirlwinds since the 1980s have created "winner-takes-all" dynamics in many sectors. As it has become easier for top performers to serve bigger markets—in fields from pop music and film to highly specialised services like litigation, financial engineering, and management—the market rewards for being number one rather than second best have ballooned.[12] (Globalisation has added to this—but the technology that drives it would have made it happen within national economies in any case.) In some countries, and particularly clearly in the United States, this has encouraged a growing concentration of profits in the hands of a few firms in the affected sectors (most obviously technology and web services), amplified by policies that make it harder for competitors to challenge dominant firms.[13] In parallel, many countries have seen the share of national income going to capital owners rising while that going to wages and salaries has fallen. All this aggravates inequality between leading and lagging regions. Those who pocket the returns from capital ownership are more likely than an average worker to live far away from where traditional economic activity is located—and so is the in-demand professional. With more inequality, wealth will tend to congregate in the most successful places—the places where the wealthy prefer to live.

This has not just meant a reversal of fortunes for those without good alternatives to the manual jobs local industry used to provide. It has also pushed apart the lives of city dwellers and those who live in towns or the countryside. If two places take different economic trajectories for long enough, cultural polarisation is as important a consequence as inequality. With economic and cultural polarisation comes political polarisation. From the Five Star Movement's success in the Italian Mezzogiorno to the support for Brexit in the parts of Britain with the weakest house prices,[14] the strongest support for antiestablishment movements is found in the regions that have lost out in the competition to attract capital and skill.

3. *The cost of staying put.* With places growing apart, economically and culturally, where to live becomes a more high-stakes choice for each individual. If your birthplace is on the wrong side of economic change, moving away from home is increasingly a ticket to success. Or, perhaps, a lottery ticket—success is far from guaranteed, but you know that unless you take the chance of moving away, you have no chance of striking it rich. The economic transformation of the last four decades favours those who move over those who stay put.

Moving is costly, so this is a change that can put opportunity out of reach for those with the fewest resources. Obstacles to relocating can take many forms. Some of those who might like to move may face external constraints: where the financial crisis caused house prices to collapse, for example, mortgage debt trapped people in their homes. That is one possible reason why the once famously mobile Americans are moving less between states than they used to.[15] Another constraint can be the lack of a social safety net, which can trap some who would otherwise leave in caring obligations.

But it is not just a matter of financial cost. Regional inequality favours those who actually move, but also those capable of moving: the movers but also the mobile. And mobility—the willingness and ability to follow where opportunity beckons rather than stay close to one's roots—requires certain psychological resources even more than it requires money. The types of people who move are different from those who stay. About Tilbury, the *Economist* wrote that unlike immigrant workers, "most residents of the town, one of England's poorest places, are as likely to commute to the capital [forty minutes away by train] as fly to the moon."[16]

Mobility reflects abilities that are really personality traits: quick learning and adaptability; a willingness to take risks, embrace the unknown, and jump on unexpected opportunity; tenacity and even pushiness; and a tolerance for what (and who!) is new, different, and uncomfortable. These traits contrast with traits like steadfastness, fondness for what is near and familiar, and loyalty to one's own. An economy where regions and places grow apart favours those who have few ties to hold them in place or who are willing to strain or break the ties they have; it disfavours those whose ties are stronger or who care more about honouring them.

It does not do, therefore, to say that people just need to move to where the jobs are, so long as they are guaranteed the financial ability to move. The way our economy prizes mobility penalises not just those who lack resources but also certain behaviours, certain life situations, and certain personality types. Being the sort of person who stays closer to their roots, through choice or inability to do otherwise, comes with a greater economic disadvantage than it did forty years ago. Compared with then, the economy today rewards individualism and independence more. It also rewards "openness to experience," one of the "big five" personality traits often used by psychologists and regularly found to be associated with more liberal political attitudes.[17] Conversely, those with a personality less "open to experience" are entitled to feel that the economy is not working for them in the way it once did.

What does this do to the politics of those who stay behind versus those who leave? It echoes the economic core-periphery split we have already mentioned. Here is a telling fact from the 2016 US election.[18] White Americans who still lived in the community where they were raised supported Donald Trump by 57 per cent against only 31 per cent for Hillary Clinton. Even those who lived up to two hours' drive away preferred Trump. Among those who had moved farther away, however, more supported Clinton.

4. Feminism is good for your wallet. The crumbling foundations of the blue-collar aristocracy are the assembly lines, docks, rigs, and trucks where the men traditionally did most of the work. As such, they are the perfect stage for displays of old-fashioned machismo (Trump's photo op with an eighteen-wheel truck on the White House lawn comes to mind). That sits less well with the skills that create value in the new service and knowledge economy. Social intelligence, a talent for caring, and similar soft skills are increasingly in demand, as are the jobs that require them: nursing, social care and childcare, teaching, and the like. In the United States, for example, one in four new jobs in the next decade is expected to come in health care, social assistance, and education, and we should expect similar developments elsewhere.[19] In many places, however, these jobs come with low status and lower pay.

This means that to be fully included in the economy of the future, more men, in particular more unskilled men, must be willing not just to take jobs in services but to work in service jobs traditionally occupied by women (sometimes given the slightly sexist label "pink-collar jobs"), and those jobs themselves must offer decent conditions regardless of who works in them. Of course men can do such jobs. But many resist them. If Trump's "Make America Great Again" means anything, it is a call to bring back the factory- and extraction-based employment of yesteryear and restore the prestige of the male breadwinner to workers who put more stock in a certain idea of manliness than in formal education. But that is not going to happen. (It is worth noting that those railing against the Western order show curiously little concern for a female-dominated industrial sector such as textile production, which has a much stronger case for having suffered from globalisation.)[20]

The inexorable logic of economic change and technology-driven productivity means that soft skills are increasingly rewarded, and traditionally "manly" skills no longer attract much pay in the job market. That may well be a psychological burden on those wedded to traditional gender stereotypes, but attempting to restore the stereotype will not help men thrive in the new economy.

What will help is a cultural transformation to make men increasingly comfortable doing what used to be seen as women's work.[21] That transformation is at least as profound as the one the other way round—letting women in where they were previously excluded—and takes an effort that is political and legal as well as psychological and cultural. For societies to navigate these changes successfully—the Nordics were early pioneers but have challenges of their own[22]—job roles must adapt not in isolation but in parallel with changing cultural expectations of gender roles in the home, and with the evolving politics and law needed to adapt the labour market to these changes. The prize is better-managed economies—and more harmonious societies.

These four effects of economic change all have a sharp end. Being a production worker is not what it used to be—not because factories (or docks, or rigs) disappeared but because technology left such workers behind. Small towns have fallen behind big cities. Those who stay put are at a disadvantage to those with the skills and the temperament to seek opportunities elsewhere. And what were once seen as masculine virtues lose out in the economic competition to those traditionally seen as feminine ones.

Each of these four changes brings winners and losers along different dimensions. But they overlap. One group in particular has been hit along all four: low-skilled white men in small towns, especially those who are tightly rooted in their communities and subscribe to traditional cultural attitudes. It is a quadruple whammy to their economic fortunes—not relative to other groups (men are still paid more than women, whites more than minorities) but compared with the economic status that working-class (white, nonimmigrant) men once enjoyed, and with the communities and the ways of life their earnings once sustained. These consequences, so often blamed on globalisation, are the product of a deep and relentless transformation of how we produce that has been driven by new techniques and ideas.

We need not be sentimental about the disappearance of these jobs. In themselves, the tasks they involved became a waste of human effort once they could be automated; we should not want people to stand in for machines and technology without good reason. But we should recognise that much else of value was lost with the jobs, and the disaffection from these structural changes goes far beyond the financial.

The psychological strains of economic decline among forgotten people in left-behind places can be heard in works of art from Bruce Springsteen's songs to the writing of Edouard Louis. At their worst, those strains are a matter of life and death. Since the turn of the millennium, the United States has been suffering an epidemic of "deaths of despair"—a surge in mortality among low-education whites from drugs, alcohol, and suicide.[23] There are worrying signs that something similar may be happening in the United Kingdom.[24] And stories of the ill health of those stuck in the economy of the past are told everywhere. Louis's book *Who Killed My Father?* blames France's political and economic system for steering young working-class Frenchmen into backbreaking (literally, in his father's case) factory jobs and leaving them inadequately cared for once their bodies can no longer do the work.

Let us not be surprised that, everywhere in the West, it is in these groups that the populist insurgency is the strongest (even if it also exists in well-to-do groups). As we will see in the next chapter, even when antisystem movements and their supporters are motivated by illiberal attitudes or authoritarian ideology, economic change is at the root of their political success.

3

Culture versus Economics

The previous chapters told a story of how economic change paved the way for today's contentious politics of the West. That is why, if we manage to restructure the economy so as to rekindle a broad sense of belonging, we may expect the insurgency against the Western liberal model to recede. But many people disagree that economic failure is the source of our political challenges. So let me offer a fuller argument in defence of my central premise, acknowledging the objections that have been raised against it. These can be grouped into three claims.

The first is that the *timings* of the political changes do not fit the economic story. In particular, this objection highlights the fact that protest movements against liberal politics and the opening of borders to trade and immigration emerged decades before the economic shock from the 2008 global financial crisis. The second claim is that the political and economic characteristics of the *people* involved do not match, because not all those who support nativist, illiberal movements are economically left behind and, conversely, not all those who are left behind vote for such movements. The third counterargument is that even if the economics and the politics do match up, cultural preferences cannot be reduced to a question of simple economic interests: if people vote for illiberalism and against openness, it is because they prefer illiberal and closed societies, regardless of economics.

Of these three claims, the first two are more straightforward to address.

In their book making the case that cultural factors lead to what they call "national populism," the political scientists Matthew Goodwin and Roger Eatwell point out that most of the challengers to the Western order have been around for decades.[1] This, they argue, shows that they cannot be attributed to the fallout from the global financial crisis of 2008.

They are quite right that at least some of these challengers have been around for decades. But even if the 2008 crisis does not explain the emergence of national populism, *earlier* economic upheavals could have caused it. Far from weakening the economic explanation of these movements, a closer look at their history strengthens it.

We tend to forget that the political reaction to the end of the postwar period of broad-based economic progress was immediate and fierce, at least in Europe. In the last chapter, I identified the beginning of the end of the economy of belonging with the secular turn in manufacturing employment in the West in the 1970s. And sure enough, the 1980s was when some of today's strongest illiberal populist movements first came into their own. Parties like France's National Front, the Freedom Party of Austria, and Norway's Progress Party made their first big inroads into the mainstream parties' earlier electoral dominance shortly after industrial employment began to decline. Consider the European Parliament, where the combined seat

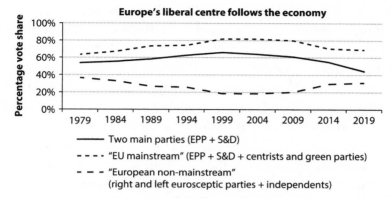

FIGURE 3.1. Vote share in European Parliament elections of mainstream parties (European People's Party, Social Democrats, and other pro-integration parties) and the anti-integrationist nonmainstream.
Source: Nicolas Véron, "European Parliament Election Results: The Long View," Bruegel, 29 May 2019, http://www.bruegel.org/2019/05/european-parliament-election-results-the-long-view.

share of groups opposing European integration was as high in the 1980s as in the 2014–19 period. Then the 1990s and early 2000s, when the economy seemed to be providing better incomes and jobs again, saw the pro-European centre gain support while the anti-European fringes declined (Figure 3.1). They can thank the downturn of 2008 for their return.

The 2019 European election was heralded in the media as a breakthrough for the anti-European Right, but when the votes were counted, mainstream parties collectively held their ground at the same level as in 2014. If anything, the breakthrough had been that previous election, when the economy was still barely recovering from the crisis. Five years of good economic progress later, trust in the European project was increasing again and anti-Europeans' electoral support had stalled—*despite* the upheaval of the 2015–16 refugee crisis.[2] The ups and downs of populist rebellions actually fit Europe's varying economic fortunes well.

While very different, Ross Perot's US presidential run in 1992 and the Republican Party's "Contract with America" in 1994 reflected the same populist convulsion that accompanied the end of industrial society. And in America, too, it went away in the good economic times of the mid- to late 1990s and the 2000s boom. It only returned with the Tea Party movement immediately after the 2008 financial crisis.

It is particularly noteworthy that the timing of the economic change fits not just when these movements appeared but also when they receded. They emerged from the economic fallout of industrial job loss and high inflation in the 1970s. They retreated in the 1990s and 2000s, which were heady economic years in most of the West. Rising employment rates and steadily growing purchasing power almost made it seem as if the good old days were back, and politics responded accordingly. In Europe, mainstream parties regained support throughout the 1990s and the early 2000s. Fringe forces attacking the system either dwindled or polished off their edges, and European leaders doubled down on the liberal rules-based internationalism embodied in the European Union project—launching the single market, creating a common currency, and integrating the postcommunist countries of central Europe (as well as the Nordic countries) into the EU system. The United States, though hammered by the 9/11 terrorist attacks and divided over its wars in Afghanistan and Iraq, nevertheless saw its domestic politics largely return to the centre, with the two main parties again receiving all but a few per cent of the vote between them.

All this goes to show that the global financial crisis and the subsequent resurgence of populist movements fit seamlessly into a sequence of political responses to economic change. Although antiliberal movements predated the crisis, there can be no doubt that it put new wind in their sails. In a fifty-year perspective, therefore, the 2008 crisis experience reinforces the economic explanation of political populism. The illiberal insurgents who first appeared in the wake of the economic troubles of the 1970s and early 1980s were beaten back when Western economies improved in the following decades, then returned with a vengeance in the aftermath of the 2008 crisis, in some countries gaining victories that had eluded them before.[3]

Let us move on to the second objection. Even if the *timing* fits, this argument goes, is it actually those left behind by the economy who are powering the rise of illiberal nativists? If not, then restoring an economy of belonging may be worthwhile in its own right but will do little to tame the antiliberal groundswell.

It might seem that this objection has more going for it than the first. In many cases, the individuals and groups who support nativist antiliberalism are not obviously those we would call economically left behind. In the United States, Donald Trump gained his largest vote shares not among the lowest earners but among lower-middle-class voters and the high-income groups who traditionally vote Republican (who are also more likely to be white than the people with the lowest incomes).[4] In the United Kingdom and the United States alike, opposition to the liberal international order does not correlate all that well with individual income—many Brexit and Trump voters are economically comfortable (such as affluent pensioners for Brexit[5] or Trump-supporting "soccer moms"). The easiest predictor of which way someone voted in these contests is not their income but their education and age: older people and those with less formal schooling were more likely to challenge the established order. In France, Italy, and Germany, education levels are also good predictors: those with less formal education are more likely to support the party of the Le Pen family or Alternative for Germany. Age, however, works the other way around in

France and Italy—the Eurosceptic fringe parties find some of their strongest support among the youngest voters. Given that these countries have a particular problem with youth unemployment, this strengthens the economic explanation.[6]

One of the most influential attempts to refute the economic narrative is that of political scientists Ronald Inglehart and Pippa Norris, who have looked at how well individual cultural and ideological attitudes match political choices.[7] They found, for instance, that people with more authoritarian values and greater scepticism towards immigration are more likely to vote for fringe parties opposed to international openness. That much is unsurprising, but Inglehart and Norris also claim that these personal values explain people's political choices *better* than their economic situation. From findings like those of Inglehart and Norris, it can be a small step for some to conclude that illiberalism is the fault of too much liberalism—a backlash that is perhaps deplorable but one that liberals had coming. If that conclusion were warranted, it would not be an economic reform programme Western societies need, but a course change to less aggressively liberal politics.

Taking aim at the best test case for the economic story, Norris has written: "The standard economic account explains populism as arising when growing inequality and social exclusion mobilize the dispossessed. But populist authoritarian leaders have arisen in several affluent post-industrial 'knowledge' societies, in cradle-to-grave welfare states with some of the best-educated and most secure populations in the world, like Sweden and Denmark—where you'd expect social tolerance and liberal attitudes instead of xenophobic appeals. . . . Why? Here's why. Populist authoritarianism can best be explained as a cultural backlash in Western societies against long-term, ongoing social change."[8] Not an economic backlash, then, but a cultural one, because even Sweden, seen by so many as the paradigmatic Social Democratic welfare state, has seen a rise in the right-wing illiberal fringe. Its Sweden Democrat party has come from nearly nowhere to win 17 per cent of the vote in national elections in little more than a decade. How can the explanation for this be what I have called the end of economic belonging?

Norris is right to take Sweden as a test case, given its image as the most accomplished incarnation of an economy of belonging—so much so that it is known in Swedish as *Folkhämmet*, "the people's home." So let us take a closer look at Sweden, because the country is no longer what it used to be, nor what it remains in the popular imagination of other countries. Here is how a team of five economists working in Sweden describes the country's recent economic changes: "The rapid rise of the Sweden Democrats followed two events that worsened the relative economic standing of large segments of the population. In 2006, a centre-right coalition of parties took power and implemented a far-reaching reform agenda of tax cuts and social-insurance austerity aiming to 'make work pay.' . . . The second key event is the 2008 financial crisis that was followed by a 5-percent drop of GDP in a single year."[9]

Could this provide a different answer to Norris's "Why?"— in other words, might it be economics after all, even in Sweden? The economists grouped data on individuals according to whether they were labour market "insiders" with stable jobs or "outsiders" moving in and out of unstable work. They further classified insiders according to how liable their jobs were to be eliminated by automation. Which group a person belonged to turns out to have made a huge difference to their post-2006 fortunes: "Over a mere six years, these reforms led to large shifts in inequality . . . incomes continued to grow among labour-market 'insiders' with stable employment, while cuts in benefits implied a stagnation of disposable incomes for labour-market 'outsiders' with unstable or no jobs. [The] deep recession drastically increased job insecurity for 'vulnerable' insiders—those with stable employment, but with jobs at higher risk of replacement by automation and other forms of rationalization—relative to 'secure' insiders."[10] And how did this pattern of diverging fortunes play out politically? The researchers' answers are definitive. On what they call the "supply side" of politics—politicians offering a right-wing populist option to voters—Sweden Democrat representatives are much more likely than those from other parties (and the population at large) to be from the groups of people who have lost out to economic change. On the "demand side," local voter support for the Sweden Democrats was strongly correlated with the negative economic impact an electoral district had suffered. The bigger the share of economic losers in an area, or the greater the loss they had suffered, the higher the Sweden Democrats' vote share rose.

This economic and political X-ray of Sweden teaches us a broader lesson about how to establish the facts about our present moment in history. It does show that ideology matters—those who dislike immigration are more likely to support an illiberal party. But as the economic findings prove, we cannot (as studies such as Inglehart and Norris's tend to do) simply correlate individuals' economic circumstances and ideological attitudes with their politics and take the relative strength of the resulting patterns as giving the answer regarding whether the causes of political choice are economic or ideological-cultural. That is far too narrow an approach.

First, because, as the Swedish study shows, the importance of economic factors emerges more clearly when we look at *changes* in behaviour over time. This is true in other countries, too. In the United States, the *swings* in support between the Democratic and Republican candidates in the 2016 presidential election track income *levels* very well. People higher up the income scale have always tended more towards voting Republican than Democrat, but Donald Trump rocked these traditional voting habits to their foundations—and more in his favour the further down the income scale you go. And so, the biggest swing from supporting Barack Obama to supporting Trump was among the lowest-income voters. Higher-income voters, in contrast, shifted markedly from their traditional Republican support towards Hillary Clinton. In other words, the *disruption* of conventional voting habits—and in particular, the electoral shift that got Trump over the line—was clearly driven by the left behind.[11]

Second, the Swedish study illustrates how the economic drivers of political choice are often more visible at the level of *places* than that of individuals. It is overwhelmingly clear that areas in economic decline (whether relative or absolute) saw more support for insurgents—this is true for Trump-voting areas in the United States, Brexit in the United Kingdom, the National Front in Italy, the Five Star Movement in Italy, Alternative for Germany, and the Sweden Democrats. (It is true in eastern Europe, too: Poland's antiliberal and EU-sceptic Law and Justice party, for example, gets more support in lagging towns and the countryside than in the economically leading cities.) In Britain, the economist Thiemo Fetzer has shown that because the dependence on benefits and public services varies from place to place, the government spending cuts that started in 2010 as part of the fiscal austerity programme hit more severely in some places than others. And the deeper that public spending fell in an area, the more voters supported first the UK Independence Party of Nigel Farage, and ultimately the choice to leave the EU. This effect is strong enough for Fetzer to conclude that austerity caused Brexit—without the spending cuts, the number of people voting to leave would have been too low to win the referendum.[12]

Economically vulnerable *communities*, then, have indisputably turned against the postwar system of liberal openness, even if it is not always the most vulnerable individuals within those (or other) communities who have done so. That by itself is a strong argument for the economic explanation—and for the political proposition that if we turn around the economic fortune of struggling places, we can change the politics, too. But to be more convincing, the economic story should ideally be able to explain why the effect of being economically left behind is more visible at the community level than at the individual level. So let me offer some conjectural reasons. One is that voters may well feel a sense of loyalty to a challenged community they identify with, and support what they think would benefit it, even if they have personally been spared economic hardship. This seems particularly plausible for geographic communities; people care about their neighbours. But it could also explain why low education is a good predictor of the antiliberal vote: someone who has achieved material success despite little formal education may resent the shrinking life chances of *others* with similar low levels of education. Another reason could be that the inequalities I have discussed make people feel vulnerable to "slipping" down the social scale in an uncertain future, despite their own currently comfortable but (perceived to be) precarious economic situation. In the United States, for example, the Trump vote was higher in places where the local economy had a high share of the kind of routine jobs experts think are more likely to be automated in the future.[13]

Elsewhere, too, the anxiety of a "squeezed middle" has seemed politically potent.[14] But this clearly economic motivation would be blurred in a study that compared people's current incomes with their political choices.

These reflections suggest an answer to the third objection to the economic story—namely, that illiberal values and antipathy to the Western social model are inherently irreducible and cannot be explained away by economic motivations. Consider Sweden again. Surveys show that Sweden Democrat voters are strongly opposed to immigration, suggesting an irreducible role for values. But the party's vote share is no higher in areas with more immigrants. (The same is true in many countries. The areas with the most immigrants are the big cities, but these tend to be bastions of liberalism. The illiberal backlash is more common in places where immigrants are relatively scarce.) And voters with anti-immigrant values became more supportive of the Sweden Democrats, compared with those with greater tolerance for immigration, only *after* the make-work-pay reforms. The real story of Sweden, then, is that illiberal values and ideology do *not* seem to be a direct, independent determinant of how people vote, but rather something that first begins to affect their political choices when triggered by economic stress.

That interpretation fits with patterns found elsewhere. When economists led by Christian Dustmann and Barry Eichengreen took a deep dive into data on individual values and voter choice in twenty years' worth of European Parliament elections, they found that the frequency of authoritarian and traditional cultural traits in an area amplifies the erosion of trust in politics caused by economic downturns. In places where liberal and modern cultural traits are more common, such trust is more likely to endure through economic swings.[15] Fetzer's research in Britain again found the same: trust in politics was more sensitive to the impact of economic circumstances where people were already predisposed against immigrants.

So the simple cultural story does not hold up. While the fact that people with authoritarian and xenophobic attitudes disproportionately vote for illiberal parties may superficially seem to say that culture, not economics, caused our current politics, digging below the surface shows that the full story is economic after all. To argue that economic hardship and uncertainty lead to greater support for illiberal politics and reduced economic openness is not to say that people simply vote with their wallets. That is the mistake made by centrist politicians who think voters can be discouraged from turning their backs on the Western social order just by being told it will make them poorer. But an integral part of the economic explanation I propose in this book is that economic grievance *expresses itself* as cultural or values-driven behaviour. It intensifies or politicises particular values and attitudes, which may have been more or less close to the surface in different individuals but would not have motivated political choice in the absence of economic pressure. What has really happened in Sweden and elsewhere is that anti-immigrant and illiberal sentiments have been drawn into political service by rising economic insecurity. Even if such attitudes existed, more or less latently, in the past, it is economic change that has turned them into a political force.

This is a contested explanation, but it is the one that makes the best sense of the economic and political developments of the West. Many studies have established that economic decline is associated with intensified illiberal values in the United States, the United Kingdom, and elsewhere.[16] And this is plausible insofar as well-documented psychological mechanisms can explain how economics affect politics the way I have suggested. Being economically left behind creates psychological and physical stress,[17] is associated with ill health,[18] and can even cause direct biological harm (such as increased susceptibility to infection).[19] Psychologists have found that when such external pressures make people feel bereft of personal control, they tend to become more protective of their own group against outsiders and more likely to desire "strongman" leaders.[20] Some explain this as resulting from a need to compensate for missing personal control; collective control by a homogeneous group or a decisive leader with whom one identifies can provide this compensation. As a result, threatening environments can trigger personal attitudes that, in political choice, align with illiberalism or authoritarianism.[21] These mechanisms also explain why the link between economic distress and illiberal voting is more obvious when looking at places than at individuals. Even those who are individually spared economic hardship can perceive themselves as threatened by broader trends. In particular, people seem to take the economic condition of their local community as a proxy for the nation's economic status, and a "perception that the economy is in a downward trajectory can lead to nativist sentiments and hostility towards outsiders," one study has found.[22]

If people project local economic stagnation onto a perception of national decline, we should not be surprised that these groups feel left behind not just by the economy but also by the policy-making elite responsible for the nation's well-being. The next chapter shows that, unfortunately, they are often right.

4

Half a Century of Policy Mistakes

The main driver behind the rise and fall of Western industrial employment acted in many ways like a force of nature. Technological innovation was the economic equivalent of a hundred-year wave, first sucking huge numbers of (mostly) men into factories, then, from the 1970s on, spewing them out again. And like a force of nature, it was and is hard to prevent—more efficient technology will eventually drive out older practices— but it can be tamed. That is what Western countries did in the mid-twentieth century, thanks to the economic radicalism of Franklin D. Roosevelt in the United States and postwar governments across the Western world.

It took the fratricidal bloodletting of two world wars as well as the shock of the huge economic crises of the 1920s and 1930s to overcome class conflict and bring Western societies to a state of national compromise. But the compromise was struck. By the late 1940s, every Western democratic country emerging from the Second World War (and a few that had stayed out of it) had recast their national economic relations according to a new social contract. That contract promised most people (first men, then increasingly women) solid job prospects even without formal qualifications, and growing wages that saw economic differences between classes diminish. It secured the social status not just of poorer individuals but also of poorer places, which could increasingly offer similar living standards to the most affluent cities. Rapid productivity growth brought rising prosperity to all, as Western societies rode the wave of expanding factory employment.

When that wave crested and broke, the unravelling of the social contract was not just a casualty of economic change but also a consequence of how governments and political leaders responded to it. Roosevelt and his peers had put in place reforms and policies that made technological progress work to everyone's benefit. In this chapter I show how their successors too often governed in ways that would worsen, rather than tame, the technological transformations that left parts of the population behind. Conversely, technology need not have doomed the postwar social contract; policy actions and omissions were part of what broke it. Those actions and omissions meant that the people who could previously have relied on factory and related work—and, increasingly, young graduates as well—have seen their opportunities shrink and their status diminish, while many places have been abandoned to a traumatic decline.

A social contract may not be a literal document in which you can check the wording of each clause to make sure it has been fulfilled. But it is nonetheless real. In a healthy society, there is a broadly shared understanding about people's rights and responsibilities, as well as largely shared expectations about who should get what in terms of economic value.

And sometimes, the social contract is as good as written down. In 1950, the United Auto Workers and General Motors agreed to wage terms for a five-year period. What was quickly nicknamed the Treaty of Detroit guaranteed GM workers specified wage increases in real terms—adjusted for the cost of living—designed to reflect the company's productivity growth and effectively locking in for workers their share of that growth.[1] GM's dominance in car production, and the auto sector's dominance of the peacetime economy, meant this set a standard for many other employers, with the helping hand of policy that exempted these contracts from any attempts by the government at wage control.

The Treaty of Detroit is a particularly clear expression of the West's postwar social contract. But other countries achieved similar outcomes based on their own historical experiences and particular institutional practices—though all gave an important role to union representation and collective bargaining. This ensured that in a very real sense, people were "all in this together." Workers could, as a rule, expect wages to grow in line with labour productivity. Since productivity growth was fast-paced, the new settlement rapidly overtook the legacy of the more unequal past, and most Western countries saw their income distributions narrow impressively for three decades after the war (Figure 4.1). High top rates of taxation contributed to making posttax incomes even more egalitarian.

Egalitarianism was only one plank of the new social contract. Another was economic security. While the broad reach of income growth was helped by the nature of the manufacturing economy and the institutions it favoured, the reduction of economic risk for individuals was in large part a political project that had started before the war and expanded after it. Governments adopted policies to remove the economic risk of unemployment, accident, ill health, and old age that individuals and

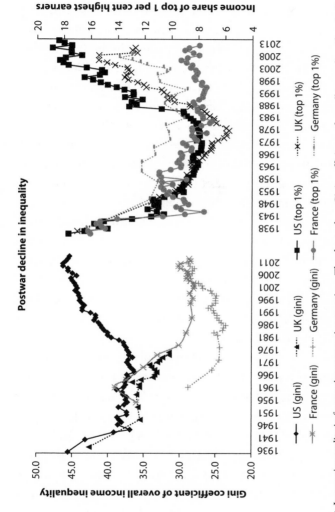

FIGURE 4.1. Income inequality in four major economies over time. The charts show Gini coefficients of overall inequality of equivalised disposable household income (US: gross household income; UK: after-tax income of tax units) and shares of the top 1 per cent of tax units (individuals in France and post-1991 UK) in gross income excluding capital gains.

Source: Anthony Atkinson, Joe Haselli, Salvatore Morelli, and Max Roser, *The Chartbook of Economic Inequality*, 2017, https://www.chartbookof economicinequality.com.

families had previously borne on their own shoulders. Together these constituted the new welfare states. (In the United States, the government stayed out of health care provision for able-bodied adults—partly as a result of the unions' desire to keep it within the purview of collective bargaining—but treated employer-paid health insurance favourably in the tax code.)

Even so, the social insurance function of the West's postwar social contracts originally worked through the mechanisms characteristic of the factory economy. It was the bargain between big industrial employers and unions that set the pace for everyone else to follow; and the welfare state was initially designed around the typical industrial job situation of a sole male breadwinner in constant (and often the same) employment until retirement.[2] But this was an ephemeral basis for such a fundamental pillar of the Western social order. The economy was changing, and what had worked for a generation after the war would need to change with it. Too often it didn't, or it changed in the wrong direction.

The technologically driven erosion of factory employment outlined in chapter 2 reversed the immediate postwar economy's tendency to improve security and equality. The war experience had motivated a fortunate alignment of economic forces, government policies, and enlightened behaviour by social institutions and businesses, which had ensured a postwar economy of belonging. This alignment started coming apart just as the end of industrial society set in in the 1970s. In part by design, in part by neglect, large portions of the West failed to update a social contract that was rapidly becoming obsolete. Some countries did better than others, however. How well or badly different countries navigated that change maps well onto how manageable or challenging a political landscape they face today.

There are three stages in the story of how policy makers have dealt with the economic upheavals of the last half century. The first is how they managed—or more often than not, mismanaged—the shift from an industrial to a knowledge economy. The second is the impact of the global financial crisis, the run-up to it and its aftermath. The third is still under way: it is about the policy response to the digitisation of economic life. If this were baseball, it would be fair to count two strikes against Western policy makers' performance already. That leaves them one pitched ball—the third big economic transformation hurtling towards us—away from being struck out.

Strike one: (mis)managing structural change. In 2015, the economist Robert Solow penned an article asking, "Why aren't wages keeping up?"[3] Solow is a giant in the economics profession whose theories of growth shaped everything that was done in that field in the second half of the twentieth century. He was also uniquely placed to give the question the full historical sweep it deserved: he published his article when he was just shy of his ninety-first birthday.

"The purpose of the Treaty of Detroit," Solow wrote, "was to freeze [the] allocation" of economic surplus (or "rent") between capital and labour.

> What happens to it now is not so much a matter of economic law. It depends on bargaining power, business attitudes and practices, social norms and public opinion. The suggestion I want to make is that . . . the share of wages in national value added may have fallen because the social bargaining power of labor has diminished. This is not to say that international competition and the biased nature of new technology have no role to play, only that they are not the whole story. Internal

> social change and the division of rent matter too. [So does the] shift toward more casual labor. . . . Casual workers have little or no effective claim to the rent component of any firm's value added. They have little identification with the firm, and they have correspondingly little bargaining power.

The shift from industry to services unleashed the strong forces of divergence described in chapter 2, but that was not all it did. As Solow argues, it also undermined the collective bargaining that had helped contain such forces in the past, because in many countries that bargaining was disproportionately carried out within the manufacturing sector. The shrinking need for workers in factories both tilted the balance of power in employers' favour and eroded the industrial sector's ability to set conditions for labour markets in the economy as a whole.

The test of policy makers in the last three decades of the twentieth century was to manage this shock to the industrial structure and its repercussions on labour markets, economic geography, and income and wealth distributions. There is no shortage of policies they could have used to counteract or remedy at least some of the costs borne by those who lost out from these transformations—or, even better, policies that might have prevented people from becoming losers in the first place. The next part of this book examines many of these options. But by and large, Western policy makers did not take advantage of them. Indeed, some of the policies they did adopt made things even worse.

Take inequality. Even as market incomes became more unequal, and in some countries increasingly favoured capital owners rather than wage earners, tax policy everywhere was changed in ways that weakened its redistributive impact. Top income tax rates were slashed in the 1980s, making the taxation of personal incomes less progressive.[4] The tax burden on capital was lightened compared with that on labour income, with corporation taxes much lower today than in the 1970s. Indirect taxes such as value-added tax (VAT)—which typically takes a greater proportion of the income of the poor than of the rich, who save more—have in many countries increased as a share of total taxes. And while the amount of wealth in Western societies has grown much faster than incomes, governments get no more of their revenues from taxes on wealth holdings than before. Where and from whom tax is levied has failed to keep up with the changing market distribution of wealth, let alone been used as a countervailing force.

Next, consider government support for the role of collective bargaining to shape the wage structure and the wage-profit split. In some countries this has been preserved, notably in Scandinavia, where collective bargaining supports a collaborative relationship between employers and employees that has contributed to easing the adjustment to technological change. Elsewhere, however, collective bargaining has been eroded by governments sometimes deliberately acting to weaken unions. The iconic case comes from the first year of Ronald Reagan's presidency, when he refused to accommodate demands by the air traffic controllers. In the standoff that followed, the union (which had endorsed Reagan as president) was crushed as the government managed to keep planes flying until striking controllers threw in the towel. The wider consequence was to immediately weaken the hand of unions across the board, as their most powerful weapon—striking—had been blunted.[5] Over time, legislation has further disempowered organised labour. A similar story can be told in the United Kingdom, where the emblematic case was Margaret Thatcher's battle with the mining unions. And these are just the most striking examples. The majority of European countries have seen declines in union membership and the coverage of collective bargaining. The consequences are clear: the increase in inequality across countries in the 1980s is tightly linked to how much unionisation declined—the steeper the fall of organised labour, the greater the increase in inequality.[6]

The third area in which economic belonging has been undermined since the 1970s is economic security. Policy has generally failed to counteract the growing economic precariousness of ordinary people's lives, even where inequality has increased only moderately (nowhere has it failed to rise at all). This is most striking in labour markets. It is paradoxical that the most liberalised labour markets in the West (typically the English-speaking countries) and the most heavily regulated ones (the "Latin" countries: France and southern Europe) have both seen the emergence of a "precariat"—an underclass of workers trapped in erratic, unpredictable, and impoverishing conditions.

In "flexible" labour markets, this is because they permit workers to be hired with little job security and no guarantee of minimum hours worked (or paid for), sometimes known as zero-hours contracts. In conjunction with the disappearance of union-regulated factory jobs, this has naturally made insecure work more prevalent. The level of insecurity can be measured by how much incomes typically fluctuate. The United States has seen two big jumps in the volatility of earnings, first from the 1970s to the 1980s—corresponding to the onset of manufacturing employment's decline—and then during the 2008–9 Great Recession. In the United Kingdom today, large monthly pay fluctuations are shockingly common: three-quarters of people in regular jobs see their monthly pay fall by more than 5 per cent at least once a year. The average decrease in a month where pay falls is 290 pounds—more than the average UK household's monthly grocery bill. Despite the widespread nature of erratic pay, social safety nets are still constructed around an idea of

stable employment with stable wages. The perverse consequence can be that means-tested benefits are linked to work
and wages in ways that make incomes even more unpredictable
for those who need the support most (see chapter 7).[7]

It may be more surprising that the most regulated labour
markets—in France and the south of Europe—have produced
precarious livelihoods as well. But the explanation is straightforward. Very strong job security and worker protection
imposed on permanent employment contracts have actually
made some work more insecure by discouraging employers
from hiring people on permanent terms. To circumvent constraints on flexibility, employers have increasingly preferred to
create temporary positions. This has created a deep division
between "insiders"—who benefit from job protection—and
a large minority of "outsiders" who can only get short-term
contracts or no work at all (these countries have higher unemployment rates than those with flexible labour markets even
in good economic times). In France, for example, more than
80 per cent of workers have typically been covered by permanent contracts. But in 2015, only 16 per cent of new hires
were. (Since then, labour market reforms have made a big
difference—I return to this later in the book.) In Spain, Italy,
and Portugal, almost all new jobs in the post–financial crisis
recovery have been on short-term contracts—sometimes as
short as one week.[8] In 2014, one-quarter of all Spanish workers were in temporary work, and seven out of ten young workers. Such "nonstandard" working conditions are a vehicle for
deprivation: 22 per cent of OECD households that have only
nonstandard work are in poverty, against only 3 per cent of
those who enjoy stable work conditions.[9]

A particular mention goes to Germany, which managed the
feat of moving from one bad system to the other. Its labour

market reforms in the early 2000s were intended to remove rigid rules and reform benefits that were thought to keep people out of work. The reforms were successful insofar as they increased both growth rates and employment. But average wages did not move—and actually fell for the lower paid. Temporary work, meanwhile, became more frequent, as did so-called mini-jobs, or very part-time positions. As a result, the bottom 40 per cent make the same as or less than twenty-five years ago (after adjusting for inflation), and the number of working poor has doubled.[10] Unionisation, too, has fallen significantly, which seems to be behind the long wage stagnation.[11] If Germany was the model for some of the southern European countries that reformed their labour markets under pressure from the debt crisis a decade later, it is not a big surprise if they achieve similar results.[12]

Despite often being seen as an example of an inclusive economy both in Germany itself and by others, the German economy now creates income inequality to equal that of the United Kingdom and the United States before taxes and redistribution—to the point where the German economist Marcel Fratzscher has said the old Germany social market economy that was built on the ruins of the Second World War no longer exists.[13] Indeed Germany, too, has produced groups of left behind—those channelled into the precarious rungs of the labour market after the early-2000s reforms, as well as large parts of the former East Germany. While huge efforts have been made to bring them up to Western levels of prosperity, they still lag behind thirty years after reunification and are fertile electoral ground for populists and extremists.

In all the countries mentioned here, the outsiders forced to accept precarious terms are either traditional marginal participants in the labour market—the young, immigrants, minorities, often women—or those whose jobs disappeared in the structural transformation from manufacturing to knowledge-centred economies. That group includes many of the French *gilets jaunes*, whose protests have posed the greatest political headache for President Emmanuel Macron's programme. The irony is that that programme constitutes the most determined effort France has seen to end the labour market's marginalisation of outsiders, following similar attempts in southern Europe in recent years.

So long as Western economies offered an ample supply of industrial jobs, which could easily absorb workers with little higher education and give them collective influence through unions, both the "Anglo-Saxon" and the "continental" labour market systems were compatible with an economy of belonging. When that changed, however, it turned out that despite their seemingly huge differences, both served to marginalise such workers and other vulnerable groups.

The result was to return the burden of risk increasingly to the shoulders of individuals, and particularly those groups and individuals least capable of bearing it. The changing nature of work was one of the key drivers, but not the only one. Many policy changes had the same effect of making individuals bear more risk by themselves—for example, the shift from defined-benefit pensions (which employers or the state have to secure) to defined-contribution pensions (where individual workers shoulder the market risk of their savings for retirement). And as I have already mentioned, benefit systems that reduce risk in a setting of stable and predictable work can increase it when work itself becomes unstable and erratic. Fluctuating labour incomes can fall foul of rigid means-testing thresholds, for example, and tax credits may amplify the instability of the labour income from the low-wage jobs that tend to be the only target of schemes to "make work pay" (see chapter 7).

All this is a far cry from the collective insurance mechanisms that the West's postwar social democracies amounted to. Greater individual insecurity was made doubly painful by the backdrop of rising inequality and elusive prosperity. This "great risk shift" (as political scientist Jacob Hacker has called it),[14] combined with an altered balance of power in labour markets and tax systems that have failed to offset the changing distribution of market incomes, all helped to weaken the postwar economy of belonging just as it came under intensifying pressure from technological change. How much it weakened differed from country to country. In particular, the European social market economies did a better job of bringing along those at the bottom than the United States (Figure 4.2)—but both individual and regional inequality grew significantly in Europe as well.[15] We should not be surprised, therefore, by growing polarisation and alienation in Western societies, nor at their political consequences.

Strike two: A great recession made at home. If Western governments' policy mistakes had been confined to mismanaging deindustrialisation, populist forces may have remained quiescent after their initial, largely unsuccessful emergence in the 1980s. But the global financial crisis in 2008 and the Great Recession that followed it added to the ranks of the economically disaffected and stoked their support. In many countries, a critical mass of citizens now turned their backs on mainstream Western politics in support of the insurgent antisystem parties—the same that had first emerged in the 1980s in some places, and similar but new ones in others. Given the depth of the economic damage the 2008 crisis caused, this is not surprising. In little more than a year, the economic outlook across the West went from rosy to abysmal. By late 2008, the US economy

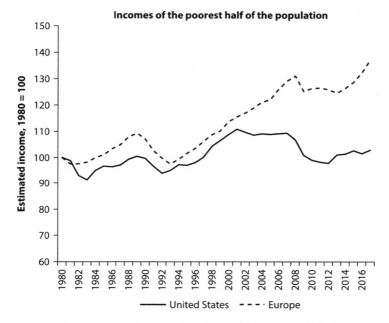

FIGURE 4.2. Evolution of average income of the bottom 50 per cent of the income distribution, 1980–2017. "Europe" covers 38 European countries, including all European Union member states.
Source: Thomas Blanchet, Lucas Chancel, and Amory Gethin, "How Unequal Is Europe? Evidence from Distributional National Accounts, 1980–2017," WID.world Working Paper 2019/06, April 2019, https://wid.world/europe2019.

was shedding jobs by more than half a million *every month*. All around the rich world, nations fell into the deepest economic slump in generations. For the first time since 1982, the entire world economy shrank.

Like the response to deindustrialisation, bad economic policies made matters worse. The immediate response to the crisis by finance ministers and central bankers from autumn 2008 to spring 2009 was admittedly praiseworthy; they acted in concert to arrest the global collapse in demand by expanding government budgets and pumping money through the economy's financial arteries in the form of quantitative easing (large-scale purchases of financial securities). This stopped the downturn from becoming a repeat of the 1930s Great Depression. But outside the most acute crisis management period—both before and after—policy making was riddled with mistakes.

During the boom, all had not been well, and it was in two of the West's biggest economic engines that trouble first appeared. In both cases, it related to a mismanaged financial system. In the United States, employment rates had started slipping from 2001, even in the middle of a full-throttle housing and construction boom. Germany, in contrast, missed out on the consumer boom entirely: while growth was reasonably strong, wages stagnated and growing numbers of people ended up in low-pay, precarious work. In the former case, a financial bubble sustained the semblance of solid growth despite worsening job prospects. In the latter, the deteriorating quality of jobs repressed wages and consumption, increased income inequality, and boosted profits. That increased the German savings rate (owners of capital save more than wage earners—especially low-wage earners). Without a matching increase in national spending, German banks channelled much of these excess savings to investments in Greece, Ireland, and elsewhere in the eurozone periphery, thereby fuelling financial bubbles elsewhere.

It is likely that falling productivity growth worldwide was also linked to the mushrooming credit markets. The alarm over this has been sounded from an unexpected direction. Over the last decade or so, the Bank for International Settlements, the International Monetary Fund, and the OECD— traditionally seen as the commanding heights of economic policy orthodoxy—and leading financial economists have all been producing research documenting that beyond a certain point, a larger financial sector (in particular banking) and more credit in the economy reduce growth, weaken productivity, and increase inequality.[16]

The reason is that while expanding financial intermediation can make the economy more efficient by providing finance for investment projects, continued expansion ends up drawing resources away from where they are best deployed. Rather than providing capital to people with good ideas and the businesses with the greatest potential for growth, an overgrown financial sector directs funding to activities such as construction, which are nicely suited to the banks' model of secured lending but offer low productivity growth. It also pulls resources into the financial sector itself: just before the 2000s boom turned to bust, almost half of new Harvard graduates took up jobs in finance.[17]

The upshot is that, for a whole decade before the crisis, with governmental blessing, ballooning credit and finance exacerbated the problems that had resulted from technological innovation and industrial decline. Much of the West gorged itself on finance as a result of unwise policy choices. A key part of the liberalising reforms in many countries from the 1980s onwards was a deep deregulation of financial services. In just one year, 1999, the United States made two terrible policy choices: exempting derivatives from regulation and removing the 1930s-era restriction on mixing investment banking with deposit taking. Meanwhile in Europe, greater cross-border economic integration in the form of the European Union's single market included finance, which could now expand more freely both within and across countries, with the removal of barriers to financial flows culminating in the creation of the euro. But financial integration was not matched by common regulation of finance. On both sides of the Atlantic, politicians seemed enthralled by the "masters of the universe" who ran ballooning investment banks. In particular, there was no attempt to discourage the most harmful forms of finance and encourage the safer forms. Between 1999 and 2008, the balance sheets of banks exploded—from €14 trillion to more than €30 trillion in the eurozone, from £2 trillion to £7 trillion in the United Kingdom, and from $5 trillion to $11 trillion in the United States.[18]

Raghuram Rajan, formerly the chief economist at the International Monetary Fund, was one of very few to warn against the financial excesses of the 2000s. In 2006, he used a speech at the annual Jackson Hole conference for the world's top central bankers to warn against the risk of financial instability, striking a sour note in what was otherwise a celebration of the supposedly masterful tenure of Alan Greenspan as Federal Reserve chair. Like Cassandra, he was both prescient and scorned; Lawrence Summers, the Harvard economist and former US Treasury secretary on whose watch the 1999 deregulatory measures were adopted, called his warning "Luddite," the term for someone opposed to progress and clinging to inefficient traditions. Summers may have expressed it most acerbically, but many shared his dismissive attitude to Rajan's warnings. This episode illustrates why the world's central bankers and regulators failed to prevent the crisis: not because there was nothing they could do, but because they did not see it coming.[19]

In this respect, the global financial crisis was a worse indictment of Western policy makers than the botched response to deindustrialisation, and the second strike less forgivable than the first. The sectoral transformation of the employment structure was the inevitable consequence of deep technological changes beyond anyone's control, and the only question was how it could be managed, not how to avoid it. The global financial crisis, however, was a direct and avoidable result of reckless policy choices. Even worse, according to Rajan, this second mistake compounded the first.[20] The growth of finance served political leaders as a sticking plaster that reduced pressure to address the challenge of structural economic change. As long as credit growth could sustain higher consumption, voters would be less worried about the loss of factory jobs, slowing productivity growth, and stagnating incomes for many individuals. But removing the symptoms of economic malaise without addressing their cause only served to store up worse problems for later.

In 2008 the day of reckoning came. Once the immediate fallout had been contained, policy makers returned to making unforced mistakes. In Europe, the excess of accumulated public and private debt was not restructured but left as a drag on growth and a risk to financial stability. There and in the United States, government spending was dialed back quickly after the initial fiscal stimulus, giving fiscal policy a contractionary rather than an expansionary effect on demand growth even though the economy was still weak. And while central banks cut interest rates and intervened in the securities market more than they had ever done before, they stopped loosening monetary policy before they had secured a strong recovery. The European Central Bank even began tightening monetary policy in 2011, helping to trigger a second recession.

The most obvious consequence of all these mistakes is that living standards in the West have suffered enormously— in most countries, incomes today are between 10 and 20 per cent below what they would have been if the precrisis trend had continued uninterrupted. Western economies have taken longer to recover from the global financial crisis than they did from the 1930s Great Depression. Tens of millions of workers lost their jobs; many also lost their savings. It took a decade to return the same proportion of people to work as had been working at the employment peak before the crisis. And British people have experienced their worst squeeze on real wages since the Napoleonic Wars.[21] Above all, those too young to have established themselves with careers and homes before the crisis have been left with much worse prospects than older generations faced at the same age (see chapter 8). Low economic growth and damaged public finances after the crisis have led governments to cut spending in ways that have often caused the most pain to those who were already the worst off. This has added people who may have been faring reasonably well until 2008 to the ranks of those bearing the cost of decades of deindustrialisation.

In a sentence: incontinent policy before the crisis brought a financial collapse, and timid policy afterwards amplified the suffering it caused.

Strike three: the task ahead. In the baseball metaphor, the first strike for many Western governments was their poor handling of deindustrialisation; and for most, the second strike was the run-up to and the aftermath of the global financial crisis. A third economic challenge is now under way, as technology has begun to deliver another shock like the one that afflicted manufacturing.

One predictable effect of the digital revolution is a new cull of jobs. Machine-driven productivity growth put paid to most physical production jobs that existed in 1970 (and as the next chapter shows, would have done so even in the absence of globalisation). Automation and digitisation are now doing the same to a swath of service jobs—including some done largely by the sort of people who would formerly have taken manual factory jobs. Autonomous vehicles are an important example. Truck driving is, by some measures, the most common single profession in the United States, and one of the few providing decently paid jobs to men with little formal education. When the self-driving truck becomes technically and commercially viable, it will make most of them obsolete.

But those "male manual" jobs are far from being the only types of work under threat. Many lower-skilled jobs typically carried out by women—in particular in retail—are also likely to be lost as online shopping keeps growing. The emergence of self-service outlets shows that even in brick-and-mortar shops, automation eliminates the need for human workers. Finally, an expanding range of tasks that require cognitive but identical repetitive efforts will be taken over by computer algorithms as these get better. Many jobs in financial and legal analysis, even medical diagnosis, are soon going the way of travel agents' and stenographers' jobs, which have been usurped by travel booking websites and digital transcription software.[22]

The other consequence of industrial automation was its effect on labour relations, and a weakening of unions' and workers' bargaining power as factory jobs disappeared.[23] This is a feature of the new services automation, too. One of the most dramatic consequences of the internet has been the creation of platforms that allow work to be organised in a fundamentally more fragmented way. We all know Uber, eBay, and Airbnb, which connect buyers and providers of transport, goods, and lodging in one-off, fragmented interactions, thereby eliminating the need for businesses such as taxi firms, shops, and hotels. The actual taxis, goods delivery, and rooms still have to be where the customers physically find themselves. But the "gig economy" facilitated by online platforms also brings with it a global market for service jobs—or, rather, for piece-rate service tasks—in anything that can be done digitally and remotely. Coding, translation, copyediting, and other high-skilled and middle-class jobs are opening up to global competition even as computerised pattern recognition and artificial intelligence mean fewer people are required to accomplish the same amount of work. Automation and globalisation are both expanding from blue-collar to white-collar work, which is set to be disrupted as much as if not more than manufacturing was from the late 1970s on.[24]

Job loss through automation-driven productivity growth and, to some extent, competition from globalisation—these are the very same forces that, in the absence of an adequate policy response, denied a large group of workers what they expected from the social contract. That means economic belonging is likely to take another hit. Unless governments adopt policies that handle this disruption better, it will potentially affect even greater numbers of people than deindustrialisation. And to the extent that researchers can predict it, it is the places most left behind by the previous wave of automation that are most exposed to the next one. That is because lower-skilled routine jobs—for example in retail, warehousing, and customer service such as call centres—are both more threatened by technological innovation and disproportionately found in places that previously lost industry or mining jobs, places like the north of England or the US states of Indiana and Ohio. In contrast, the places with a high proportion of knowledge economy jobs—think Oxford or New York—are not just doing better already but are also more secure because such jobs tend to be harder to automate.[25]

In baseball, it's three strikes and you're out. Unless governments do a better job of rising to this third challenge than they did to the previous two, it is the Western liberal order that is likely to strike out.

5

Scapegoating Globalisation

In 1997 a soft-spoken Harvard economics professor named Dani Rodrik published a short book called *Has Globalization Gone Too Far?*[1] In it, he pointed out some ways in which freer international trade and financial flows could, in theory, leave workers worse off, using conventional models and arguments from mainstream economics. Rodrik inadvertently became a cult hero for an emerging antiglobalisation movement that was then largely made up of young leftists protesting against the global elite when it gathered at summits in Seattle, Quebec, and Genoa. It was different among professional economists. Rodrik recounts that while they could not fault the economic arguments of his book, they accused him privately of "providing ammunition to the barbarians"—the politicians, then still on the fringes, opposed to breaking down barriers between countries.[2]

The problem with silencing analysis that might give ammunition to the "barbarians," however, is that it leaves you unprepared should the barbarians go on the offensive. The political centre would be stronger today had it listened to warnings from people like Rodrik earlier. Instead, populists have for too long been the only ones to articulate the economic harms perceived by large groups of people, who have understandably chosen to believe them rather than the established policy makers who ignored them and their concerns. When Donald Trump talks about "forgotten people" or Marine Le Pen about "la France des oubliés," they have a point.

But remembering the forgotten does not mean accepting the populists' analysis of what happened to them. *Pace* Rodrik, the problems of the left behind are not caused by globalisation going too far, but by the technological changes and policy mistakes outlined in the preceding chapters. The suspicion that globalisation is to blame, however, is hard to resist. In forty years, the global economy has changed beyond recognition. The two decades before the global financial crisis in particular were a heyday of global economic integration. Global exports grew roughly twice as fast as global economic output, spurred on by a series of deals to lower trade barriers. Financial flows between countries grew much faster still. And many countries experienced the most rapid increases in immigration since the Second World War.

Some of this was the result of improved technology: the falling costs of transport, travel, and communication across borders. It was also a product of policy choices to lower economic barriers between countries. In 1993, Europe's single market was launched. The following year, the North American Free Trade Agreement came into force. In 1995, the World Trade Organisation was created, and with it the first permanent institution with powers to police global trade rules. Six years later, China joined the World Trade Organisation, setting off a stunning decade of economic growth powered by a tsunami of Chinese manufacturing exports throughout the world. In parallel to trade liberalisation, previous limitations on moving money and people between countries fell away. The most extreme instances of this were the twin European policies of a single currency and of free movement of people between European Union member states.

It would be astonishing if this rapid economic integration had not had a big impact on our lives. It has certainly created losers as well as winners. But a close look at all three forms of globalisation—trade, immigration, and finance—shows that it is an illusion to think that the era of belonging in Western economies could have been preserved by preventing global economic integration, or that it can now be restored by unravelling the economic threads with which the world has been woven together. For the most part, all three dimensions of globalisation just listed serve as scapegoats instead, distracting from the real priorities governments ought to address.

Scapegoat number one: trade. Start with trade, by far the most discussed aspect of globalisation. The story that emerging countries "stole" the West's manufacturing employment depicts a zero-sum world where well-paying factory jobs lost in one country are captured by another. The rise of this narrative of conflict should have been foreseen. The distributional effects of freer trade—in particular, that low-skilled labour loses out when a relatively rich country lowers its trade barriers with poorer ones—are among the most basic predictions of "classical" trade theory. The logic is clear, so why did it take so many by surprise?

Perhaps because, until recently, it was entirely natural to associate freer trade with *greater* fairness, prosperity, and political harmony. That was the key lesson of the breakdown of the global economy in the 1930s, which was followed by the catastrophe of the Second World War. And the trade liberalisation that started immediately afterwards (the volume of US exports roughly doubled each decade after the war) at first brought greater social cohesion and shared prosperity. Openness *was* visibly working for everyone.

This was partly because this openness was not at first of the "classical" type, where countries exported different products according to their "comparative advantage"—rich countries exporting goods made with capital or skilled labour, poor ones those depending on low-paid, unskilled labour and land use. Instead, the first phase of postwar trade globalisation involved trade in similar products between similar countries: for example, French workers building cars sold to German customers, and vice versa. It was not until the 1980s that economists developed a new theory that explained such trade by economies of scale and the value of product variety rather than differences in resources—and showed that when similar countries trade with one another for these reasons, it does not have the distributional implications of "classical" trade between dissimilar countries. These new theories reflected the postwar experience that greater economic openness was bringing prosperity for all.

But the antiglobalisers beginning to emerge at the same time were quick to jump on one fact. Just as economists had developed a new theory to explain the changed patterns of global trade, those patterns were changing again. Until the mid-1980s, virtually all trade took the form of sellers in one country shipping raw materials or finished goods to buyers in other countries. But now it was becoming common for the exporter and the importer to be identical, since companies own production sites in many countries and ship unfinished goods across borders for different stages of the production process. Such "cross-border supply chains" hardly existed in the 1980s. Today they account for more than half of all international trade and are the reason why giant multinational companies have become such big players in the global economy. They have also allowed a shifting of the stages of the manufacturing process that require lower-than-average skill in rich countries but higher-than-average skill in poorer countries, raising the skill levels demanded in both.

Trade globalisation has clearly been a boon for many poor countries, which have obtained an extraordinary lift in living standards, and seen hundreds of millions of people pulled out of poverty, from joining cross-border manufacturing supply chains. So the high-humped back of the elephant chart, at least, owes a lot to trade globalisation. China alone went from supplying virtually zero to producing one-sixth of the world's merchandise exports in four decades. Emerging economies as a whole had about ninety million more manufacturing jobs in 2014 than they had in 1985.[3] Suddenly, the rich country/poor country pattern of global trade was back, and poor countries made good use of their large supply of low-wage labour to expand manufacturing jobs.

This does not, however, mean that the West *lost* ninety million manufacturing jobs that it could have retained had they not gone to China or other emerging industrial producers. If there really were a fixed number of such jobs to go around, it might seem reasonable to hold on to them by any means necessary. Such "factory fetishism"—a sort of economic machismo that sees manufacturing dominance as the best measure of productive virility—is at the heart of Donald Trump's "America First" doctrine.[4] But it is a flawed view of the economy: if industrial employment is bound to shrink because of more productive

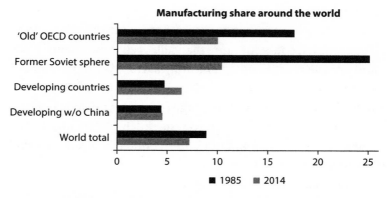

FIGURE 5.1. Factory employment as a share of total employment, by global region. *Source:* Adrian Wood, "Variation in Structural Change around the World, 1985–2015: Patterns, Causes and Implications," WIDER Working Paper 2017/34, Helsinki: UNU-WIDER, 2017.

technology, increasing one's manufacturing dependence just stores up bigger problems for the future. Figure 5.1 shows that manufacturing jobs' share in total *global* employment fell from about 9 to about 7 per cent in the three decades after 1985 (even though the absolute number of factory jobs worldwide actually rose from about 175 million to 220 million—reflecting that the global population was growing fast). The secular fall in manufacturing employment we have seen in the West is also a global phenomenon.[5]

Fighting over a shrinking pie is no route to prosperity. Those promising to make their countries great again by rebuilding trade borders, however, would disagree; and they could argue that if the world can sustain ever-fewer factory jobs, it is all the more important to claim them for one's own country. So let us take that argument at face value and measure, as far as we can, how much of a difference governments could have made to Western factory employment today had they refused to engage in trade liberalisation after the 1980s.

In 1985 the countries then in the OECD (broadly the "old West") had about sixty million manufacturing jobs, a number that then fell by eighteen million in the next three decades, according to economist Adrian Wood.[6] How much of this fall was the result of more efficient technology reducing the need for human labour as described in chapter 2, and how much was because goods that were previously produced at home for home markets were now being traded across borders?

The most famous studies of this question focus on the US labour market and were carried out by the economist David Autor and his colleagues. These studies have struck a chord with an elite already primed by the elephant chart, thanks to their pathbreaking measurements on the "China shock"—the effect on US manufacturing of China's entry into the world trading system.[7] They looked at the period 1999–2011, during which the number of Americans working in factories fell from more than 17 million to about 12 million. On their best estimates, 560,000 of these jobs disappeared because of direct import competition from China. Adding in industries that were not directly exposed but connected to those that were brings the fall in manufacturing jobs to about one million—a big number but only about 6 per cent of 1999 factory employment, and one-fifth of the decline. Other factors than the China shock must have been behind the remaining four-fifths—above all, the automation I have already discussed. This is not to deny that trade has caused suffering to those who lost their jobs because of it, but to point out that those victims are few compared with the many more whose jobs have gone because they were rendered obsolete by technology. They will not be helped, and could very well be hurt, by reversing globalisation.

What about the rest of the West? The United States is not so much representative of rich countries as an extreme case.

During this period, employment rates fell more there than almost anywhere else (both in manufacturing, which declined everywhere, and in overall employment, which increased elsewhere even when it fell in the United States). That includes countries that are much more open to trade than the United States. So if trade with China caused only a small fraction of the loss of American factory jobs, one would expect that this fraction was even smaller elsewhere. And that is exactly what is borne out when the Autor-Dorn-Hanson methodology is applied to other Western economies.[8] The overwhelming conclusion is that only a tiny fraction of Western factory jobs can truly be said to have "gone to China."

That tiny fraction becomes somewhat bigger if we add in trade with other poor countries. But so far we have only looked at one side of the coin. More open trade does not just threaten jobs; it creates jobs, too—even factory jobs. Two other economists, Robert Feenstra and Akira Sasahara, have pointed out that the Autor team's methods should be extended to account for the boost trade gives to manufacturing *exports*, not just the way it displaces domestic production with imports. It turns out this boost is substantial. For the United States, more open trade with *all* countries created almost as many factory jobs to serve bigger export markets as it eliminated because of competition from imports.[9] Calculations for Germany show that new export opportunities created *more* jobs than import competition took away—in other words, less globalisation would have made the challenge of disappearing industrial jobs worse.[10] To be clear, all this research focuses on manufacturing jobs *only*, ignoring service jobs that have come about because of trade. But it shows convincingly that, even taking factory fetishism more seriously than it deserves, trade accounts for at best a very small part of the decline in rich-country manufacturing employment.[11]

So what? the globalisation sceptic may say. Every factory job counts, and even if we could not prevent nine out of ten from being automated away, we should have held on to the tenth that was offshored. But this assumes that preventing a job from being offshored would have ensured its survival at home. That assumption is wrong. At least some of these jobs were destined to disappear as a result of technological innovation. When Western firms started setting up factories in countries with cheap labour such as China, Mexico, and eastern Europe, it was because it rendered profitable certain methods of production—using labour intensively but not very productively—that were becoming uneconomical in the West. Without offshoring labour-intensive production tasks to low-wage economies, the pressure on companies to invest in more labour-saving technological upgrades at home would have been even stronger. Indeed, the high-income economies that have retained the strongest manufacturing sectors—Korea, Germany, Japan, Sweden—are those that have invested the most in industrial robots.[12] Perhaps a greater share of the world's industrial *output* could have been sourced in the West today if it had denied poorer countries a place in supply chains, but the effect on *jobs* would have been marginal (and less trade would also have meant fewer new factory jobs created in manufacturing for export).[13]

While I have focused on jobs, the same goes for wages. The increase in income inequality in Western countries can only be attributed in small part to trade, which is unsurprising once we know that the impact of trade liberalisation on jobs is also dwarfed by other factors.[14] Most of the rise in inequality happened in the 1980s, when trade with poorer countries had not yet become a significant feature of Western economies. Economists Arvind Subramanian and Martin Kessler have shown that such globalisation only started in earnest in the 1990s,

The timing of trade globalisation

FIGURE 5.2. Average income per capita of three major economies' trading partners, as a ratio of their own income levels. "EU" is 27 European Union member states as of 2013.
Source: Arvind Subramanian and Martin Kessler, "The Hyperglobalization of Trade and Its Future" (Peterson Institute Working Paper 13-6, July 2013), https://piie.com/publications/working-papers/hyperglobalization-trade-and-its-future, with updated data provided by the authors.

as illustrated by Figure 5.2, which traces the relative average income of the trading partners of the United States, the European Union, and Japan, weighted by their share of trade.[15]

For decades, the United States' trade partners consistently hovered around two-thirds of American income per capita, until 1991, when poorer countries began to increase their share in US exports and imports. Europe's trading partners were even richer—richer than the European Union itself on average—and stayed richer until the end of the 1990s. Both patterns reflect how, until very recently, the world's rich countries traded largely among themselves, and it was not until the last few years of the twentieth century that this changed to any significant degree. "Hyperglobalisation" really got under way around 1990, by which time the most dramatic widening of income inequality in the West had already happened, and the proportion of Western factory jobs had long since passed its peak. The increase in the flow of manufactured goods from poorer to richer countries was more of a scapegoat for the end of belonging in the West than the cause.

What is true, however, is that the Western factory jobs that are added or retained in a world of freer trade are different from those that they replace. They differ in two ways, both of which resemble the effects of automation and other technological advances. First, they require higher skill levels.[16] Second, the new jobs are often in different places from the old ones. The consequence is that the new and often better job opportunities created by trade, even in manufacturing, are not always available to those who depended on the old ones. The most important conclusion from the "China shock" research is that import competition has very concentrated geographical effects, with substantial negative and long-lasting consequences for the places particularly exposed to it. Autor and his colleagues found that wages and employment could remain depressed for more than a decade in places particularly badly hit by new imports.

That may help explain the earlier neglect of left-behind places by policy makers: the more localised the costs, the less noticeable to anyone else. But it does not support the belief that trade has been bad for rich countries. Nor does it even mean that those particular places could have avoided decline were it not for globalisation. What it does show is that the groups and places least well equipped for the (much more dramatic) technological transformation of Western economies from low- to high-skill manufacturing, and from industry to services, were also the most exposed to an opening global economy.

But removing that exposure would not have undone or halted the technological transformation, so less economic integration would not have helped them. Indeed, as I have just pointed out, it may well have intensified the process of automation and other labour-saving, skill-demanding changes. The challenge of managing this transformation would have been no easier with less globalisation. The old jobs could only have been sustained in large numbers by paying low enough wages to remain economical in the face of continuing technological advance—in other words, resembling more and more the factory jobs in poorer countries that antiglobalisers complain about.

Scapegoat number two: migration. What about another dimension of globalisation, migration?

Even more than the liberalisation of trade, the movement of people across borders has been a political powder keg on both sides of the Atlantic. In Europe, it finally ignited with the refugee crisis in the winter of 2015–16. In the same period, Donald Trump successfully campaigned for president by tapping into the growing xenophobia nourished by the 9/11 attacks and a doubling of the immigrant share (especially from Mexico) in the US population since the 1980s. There is no doubt that immigration plays an outsize part in the usurpation story. And while antipathy to immigration is more complex than that to trade, it has an undeniable economic component. Where imports are seen as moving "our jobs" offshore, immigrants are accused of undercutting the livelihoods of "hardworking people" in their own communities.

The economic objections to immigration seem plausible. But it has proved extraordinarily difficult to demonstrate objectively the negative effects immigrant workers are popularly perceived to have caused. Despite huge amounts of research, there is vanishingly little evidence that immigration has depressed wages for native workers more than marginally, if at all, and a lot of evidence that it has had no effects, or even contributed to higher wages.[17] In the infrequent studies that do find a negative effect on wages for the lowest paid, the impact is small. How small? Very small—in the United Kingdom, for example, the effect of immigration in the semiskilled sector "amounts to a reduction in annual pay rises of about a penny an hour" since the 2004 European Union expansion to formerly communist countries.[18] There is even less evidence that the natives' employment prospects (as opposed to their wages) have suffered at all because of immigration. On the contrary, natives tend to respond to immigration that could put downward pressure on low-end wages by shifting into better, higher-paid occupations. In Norway, for example, native workers moved into jobs requiring knowledge of the Norwegian language as East European migrant workers filled up less language-intensive jobs.[19]

There is also little substance to the worry that immigration has been a drain on public finances in host countries.[20] Societies that accept more immigrants from the very poorest countries tend to have less generous public welfare systems in the first place. Migrants from relatively better-off countries, such as those moving from central and eastern Europe to western Europe, are preponderantly of working age and often more highly skilled than the average native person in the host country. They consequently improve the public finances by paying more in taxes and drawing less in benefits. What has happened in a country like the United Kingdom, however, is that the authorities have neglected to use some of these additional revenues to expand public services like health and schooling in places where immigration has created pressures on those services for the local population. Insufficiencies in schooling or delays in how quickly patients can see a doctor are then blamed on the very immigrants who produce the resources that could fund these services better. But the fault is one of domestic resource allocation rather than immigration itself.

Beyond the effects on wages or budgets, there is emerging evidence of more complex economic consequences of immigration. These are potentially significant and often positive, but they rarely register in the public debate. They include the fact that immigration can boost productivity[21] and that the cross-border networks created by immigrants' personal and cultural ties boost exports to their countries of origin or inward investment from them.[22] A full accounting of the economics of immigration would need to include effects such as these, which tilt the ledger further towards net benefits for the host country.[23]

Yet all the data and evidence have very little traction with those who are opposed to immigration. Why is this? The most important reason is that compared with trade, immigration presents a challenge that is culturally much more raw. Immigrants are people, and people shape communities in ways that imported goods do not. Another reason is intellectual. It is easy to assume that a greater supply of workers might depress wages, all other things being equal. It takes a more sophisticated perspective to appreciate that all other things are not equal, and to recognise the many ways immigration can therefore boost productivity, wages, and public-sector balances.

But perhaps the most important reason is that—as with trade—rates of immigration have risen strongly almost everywhere at exactly the same time as the economy of belonging was withering fast. Many big cities and other successful areas have thrived on openness with the outside world, largely making a success of rising immigration, and as a result have an above-average tolerance of it. Meanwhile, many of the West's former industrial strongholds saw a massive decline for reasons unrelated to immigration but coinciding with it. As discussed in chapter 3, stress and economic insecurity predictably trigger hostility towards outsiders and a more intense concern with preserving narrower communities and known traditions.

This explains the paradox found within one country after another: it is often in places with few immigrants that people dislike them the most. With some exceptions,[24] immigration has been concentrated in the economically more promising places, such as the big cities—where there is work—which means that the places with the fewest immigrants are often those places that have fallen most behind economically. The hard times these areas are experiencing make them fertile ground for the antiglobalisation populists, so that when immigrants do arrive, there is a backlash as the population of foreigners rises from almost zero to a modest but still significantly lower share than in the cities (a small but *proportionately* large increase). Populists tap into and articulate fears and insecurities that are understandable reactions to local economic pressures and the resulting feeling of no longer belonging to a national whole. Again, the damage blamed on immigration is mostly the damage caused by the lack of domestic policy action to stop exposed groups and places from falling behind.

Scapegoat number three: financial globalisation. Finally, we come to financial globalisation. Even if there has been no shortage of opprobrium heaped on financiers, financial globalisation has been the least politicised of the three faces of globalisation.

Yet of the activities that have freely crossed borders since the 1980s, finance is unambiguously the one with the hardest case to answer, in terms of the harm caused to ordinary people. As I have already discussed (chapter 4), the evidence is now strong that beyond some threshold, an expansion of finance can bring instability, inequality, and lower productivity growth. What is hard to disentangle, however, is how much of this comes down to overgrown banking and financial excess anywhere—the phenomenon of "financialisation"—and how much to financial *globalisation* or cross-border finance specifically.

The scale of international financial flows is simply breathtaking, and it dwarfs all the developments in trade and migration.[25] On the eve of the global financial crisis, banks globally had invested or lent more than $22 trillion to countries other than their own. That does not count the deepening direct links between financial institutions other than banks, which amounted to another nearly $13 trillion. The total $35 trillion of cross-border financial claims had more than trebled from $10 trillion in just eight years since the start of the millennium, and doubled in the decade before that: a sixfold increase in international finance since 1990 (Figure 5.3).[26]

This, however, is only one side of the bigger story. In the majority of countries, domestic finance swelled in parallel with its growing international reach, with the financial sector's domestic and international business feeding off one another. For smaller countries—such as Iceland and Ireland—getting in on the action as intermediaries for global financial flows went alongside huge lending booms at home. Bigger countries' banks used large domestic balance sheets as ammunition to expand abroad. Like dough rising above the edges of a bowl, credit supply simultaneously expanded at home and spilled over national boundaries.

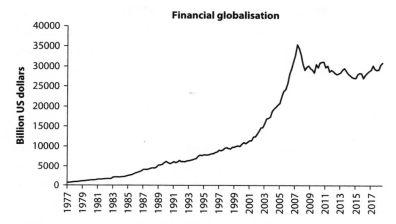

FIGURE 5.3. Gross cross-border claims of financial institutions, in billions of current US dollars.
Source: Bank for International Settlements, Locational Banking Statistics, https://stats.bis.org/statx/srs/table/a1?m=S.

These cross-border banking links served as transmission lines for the global financial crisis of 2008. The enormous exposure of national banking systems to risks in other countries was ill understood ahead of time, and this explains much of why the crisis and its immediate global impact were so unexpectedly virulent. There were concerns raised that some countries exported too much of their savings and others lived dangerously beyond their means, so-called macroeconomic imbalances. But as historian Adam Tooze has explained, the real but unnoticed danger was the amount of finance that went both ways between countries: "One could net the flows out to identify how much, on balance, flowed one way rather than the other, but that would give no idea of the scale of the commitments on each side. It would be akin to noting that two elephants on either end of a circus seesaw leave a net balance of zero. It would be true, but it would not give a very adequate description of the forces in play."[27]

What blame, if any, does this breathtaking financial globalisation merit for the plight of the West's left behind? Two accusations could be made. One is that the growth of finance, both in overall size but also in the way financial industry practices have insinuated themselves into other economic activities, has undermined the Western economy of belonging. But we have to distinguish here between domestic *financialisation*—a name for the financial sector's expansion in size and scope—and financial *globalisation*. Chapter 4 already showed the ways in which financialisation aggravates the economy's post-industrial tendency to leave some people behind. But it does so through largely domestic mechanisms: reckless domestic bank lending creates financial instability; financialisation diverts resources away from the most productive investments; and financial engineering shifts the balance of power and the division of national income in favour of domestic capital owners over domestic workers, which also increases regional inequality. Financialisation has all these effects. But it would have them in a perfectly closed national economic system, too.

This is where we come to the second accusation, which is that financial globalisation is the *cause* of domestic financialisation—either directly or by stunting national policymakers' ability to regulate it (or both). Once capital and money can flow unhindered across borders, the argument goes, it becomes impossible for governments to prevent the expansion of finance at home—because no government can risk seeing capital flee. As a result of financial globalisation, in other words, every national economy becomes more exposed to instability, distortions, and lower taxes on capital (resulting in either poorer public services or more taxes on ordinary workers), because it renders domestic policy makers powerless to prevent these ill effects. This suspicion of global finance has a long history and sometimes expresses itself in unsavoury and even danger-ous ways. Conspiracies about international cabals of financiers secretly controlling puppet politicians have persisted through time, often descending into outright anti-Semitic attacks on Jewish financiers from the Rothschilds to George Soros. It is not a coincidence that financial crises tend throughout history to be followed by rising support for right-wing extremism.

But there are honest and decent ways of making the argu-ment that reducing barriers to financial flows across borders reduces governments' ability to mitigate finance's corrosive effect on the economy of belonging. Here are two examples.

First, if capital can move between countries with ease, workers and governments may worry that efforts to increase either wages or taxes on capital will lead owners of capital to shift their money abroad and leave less to invest in domestic companies—meaning there would be fewer or worse jobs and less domestic capital left to tax. As a result, the mere existence of capital mobility reduces workers' bargaining power and gov-ernments' power to tax.

Second, globalised capital complicates monetary policy. If money can move from one country to the next based on wher-ever the short-term rewards for investment are higher, central banks will struggle to guide interest rates where they judge best for their domestic economy. Local borrowing costs will instead depend on the global monetary situation, with funds flooding in or out as a result of attempts by local policy makers to create tighter or looser financing conditions than those that prevail abroad.

There is no shortage of signs that both theoretical possi-bilities have come true in practice. During the most intense period of financial globalisation, capital taxation has indeed been lightened, wages have stagnated, and large cross-border capital flows have destabilised economies while national authorities look on, seemingly impotent. Even this does not prove, however, that financial globalisation made governments powerless. There is another possibility: that governments could have prevented these outcomes even in the presence of globalised finance, but that they failed to use the power available to them. In chapters 9 and 10, I propose a number of policies that have remained at national governments' disposal and that could have blunted the harmful effects of cross-border finance. If that argument holds true, it is wrong to blame globalisation for something that national policy makers could have avoided had they acted differently in domestic policy.

That conclusion applies to globalisation more broadly. In trade, migration, and finance, the picture is similar (though it is admittedly less clear for finance). Once you kick the tires on the usurpation story—the claim that globalisation shafted workers in the Western world—reality turns out to be more complex. In each case, and most strongly for finance, there are signs that cross-border economic integration did indeed have harmful effects for some segments of Western societies, though the evidence is that most of the harm done to them was due to other causes, such as technological change. For some, even this qualified finding amounts to a guilty verdict on globalisation. But all of these effects took place in a *domestic* policy environment that for decades accepted them with a shrug—or even cheered on the economic transformation they reflected. This indifference throws doubt on the notion that globalisation left national governments unable to address the end of belonging. It is closer to the truth to say they simply did not try hard enough.

Since the 1990s, Rodrik has supplemented his warning about the economic effects of globalisation with one about its political consequences. Not only may economic openness harm certain groups; the way in which countries agree to lower barriers between them may also prevent them from adopting domestic policies that address those harms. Therefore, he argues, we ought to "reassess the balance between national autonomy and economic globalisation."[28] He argues that globalisation presents a "trilemma" in which we can only have two out of the following three things: globalisation, national autonomy, and democracy. That is because the harms of globalisation will trigger popular demands that—unless we neuter them by disabling democratic responsiveness—must be met at the national level (in which case globalisation has to be reversed) or at the global level (in which case democracy must be global, too, and shift sovereignty away from the nation-state).

This is too stark. It takes as a given that globalisation prevents governments from implementing the domestic policies necessary to remedy any ill effects of globalisation itself, or to address the similar but much bigger challenges posed by the technological shift from industry to services and from low-skill to high-skill work that globalisation is blamed for. "If governments feel themselves powerless to institute the tax policies and regulations needed to address the dislocations caused by economic and technological shocks, the solution is not just to seek more national autonomy but also to deploy it toward such reforms," Rodrik writes.[29] But we should not accept that politicians are right to feel powerless—at least not until they have tried such policies and failed.

The previous chapter illustrated the fact that too often they have not even tried. In the rest of the book, I set out a whole range of policies that can address the shocks that have been tearing Western societies apart at their political, cultural, and economic seams. Our current level of globalisation does not stop governments from deploying these policies, but largely they have not been tried, or if they have, it has not been in sufficient scope and scale.

Rodrik calls for "an alternative globalisation . . . a globalisation that recognises the multiplicity of capitalist models and therefore enables countries to shape their own economic destinies."[30] But *alternative* forms of globalisation need not be any less *globalised*. What I hope to show is that better policies are there for the taking, without giving up one inch of the lowering of economic borders we have achieved since 1945.[31] More than this, I want us to be more ambitious still: the best domestic policies can create the conditions in which yet further globalisation will be beneficial and be recognised as such—and enjoy popular support even from those who today oppose it most passionately.

PART II

What Is to Be Done?

6

Economics, Jobs, and the Art of Car Maintenance

The political divisions we are experiencing in the West today are the product of the end of economic belonging. I have argued in the first part of this book that the converse is also true: we can disarm the current assault on liberal principles, democratic institutions, and international openness by restoring an economy of belonging. I now turn to the big question of how to do so. In the chapters that follow, I go through a range of economic issues to show how better policies—policies that will bring everyone along rather than leaving people behind—are there for the taking if policy makers are willing to be economically radical in their defence of centrist politics.

These include policies to correct power imbalances in labour, goods, and services markets; a macroeconomic policy fit for purpose; a financial system that works for the whole economy; a reformed tax system that works for the left behind and not against them; and policies to help those regions which are struggling to catch up and thrive as they once did. Put together—and because they reinforce each other, they will work better together than in isolation—these policies are our best chance to rebuild economies where everyone belongs. In such economies, deeper (but better) globalisation can also be made to work for everyone.

But as the first part of the book showed, central to the backlash against the Western political order is the disappearance of good jobs for many people. So an economics of belonging must first of all explain what makes an economy provide decent jobs for all. The answer starts with a story that taught me how sometimes a trivial economic transaction can reveal the profound forces that shape our economic lives. In this case, it was the humble car wash.

Around 2005, while living in New York, I was discussing over lunch with a visiting Norwegian economist the contrasts between the economies of the United States and Norway. We hit upon having your car cleaned as an everyday activity that captured an important difference. In New York, you can hardly slow down at a crossing before a team of two or three workers— almost always immigrant or minority men—descends on your car with detergent, cloths, and polish and proceeds to rub it down by hand. In Norway, as my interlocutor put it, "that's a technology that went out of use in the 1960s." For decades, the only option was to watch the garage-size machine spray detergent on the windshield while it moved three huge, blue spinning brush rollers along the sides and roof—or, of course, clean your car yourself.

Car wash by hand or by machine: this simple service crystallises the difference between two varieties of capitalism. In one, wages are sufficiently low that businesses can be competitive while employing a lot of labour to carry out tasks manually. In the other, the only way to keep up with the competition is to invest in machines to replace humans for the same tasks. It is easy to see how both types of market economy can threaten to leave some people behind—the first by maintaining a large population of low-paid labour, the second because of technological unemployment. Yet those who fear for the left behind are too often focused on the second. One of the biggest failures of many Western economies has been to encourage a labour market of the first kind out of fear of the consequences of the second. But the societies that have been most successful at protecting the economy of belonging—the European Nordics—have actively prevented the use of low-paid labour and instead embraced automation. This chapter shows how to incorporate the ingredients of that success in an economics of belonging for other countries, too—and how to retain them in the Nordics, where social and technological changes are chipping away at the successes of the past.

Every time something is done by humans that could be done by machines—in particular something that elsewhere *is* done by machines—we should stop and ask why. Using human labour unnecessarily is, after all, a missed opportunity for greater prosperity and well-being. As a matter of definition, the more labour goes into producing a particular good or rendering a particular service, the less productive is each hour's work in that activity, and it is ultimately only from greater labour productivity that higher incomes can be paid. An economy that encourages business to eschew capital upgrades in favour of employing low-productivity manual labour is therefore one that accepts leaving a large population behind on low wages. But the capital-intensive alternative, too, brings the challenge of how to secure enough high-productivity employment to absorb those whose work is displaced by machines.

The choice of machine wash versus hand wash therefore illustrates a broader question of profound importance. What determines whether an economy opts for automated solutions or cheap human labour?

The first part of the answer is the level of wages relative to the cost of machines. The more people have to be paid, the more likely it is that the profit-maximising choice for a service station is to automate the car wash. If, instead, wages remain sufficiently low that extensive hiring is affordable, automation will look uneconomical. And what is true for the car wash is true across the economy.

But the very same mechanism also works in reverse. More automation leads to higher labour productivity, and that, in turn, allows for higher wages. For each car to be cleaned, much less labour is required in a machine wash than in a hand wash. So not only do rising wages encourage investment in machines, but that investment itself also leaves a greater surplus from which to pay a higher wage for the (reduced) amount of labour still needed. Conversely, lower investment makes for lower productivity, lower wages, and therefore a greater incentive to put human hands to the work that machines could otherwise do.

The second part of the answer is inequality. Tasks that do not require a lot of skill—like cleaning a car—take about the same amount of manual labour whoever carries them out. Without specialised equipment, after all, even an experienced cleaner doesn't wash a car all that much faster than the car's owner. That means that the more equal wages are, the less point there is in paying others to carry out such tasks for you. If it takes twenty minutes to clean a car by hand, and the cost is the same as what you make in twenty minutes of work, there is little reason to outsource a task you might as well do yourself. If, however, that cost is equivalent to just minutes of your salary because the car cleaner makes so much less than you, things look very different. The demand for unskilled, labour-intensive work depends on the unskilled wage relative to the wage of higher-paid labour—in other words, wage inequality—as well as relative to the cost of machines.

For a very long time, it has been conventional wisdom that inequality is the price you pay for faster growth and that high wages discourage investment and productivity. This argument often came in tandem with the view that letting the wage distribution go where the market took it was necessary to ensure that even the least skilled workers could find jobs, and that unequal wages were best addressed through redistributive taxes and transfers rather than interfering with the labour market. These views went a long way to legitimise the rise in inequality and the decline of unions in many Western countries. But the carwash example hints that they may be missing something. And along Europe's northern rim, we find living examples of how things can work very differently.

The Scandinavian triplet of Denmark, Sweden, and Norway are well known for pulling off both prosperity and egalitarianism. What is much less well known is that their wealth comes not *in spite of* equality, or as some fortunate fluke, but as a consequence of a wage-setting system that produces relative equality even before any state redistribution.

Karl Moene, a spiky-haired and leather-jacketed economics professor at the University of Oslo with a puckish gleam in his eyes, has made the Nordic economic model the object of a lifetime of study.[1] This is how he explained it to me in a 2018 interview:

> The economic growth per capita in Norway and Sweden since 1930 till today has been higher than in the US, even when you exclude oil in the Norwegian case. . . . This is a period where wage equality has been at a record high, taxes

have been record high, where welfare spending has been much more generous than in other countries, and you have very strong social organisations in the labour market . . . comprehensive unions [and] very strong associations of employers. So this has been a system that many American economists would consider a recipe for catastrophe, but it has worked quite well. Why is this? I think if you are going to put it in a few words, it is that it helps modernisation, it helps make the most modern industries, the most modern enterprises more profitable.[2]

The wage compression achieved by the Nordic labour market, in other words, is an engine of productivity growth: "[The distance] between the most productive enterprises and the least productive enterprises within sectors is much more narrow in Scandinavia than, say, the US. And why is that? Well, because you can't have very low productivity with these high minimum wages, and since you have low maximum wages, you make investment in these modern enterprises much more profitable."[3]

The car wash illustrates this at the low end of the labour market. Car washes use a lot more manual labour in the United States than in Norway. This is not just a matter of anecdotal impression; it is backed up by job statistics. More than twice the share of workers in the United States (2.55 per 1,000) spend their day rubbing down car hoods compared with Norway (1.12 per 1,000), for a comparable number of motor vehicles. The reason is that wages at the low end are higher, and the whole wage distribution more compressed, in Norway than in the United States. The average American car cleaner makes $25,700 a year, whereas his Norwegian counterpart makes about $45,000 (or the equivalent of about $37,000 after adjusting for the higher prices in Norway).[4]

Moene adds that compression from the top is important, too—not to discourage companies from using low-skilled labour but to encourage them to hire high-skilled workers, who can make the most of the latest technology: "[When wages] in the most modern enterprises are lower than they otherwise would have been . . . you get more investment in these modern industries. . . . When the IT revolution came, it was much more beneficial to Scandinavian economies than most economies elsewhere because it was very profitable to [adopt, since] people who were skilled, who can benefit from it, had a low cost."[5] Over the long run, in Moene's analysis, higher and more egalitarian wages have pulled the Nordic economies away from low-end sectors and jobs like manually washing cars and into sectors and jobs where higher-skilled workers work with more and better technology. The resulting productivity growth adds enough value to sustain the higher wages.

There is much to admire about this system. But is there also something to emulate? The institutions governing wage setting in the Nordics grew out of their nationally specific social conflicts over economic interests and their particular political history of resolving them. In addition, national culture shapes how the people making up those institutions behave and interact. None of this could simply be copied and pasted into the different historical, cultural, and institutional landscape of another country.

But that may not be necessary. The economic mechanism illustrated by the car wash follows from the wage structure, not directly from the institutional landscape that produced the wage structure. If the Nordics owe their cohesive form of prosperity to a compressed wage distribution derived from their unique collective bargaining system, other countries could hope for similar results from more equal wages even if those were achieved through other means.

The question, then, for a country without Nordic labour market institutions and traditions is how to mimic its effects on the wage distribution, in the hope of shifting away from business models based on low-wage labour. Surprisingly enough, the best stab at an answer came from George Osborne, the United Kingdom's Conservative chancellor of the exchequer (finance minister) from 2010 to 2016.

Presenting his last but one government budget in July 2015, Osborne announced a substantial rise in the legal wage floor for workers aged twenty-five years and older, mandating what he dubbed a "national living wage" above the regular minimum wage. Not only that, he explicitly tied it to the rest of the wage distribution by aiming for the national living wage to hit 60 per cent of the median market wage after five years.[6] This was a policy aiming not just to lift the floor but also to compress the distribution—if modestly. I argued at the time, half (but only half) tongue-in-cheek, that this was a "vote Thatcher, get Scandinavia" strategy, which sought to encourage productivity by making low-skilled labour more expensive through legal fiat rather than union bargaining. While Osborne never explicitly stated this, the UK government later confirmed that this formed part of its thinking. One minister stated, "Requiring a pay increase can prompt employers to make the investments that they otherwise do not necessarily feel they need to make."[7]

Can this trick work? The United Kingdom's particular experiment is still inconclusive, because the higher wage floor came into effect just when Britain voted to leave the European Union. That huge shock to the economy inevitably affected investment decisions, which makes it hard to untangle the effects of the national living wage itself. But the signs are that it will work as intended. It has clearly been successful in lifting wages at the low end. In the first year after the wage floor was raised, the bottom 10 per cent of earners saw a more than 4 per cent pay rise (more than 6 per cent for the bottom half of that group) compared with a 2 per cent rise at the median.[8] This has not led to job losses in low-wage sectors, with employers reporting they aimed to raise labour productivity to make up for the higher wage costs.[9] That productivity increase has been elusive, however. This issue is also clouded by Brexit, which has made employers cut down on investing in skills and training.[10] But we know that the introduction of the United Kingdom's original national minimum wage in 1998 did in fact have positive productivity effects on those industries most reliant on cheap labour.[11]

There is every reason to expect the same from the national living wage and, more generally, from ambitious minimum wage increases elsewhere, mimicking what the Nordics have achieved through centralised wage bargaining. The incentive to substitute machines for costly low-productivity labour is the same regardless of the source of that higher cost. And there are other indications that compressed wages are good for productivity.[12] For such an effect *within* firms, there is evidence that *un*equal wages demotivate workers and therefore hold back productivity.[13] Higher wages at the low end seem to motivate people to work harder or better; they help reduce absenteeism, shirking, and lack of discipline; and they improve ability and skill by mitigating the psychological effect of economic insecurity on workers.[14]

But most importantly, there is hard evidence that higher minimum wages drive out business models based on employing a lot of low-productivity labour and favour more capital-intensive competitors—the most important long-term effect of wage compression in Scandinavia. In the United States, one study found that minimum wage hikes increased the rate at which restaurants shut down and new ones opened, and it was chain restaurants with more capital-intensive and therefore higher-productivity operations that replaced local ones that had made use of cheap labour instead of technology. And for those who do not like chains, a more palatable example is that restaurants in France are more productive than those in the United Kingdom, because higher personnel costs have prompted a more efficient use of labour and hence a lower staff requirement for similar sales.[15]

Minimum wages can therefore act as a substitute for collective bargaining in lifting the low end of the wage scale. The same can be said of work conditions: precarious and insecure work creates the same incentives for employers as low wages—to choose easily disposable labour rather than productivity-enhancing investments with a similar negative effect on workers. Take the example of zero-hours contracts, where workers have to be willing to accept shifts at short notice (or risk not being given new ones) but are not guaranteed a minimum amount of work. This may make things easier for employers in the short run, but it also removes their incentive to improve shift scheduling and redesign production processes to make things more predictable—and ultimately more productive.

A massive body of empirical research has refuted the old argument against minimum wages that they put low-skilled people out of work and therefore hurt those they were supposed to help. While wage floors clearly eliminate some uses of low-productivity labour—and as I have just discussed, that is something worth aiming for—they are usually offset by new, more productive, and therefore higher-paid, jobs.[16] And in any case, the overall number of jobs can also be influenced by the right policies, as I will discuss shortly.

In sum, for a government that dares to be a little bit radical, a straightforward strategy is available to move an economy from a low-productivity, low-wage, bad-job model to a high-productivity, high-wage, rewarding-work one. A bold policy of ambitious legal wage floors and working conditions can go a long way towards mimicking the Nordic experience. Not all the way, however. Recall that for Nordic employers there is the added benefit of wage compression from above, which makes high-paid labour cheaper than it otherwise would be. That redoubles the incentive to invest in technology by lowering the cost of hiring skilled workers needed to manage it. Raising minimum wages and work conditions through legislation is no substitute for that "upper" part of the Nordic labour market model. The full effect of wage compression would only be had with additional policies to lower the cost of high-skilled workers. Short of measures to cap high pay, or limit the permissible pay differences within companies, the most plausible way to achieve this is to increase the supply of those workers—which is in any case necessary to address the danger that automation eliminates the jobs of low-wage workers but brings nothing in their place.

Achieving growth by shedding jobs based on cheap labour offers the promise of greater productivity and higher wages. But it also poses the question at the heart of the economic changes in the West over the past four decades—as well as the next decades facing us: What happens to those workers whose tasks are eliminated? Lifting the lower end of the pay scale does not help those who are left without a job.

The Nordic countries' experience proves that the quick uptake of labour-saving technology need not, however, leave people without jobs. They combine strong productivity and egalitarian wages with some of the highest rates of workforce participation and lowest rates of unemployment in the Western world.[17] Why is this? Why has the automation-friendly Nordic labour market model not left people behind as much as in other countries? Aside from wage equality, there are three more ingredients in the Nordic secret sauce. To ensure that new and better jobs replace all the low-productivity ones that wage compression eliminates, there must be, first, sufficient demand growth for productive businesses to expand with confidence; second, a functional financial system that can fund their expansion; and third, the ability of labour and capital to move easily from declining companies and sectors to growing ones.

Wage egalitarianism changes the composition of jobs in the economy—towards more capital-intensive, high-productivity tasks on average—but the total number of those jobs depends on the overall demand. If macroeconomic policy tools such as government budget balances and central bank interest rates are used aggressively enough, they can generate demand for workers in new and better-paid jobs. And if the financial system functions as it should, the businesses that create such jobs will have access to enough capital to expand. Scandinavia has historically done well in both regards. Many other countries have not; their record with the left behind owes much to timid demand management and flawed financial systems that have left large regions starved of capital. Later in the book, I show that there is no shortage of policy instruments to keep aggregate demand strong (chapter 8) or to improve financing so that high-productivity employers can expand (chapter 9). The problem is rather policy makers' lack of boldness in using the tools at their disposal.

But even such a policy of aggressive job creation can only work if workers can actually fill the new and more productive roles. That means they must be able as well as willing to perform the new jobs—which will typically require more skill, as they tend to be more capital-intensive—especially when relatively egalitarian wages reduces the direct financial incentive to

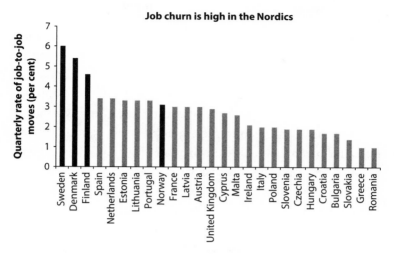

FIGURE 6.1. Rate of job-to-job moves per quarter, as a percentage share of total employed workforce. Average of yearly observations 2011–17.
Source: "Job-to-Job Transitions by Sex and Age—Annual Averages of Quarterly Transitions, Estimated Probabilities," Eurostat, accessed 6 December 2019, http://appsso.eurostat.ec.europa.eu/nui/show.do?dataset=lfsi_long_e07.

undertake training, education, and skills improvement. It also means that the labour market must do as much as possible to smooth the move of workers from one job to another as low-productivity roles become obsolete.

The Nordic nations excel at both. They rank highly for adult cognitive skills, an important key to employability in a shifting economy.[18] And measured by how easy it is to jump from one job to another, the Nordic labour markets are exceptionally well oiled. Swedes, Danes, and Finns move between jobs more often than all other European workers.[19] As Figure 6.1 shows, the frequency of job-to-job moves in Denmark and Sweden is close to 6 per cent per quarter, or nearly 25 per cent per year; it is 18 per cent per year in Finland. All this means that very few workers lack the basic cognitive skills needed to learn a new job, and that there is little friction as they go from one job to another.

How have Nordic labour markets come to function so smoothly? It might seem tempting, but fatalistic, to put it down to the cultural particularities of small, traditionally homogeneous and peaceful countries—fatalistic because this suggests it is hard for other economies to achieve the same. But the explanation that stares us in the face if we look in the right place shows that there is every reason to think the Nordics can be emulated. Simply put, it comes down not to culture but to money—to the resources Nordic countries have chosen to invest in these priorities.

Take skills first: the five Nordic countries are in the top six on the OECD league table for the share of national income spent on education, from primary to tertiary. The Danish and Norwegian governments both spend more than 6 per cent of gross domestic product on education; all the others come in above 5 per cent.[20] These countries have a broadly skilled population because they pay for it (Figure 6.2).

The same can be said for job-to-job mobility. The Nordic economies are characterised by what Denmark calls "flexicurity"—flexible rules for hiring and firing, but with policies and institutions in place to improve the chances of getting a new job. In Sweden, for example, employers' organisations are held responsible for worker reallocation schemes to find new jobs for workers who are let go. But above all, governments put significant resources into helping people into work. Denmark has by far the highest rate of public spending on "active labour market policies" among rich economies: the government spends about 2 per cent of national income on helping workers find new jobs, mostly on training and on creating sheltered or supported job opportunities or rehabilitating workers.

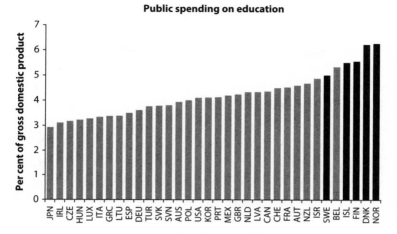

FIGURE 6.2. Public spending on education from primary to tertiary level, per cent of gross domestic product, 2015 (Denmark: 2014).
Source: "Public Spending on Education," OECD Data, accessed 6 December 2019, https://data.oecd.org/eduresource/public-spending-on-education.htm#indicator -chart.

Sweden and Finland come in next with about half as much. At the bottom of the list comes the United States, which spends a meagre 0.11 per cent—one-tenth the amount spent by Sweden or Finland; one-twentieth of that spent by Denmark.[21]

Where does this leave us? Anyone who sees the Nordic experience as a model must accept that it is hard to replicate the institutional setup and cultural attitudes that have favoured high and egalitarian wages there. Even so, bold minimum wage policies can go a long way towards mimicking their effects, so long as the other two elements of the Nordic model—high skill levels and easy flows between jobs—are also in place. The good news is that these latter two are much easier to transfer than the first. A broadly skilled population and high job-to-job mobility are found in the countries that have chosen to devote resources to these purposes. If other countries prioritise accordingly, they can choose to direct their resources the same way, and expect similar results.

There is a coda to the story about the car wash. Around the time I had that chat over lunch, manual car washes began appearing in Norway again. Suddenly it became possible to have your car cleaned by hand—to be precise, by the hands of immigrant workers—and at a cut-rate price. Scandinavia's ability to put a high floor on pay and work conditions has been slipping, in part because incoming migrant workers often elude the established system of centralised bargaining. In response, governments have looked for new ways to prevent low-pay work. Norway, for example, has introduced a policy of legally extending collective bargaining wage agreements to all workers regardless of union membership in those sectors particularly exposed to wage pressure and where unions have less presence. In effect, this has established a legal minimum wage for some jobs, such as cleaning. Ironically, Nordic countries are being forced to "mimic" their own model through new means.

The Nordics are also struggling to maintain their ability to keep everyone in work. In Denmark, Norway, and Finland, prime-age employment rates are lower today than ten years ago. The Nordic labour markets have been successful over many years in maintaining an economy of belonging, but even this success does not sustain itself. The Nordics, too, risk leaving people behind—in bad jobs or no jobs at all—if policy makers do not watch out.

7

Economic Policies for Empowerment

The end of belonging is fundamentally a story about power. Rising inequality of income and wealth, the changing status of different types of work, and the diverging fortunes of different regions in the same country—all these are consequences of a changing balance of power and lead, in their turn, to deepening power differences. For those left behind by the economy, this is experienced as losing influence over their own lives. That is why slogans such as the Brexiteers' "Take back control" are so powerful. Crucial to an economics of belonging, therefore, must be a vision of a restored sense of control and an end to dependence in people's lives.

The dependence of the left behind takes many forms. The most striking is in the world of work, where members of a growing class of people work as much as they can yet struggle to make a decent income, let alone to improve their lives. Compared with the better placed, they enjoy less security and predictability of whatever income they do earn. They are more likely to be sick, be in pain, or suffer social problems. They have few, if any, alternatives or ways out of their situation. They are, in a word, left behind in a state of *precarity*—a term that captures well the many dimensions of economic pressure: scarcity, unpredictability, dependence, and vulnerability to exploitation.

Aside from economic hardship, this causes psychological harm that has political repercussions. As I discussed in chapter 3, people tend to compensate for a feeling of loss of personal control by doubling down on group identity, which nativist and populist politicians can exploit. And this works in reverse as well: the psychological impact of precariousness aggravates the economic dynamics that leave people behind. The stress of insecurity worsens individuals' decision-making by eroding their cognitive abilities and their aptitude for long-term planning and commitment[1]—precisely the sorts of skills that jobs in the modern economy increasingly demand.

In some countries, this new "precariat" has added to the ranks of a deprived and vulnerable group that had shrunk but never quite gone away; in others it constitutes the bewildering return of a problem that had entirely disappeared except in the historical and literary memory of a distant past. It is the worst manifestation of economic dependence and disempowerment.

It is not, however, the only one. An economy that produces better jobs, through the policies set out in the previous and next chapters, would certainly help to lift incomes. But higher incomes are at best a necessary condition for empowerment, not a sufficient one.

The flip side of dependence at the bottom is the opportunity to abuse power at the top. That opportunity manifests itself not just in labour markets but wherever competition is missing in markets for goods and services, and only one or a few companies offer a product or an opportunity. The threat of abusive market power is real across many Western countries, and in many parts of the economy. It is present in small places where all the jobs within a particular line of work are with the same employer,[2] but also where big corporations dominate a market and make things hard for new entrepreneurs. It is manifested in the harnessing of private data for manipulative purposes, and in the new digital platforms in sectors ranging across retail (Amazon), transport (Uber), hospitality (Airbnb), and many others, where they dominate business flows and can therefore make or break smaller players.

Market power can of course harm anyone, not just the groups we think of as the left behind. But the left behind are always the most vulnerable to rigged markets, and emerging forms of market concentration threaten to create new groups of left behind as technology continues to transform our economies.

An economy of belonging cannot rely on broad-based prosperity alone (though it would certainly help), but must address precariousness, insecurity, and unequal power directly. That is the goal of this chapter, which outlines a set of policies that aim to give ordinary people real control over the economy that surrounds them: within the workplace, in the precarious labour market more generally, in monopolistic markets for goods and services, and in the new digital technologies. The way to achieve such control is through greater power to bargain and better alternative options, as well as legal protections against market abuse. Together, they can help move more people from situations of insecurity and dependence to a degree of self-sufficiency and independence.

1. An empowering welfare system. The welfare systems built up in the mid-twentieth century were not just about income security. They were also about freedom and self-empowerment.

By reducing economic insecurity, the Western welfare states reduced economic dependence. This held out the promise, and to a greater or lesser extent the reality, of allowing everyone to participate in the economy with a reasonably similar social status.

It is hard to argue that welfare systems achieve that purpose today in most Western countries. Originally designed around the industrial society norm of full employment of male breadwinners in lifetime jobs, they have struggled as much as industrial society itself to adapt to the technology-driven transformation of Western economies. This tie to the old industrial economy is evident in two principles woven into the very tissue of Western benefit systems to decide who is deserving of benefits: a desire to reward effort in those judged able to work and an assumption that those who are able can be neatly divided from those unable to work.

These principles are ill suited to today's economy. "Rewarding effort" tends to mean that benefits are designed to top up wage income at low levels before being withdrawn through means testing as incomes rise higher. But in an economy where incomes have become more volatile—because of the instability of work itself—this can have the perverse consequence of amplifying the instability of incomes further. It also discourages job moves by worsening the temporary income loss in between jobs. Meanwhile, benefits targeted at those unable to work struggle to deal with the fact that disability is increasingly caused by mental health problems, which are harder to assess than visible physical handicaps.[3]

Means testing creates another problem. Withdrawing cash benefits from those whose wages increase above the level where they are deemed to deserve top-ups acts as an additional income tax. Once you take this effect into account, those around a quarter of the way up the income distribution face extremely high effective marginal income tax rates—easily 70–80 per cent or more—in most Western countries.[4] In January 2020, the British bakery chain Greggs was cheered for giving its mostly low-paid employees a New Years' bonus of £300. But typical Greggs workers only took home £75, with three-quarters of the bonus lost in income tax and the withdrawal of means-tested benefits applying at their wage levels. If such rates were imposed on high earners, there would be a furious reaction pointing out how prohibitive this is for those who want to work more or qualify themselves for better jobs (indeed, the highest UK earners keep more than half of their bonus after tax). Yet for low earners, for whom the benefit system creates a low-income trap, no such outrage can be heard.

All these flaws in a benefit system built in a different era come together to create one big problem: they increase the cost of leaving a job as a protest against poor treatment or in search of a better one. In the words of the social scientist Albert Hirschman, they have blocked the possibility of "exit" as a way of influencing employment conditions. Adding to the cost of exit turns part of the welfare state into a cause rather than a remedy for the problem of dependence and disempowerment. Only one radical welfare reform can fully address this central obstacle to an economy of belonging. Proposals for it have been on the table for at least 250 years, and it has been controversial for just as long. The most common names for it are universal basic income (UBI) and negative income tax (NIT), and it would completely sever the welfare state's tie to the employment practices of industrial society.

UBI consists of an unconditional flat cash payment to all citizens[5] and an income tax levied from the first cent or penny of other income. Because the basic income itself would not be withdrawn, the combined tax and benefit package could be truly progressive, yet without the extreme marginal tax rates effectively imposed on lower-middle earners in current systems. The lowest earners would receive more in UBI than they paid in taxes, but at higher income levels taxes eventually claw back the flat payment. As the name "negative income tax" suggests, this could be operated through the tax system, so that all taxpayers would see the same flat sum deducted from their tax bill. Those who earn so little that the deduction is greater than the amount they owe in taxes would then receive the difference in a direct cash payout.

UBI/NIT is currently experiencing a renaissance in terms of public interest, but too often on the basis of weak arguments. For example, it is recommended by some who think technology and automation will leave most people unable to find jobs in the future, and see unconditional benefits as the necessary response. But if economic history teaches us anything, it is that new jobs will always appear when technological changes make old ones obsolete. (As the previous chapter explained, the question is not whether there will be jobs but what kind of jobs they will be.) Nor is it convincing to advocate UBI/NIT principally in order to prevent poverty; means-tested systems can do that in a more targeted and therefore cheaper way. The real reason for introducing a basic income is to reshape power relations in the labour market and outside it. It is a badly needed reform that is uniquely able to eliminate the disempowering insecurity and dependence that keep an economy of belonging out of reach.

The certainty of a regular, if modest, payment coming into everyone's bank account every week or month would have two important effects. First, it would give people in precarious situations the basic security they need. As experiments with UBI have shown, it would demonstrably ease the stress and anxiety of insecurity, allowing people to plan and organise their lives better, and it would let them keep the rewards from (and hence the incentive for) doing just that.[6] Second, in the workplace, it would ensure that everyone had an alternative to accepting terms that trap them in poverty and precarity. The security of a basic income would allow people to reject dangerous or underpaid employment, or the extreme irregularity that makes it impossible to eke out an income from strings of limited, short-notice shifts. And, of course, no price can be put on the modicum of dignity granted by the ability to say no.

Righting the balance of power in the workplace would force employers to take some risk back from workers. Workers who can say no must be offered better conditions, whether that means higher wages, more predictable shifts, or other improvements. As with the effect of wage floors discussed in the previous chapter, the probability is that employers would, as a result, organise work better and therefore more productively.

Compare this with what today passes for the gold standard of welfare policy to combat economic precarity: the in-work or "earned income" tax credit. It was a staple of the "third way" of centre-left politics dominant under Bill Clinton and Tony Blair, who saw it as a way to compensate for wage inequality without restraining the markets that have given rise to it, and it remains a central plank of many Western benefit systems. The intention of the policy is to reward people for leaving the ranks of the jobless, even if they can only get low-paid jobs, and to top up their earnings to offset low wages.

This is at best a sticking plaster for the groups that have been left behind by economic change. It does nothing for those out of work, by design. But it also risks aggravating the problems of unstable incomes and the low-income trap, which it can at best shift up to a slightly higher level of income (the point where the tax credit itself is withdrawn). But the worst aspect of in-work tax credits is they effectively subsidise low wages, which ends up pushing wages even lower.

Studies show that higher in-work tax credits lower wages by as much as one-quarter to half of the subsidy, and the impact is worst for the least educated with the fewest opportunities.[7] What is particularly insidious is that they also lower wages for workers who are ineligible for the tax credits but compete for jobs with those who receive them (when tax credits are targeted on parents, for example). Much of the increased income enjoyed by those in receipt of tax credits is therefore, in effect, paid for not by taxpayers but by other low-paid workers.[8] That also means employers, whose wage costs fall, are incentivised to make more use of cheap labour, contrary to the policy recommended in the previous chapter. (In-work tax credits may do better in an economy with the ambitious minimum wages I argued for in the last chapter: In the United Kingdom, a higher legal wage floor than in the United States seems to counteract tax credits' downward pressure on wages.[9] But above the legal floor, the downward wage pressure would remain, as would the other downsides.)

The contrast between in-work tax credits and a basic income is financially significant. The former allows employers to pay less because it gives workers an incentive to accept lower pre-tax wages. A basic income has the opposite effect: by making it easier for workers to leave their jobs, it forces employers to increase wages to retain them. How much more? One US study calculated that an additional $1.00 spent by the government on a higher in-work tax credit would increase workers' average after-tax incomes by only $0.73 cents because wages would fall (with some workers ending up with overall less income than before). In contrast, an additional $1.00 spent to fund a negative income tax would increase after-tax income by a full $1.39 because wages would also rise.[10]

The other important effect of introducing a certain, regular payment for all is to make it much easier to shift between jobs. This, as the previous chapter made clear, is an essential part of the new economy, and those countries which have best adapted their economies of belonging to technological change have the highest frequency of job changes. A UBI/NIT removes one important reason why those in the lowest income groups may not move jobs: the risk of running out of money in between stints of employment. It allows people to take the time needed to search for better work, or to seek training to improve their skills and job opportunities.

Naysayers have two principal objections to basic income reforms, to the extent that they agree the benefit system should promote empowerment at all (rather than simply top up low incomes). One is that they create an incentive not to work. One can see why, in theory, this should be so. To put it callously, the sharpest reason for getting a job at all is that if you do not work, you starve. An unconditional income, even for those who choose not to work when they could, removes this incentive. Yet to think there are many people who would leave their job if only they could survive without it is to ignore the many other reasons people work, such as social status, a sense of meaning, and enjoying the job itself. It ignores as well the difference between merely surviving and living well.

Furthermore, a UBI would create the opposite incentive— to work *more*—for those groups currently punished for higher incomes by the withdrawal of means-tested benefits (such as the Greggs workers mentioned earlier). If we are guided by the evidence we do have, it is clear that giving people a greater *ability* to choose not to work does not lead them to work less in practice. The one true case of a universal guaranteed income—Alaska's "Permanent Fund dividend," which pays each resident a yearly flat-rate amount from the state's accumulated oil royalties—has been found to have "no effect on employment."[11] The same has largely been true whenever basic income has been tried on an experimental basis, such as in Finland in 2017–18.[12]

The other objection is that a meaningful negative income tax scheme is too expensive. Proper calculations show that this need not be the case. Enormous yet unnoted resources are already expended in most countries' tax systems in the form of tax-free allowances that disproportionately favour higher earners. This is partially because one has to earn a certain amount of money to use the full allowance, but mostly because higher earners save more tax from the tax-free allowance because their marginal tax rate is higher. The money spent on such allowances could fund a negative income tax instead. As an example, Britain's New Economics Foundation has calculated that simply abolishing the tax-free allowances for British income taxes only (and not the separate allowances for social security taxes) could fund an unconditional cash payment to all UK adults of about £2,500/year, as well as a boosted child benefit. This would amount to a payment of about £6,700/year for a couple with two children.[13] In a study of Italy, the United Kingdom, France, and Finland, OECD economists found that a UBI at this level or higher was affordable without raising tax rates.[14]

So a modest UBI/NIT is certainly feasible. Nevertheless, to fully end insecurity and restore a sense of economic belonging for all, let alone protect that sense in the face of continuing technological transformations, a more radical version would be required—that is to say, a more generous and better-funded one. Even this is a realistic radicalism. In chapter 10 I propose a number of tax reforms that could provide additional resources for a substantial basic income even while making the economy work better for the left behind.

2. Power in the workplace. As I pointed out in chapter 4, there is strong evidence that the Western social contract was eroded partly because labour unions lost influence. From 1985 to 2017, union membership across developed countries fell from 33 per cent of workers to 16 per cent, while the share of workers covered by collective agreements fell from 46 per cent to 32 per cent.[15] To return to Hirschman, that means workers have been losing "voice" in the workplace at the same time as their power of "exit" has been weakened.

Unionisation fell over the same period as the income share of the highest earners and overall inequality went up. This is not a coincidence. International Monetary Fund economists have found that episodes of particularly steep union membership declines were followed by shifts of income to capital from labour, to the financial sector relative to the rest of the economy, and to top earners from everyone else.[16] A forensic study of the United States, meanwhile, shows that one reason for rising inequality there is that over time, American unions have disproportionately lost their lower-skilled members— mostly because such workers were overrepresented in sectors that both tended to be highly unionised and have shed jobs the fastest. The result is that union membership has declined particularly sharply among those whom it helps the most.[17]

Well-functioning unions with broad membership alter the bargaining power of their members against employers to compress wage distributions. Not only that: in the Nordics, where unions still largely fulfil this function (see chapter 6), they also push employers and government to help train and give new skills to their members so they can adapt to changing technology.

Where unions function well, policy makers should allow them to play their role. But unions can sometimes be a barrier to change: they can be wedded to the industrial structure that used to favour them even if it is outdated, or prioritise narrow influence over particular policies for their own members' benefit rather than shaping the labour markets at large. Labour protections and worker empowerment can no longer be tied to industrial-era lifetime employment, since technology has put an end to industrial-era lifetime employment as the main basis of economic activity. That makes it harder for unions both to retain high membership and to play their traditional function in the economy of belonging.

The aim of policy should therefore be to restore or preserve the *function* unions have fulfilled at their best, not necessarily the institutional form in which they did so in the past. Sometimes, that may involve creating alternatives for unions rather than strengthening them. There are a number of policy tools that can ensure this.

Administrative extension of collective bargaining. Where unions have declined in reach but still play a constructive function, governments can widen the effect of union-employer bargaining beyond the scope of union members. Through legislation or executive decrees, terms agreed to in collective bargaining in one part of a sector can be made to apply to the sector as a whole, in effect making the union give voice not just to its own members but to all those in a similar situation. This is a way to put in place what are effectively legal wage floors and minimum standards (even if differentiated by sector), which, as the previous chapter showed, can have positive effects on productivity as well as on workers' well-being.

Unions sometimes resist such policies, as they allow workers to "free ride" on collective bargaining and make it more challenging to recruit them as members. This explains why the strongly unionised Nordic economies, almost uniquely in Europe, do not have national legal minimum wages. But it illustrates that unions can sometimes make the best the enemy of the good; and conversely, that administrative extension is most appropriate precisely when unions struggle to cover the relevant mass of employees. Even Norway, a country with high union coverage, has recently chosen to use administrative extension in some sectors that unions struggle to cover, including construction, cleaning, and hospitality (and to good effect: see chapter 11).

Requirements for institutional representation. In order to either help unions fulfil their function or to create an alternative way to fulfil it, governments can require that employees have a voice in company decisions. Looking at Western countries, they fall into three groups: those that have no legal requirement for worker representation; those that only require it in government-controlled companies; and those that mandate worker representation in all companies above a certain size (usually well below one hundred employees). Decision-making rights for workers in and of themselves contribute to securing some degree of agency and control, and for that reason alone they are needed for a true economy of belonging.

But what do they do to economic performance? There is evidence that employee involvement in decision-making helps make a company more innovative[18] and that it can encourage employees to embrace technology adoption that improves productivity.[19] Conversely, there is little evidence of negative effects on company output from worker representation (though there is some that it hurts listed companies' stock price, perhaps because of investor skepticism). The countries with the strictest requirements for employee representation mostly perform well on productivity (they include the Nordics, the Netherlands,

Hungary, and Slovenia). The International Monetary Fund has found that trust between workers and management makes labour markets work better, and worker empowerment is likely to boost that trust. For all these reasons, policies that improve employee representation in decision-making can potentially boost an economy's productivity as well as enhance workers' autonomy, agency, and sense of control directly.[20]

Statutory rights for nonemployment work relationships. Internet platforms such as Uber and TaskRabbit have made it possible to procure and offer work in a much more fragmented way than through traditional employment relationships. The "gig economy" may not yet be as extensive in proportion to the entire economy as the media attention would lead you to believe, but it constitutes a significant share of new jobs since the Great Recession of 2008, and it is likely to continue to grow as it becomes practical to outsource more and more tasks as "gigs"—including cognitive ones.[21] That model is, moreover, well suited to technological developments that will require more frequent job changes.

But a fragmented workforce is a workforce with less of an organised voice or none at all, so there is a trade-off between flexibility (and the productivity that may come with it) and worker autonomy. Policy should aim to overcome this trade-off, which means finding ways to accommodate the new forms of freedom and flexibility the gig economy increasingly offers without returning to the exploitable informality of old piece-rate labour markets. In broad terms, the goal must be to ensure that workers enjoy the same balance of power vis-à-vis those they work for, regardless of their type of contract or the state of unionisation in their line of work. (Again, policies that achieve this may not always be in the interest of existing unions if it shows them up as obsolete.)

A central part of this is that the rights of workers must be *portable*. The various welfare entitlements given to workers must not themselves be tied to any particular employment but be designed in such a way that they are sustained when changing employment or in between employment. The more portable people's rights are, the easier it is to move to a better job, which brings greater prosperity not just to the worker himself or herself but also to the economy at large.

How can this be achieved? Three broad strategies are conceivable, all with the potential to make a big difference. First, unions designed specifically for gig workers could and indeed have been set up. An example is the Independent Workers' Union of Great Britain, which has pushed court cases in the United Kingdom to get gig workers classified in categories that give them stronger workplace rights.[22] Governments can legislate to help such unions organise and engage in collective bargaining.

Second, the platforms that allow gig work to be distributed can themselves be legally required to let their individual workers organise and engage in contractual bargaining with them. They could even be required to provide confidential organising and communication functionalities in the apps their workers have to use.

Third, governments could overhaul their own labour and welfare laws so that whatever benefits and rights workers are entitled to through the welfare system are the same for the same amount of work, regardless of whether it is done for a single employer, for a platform, or as conventional self-employment. This could automatically make public benefits portable, which would also prevent any penalty in the benefit system for switching jobs. As I have discussed, easy job switching is an important ingredient in boosting broad-based prosperity.

3. Power, monopoly, and market abuse. One of the most deprived areas of the United States—the coal-mining country of West Virginia and Kentucky—owes much of its deprivation to a particularly insidious form of monopoly power. Traditionally, many coal miners in those areas have lived in private company towns, where mining companies themselves have run and managed everything, and not to the mine workers' benefit. Physically isolated, workers could not go elsewhere to meet their needs, and they were even frequently paid in company "scrip," private money that could only be used in the company store. The result was to extract most of what miners were paid, a practice that continued well past the Second World War: "The greatest drain on the miners' wages was the company store. . . . Coercion, the scrip system, and the physical distance often combined to force the miners to deal at the company store, and through the monopolistic control of food and clothing and tools and powder, the coal companies were able to render wage rates and wage increases meaningless."[23] The scandal of a company town's controlling every part of people's lives is a reminder that the economy of belonging was never fully established in the United States—and should serve as a warning that market abuse is a potent force of disempowerment. Unfortunately, it is again on the rise in parts of the West, and the digital revolution makes it a growing danger everywhere.

At times, Western policy makers across the political spectrum have seen market power as an evil to be contained, if not eliminated. From 1890 to 1950, for example, the United States passed ever-stricter legislation on monopolistic companies and conduct, often under Republican presidents.[24] Theodore Roosevelt, the early twentieth-century president (and uncle to Franklin), was known as a "trust-buster" for his policies against the trusts or cartels of monopolistic businesses that dominated the economy. In recent years, the trust-busting torch has passed from the United States to Europe. In what the economist Thomas Philippon calls "the great reversal," Europe now enforces market competition better than the United States, with the result that Americans are more likely to be left at the mercy of high prices and abuse of market power than Europeans.[25]

Here are three ways in which monopoly power is working against an economy of belonging or risks doing so in the future.

First, when there is less competition, prices are higher and businesses charge bigger markups on their costs. That is good for them and those insiders who get to share in the greater profits with less effort, but bad for those consumers and outsiders who face higher costs and lower wages. In the United States in particular, the market share of the biggest companies has gone up in the last few decades in industries ranging from finance and agriculture to hospitals and railroads. President Barack Obama's economics advisers showed that this had increased inequality, because companies with market power paid much better than those that were struggling. Much of the increase in US income inequality over the last decades has come not from inequality between the low and high paid within each company—between, say, the janitor and the CEO, though that has increased, too—but from a growing difference between what a janitor at a successful company is paid and what a janitor at an unsuccessful one is paid.[26] In Europe and Japan, in contrast, concentration has not increased as much, perhaps because competition regulators have been more active.[27] But everywhere, the rate at which newcomers enter markets to challenge established companies seems to be falling, which also reduces competitive pressures and therefore makes pro-competitive policy all the more important.[28]

Second, location can be a factor affecting market power. In small places, a supermarket chain, call centre, or delivery warehouse may offer the only jobs available to people with low formal skills. It is then hard to challenge poor working conditions. In the United States, employers have reduced competition for staff further by introducing "noncompete" clauses in employment contracts, making it harder for workers to take another job even when one exists.[29]

Third, the digital revolution threatens to worsen the imbalance of power further, inside production relationships, within labour markets, and against consumers. In production, because if bigger companies can make better use of digital technologies to reduce their costs and outcompete smaller ones, their market share becomes even bigger. In labour markets, it seems inevitable that the digital revolution will continue to upend traditional work structures. Not only will many jobs—such as driving or retail—become scarcer, but fragmented flexible working will increasingly take the place of regular full-time employment. Internet platforms will play a part in this—not just the well-known ones such as Uber and TaskRabbit but across the economy. The concept of the internet platform is now a well-established model to intermediate between buyers and sellers of services, as it makes it easy to solicit and offer work outside permanent work relationships. But that also means platforms will to a large extent regulate the conditions under which people work and the terms on which new businesses can bring their products and services to market. What is more, platforms have a built-in tendency toward monopoly, because a platform becomes more competitive against others the more users it has. And finally, the digital revolution risks harming consumers because of the enormous power personal data harvesting brings. Knowing people's personalities makes it easier to exploit any vulnerabilities they may have to manipulative advertising—a risk, as we have seen, in politics as well as in commerce.

No single class of policy can stop all these forces of concentration and power inequality. Certainly traditional competition and antimarket abuse policies must be intensified and enforced, and made to work efficiently against digital companies. The traditional menu of policies goes well beyond fines, and policy makers should not be afraid of breaking companies up or, short of that, "behavioural regulation," which is to say legally ordering a company (not) to behave in certain ways. But to transform markets more profoundly to restore a more equitable balance of power, it is necessary to empower those at the wrong end of market abuse.

In the realm of personal data, governments should define strong and enforceable ownership rights for those the information is collected from, so that they have effective control over what happens to their data and can be paid for its use. In the labour market, the policies I outlined earlier in the chapter go a long way towards rebalancing power by making independence safe for workers. The same independence principle should be extended to policies to help smaller businesses compete without being taken advantage of by dominant competitors or monopolistic platforms. A good example is the European Commission's probe into Amazon, which is accused of using its sales platform to get data on successful small businesses before demoting them in search results in favour of its own sales.[30]

Similarly, governments should, as far as possible, neutralise the anticompetitive effect of scale, by minimising the fixed costs of running a business. Digital automation can do a lot of this: witness Estonia, where all interaction with the government is digitised on the basis of "the 'once only' policy, which dictates that no single piece of information should be entered twice."[31] Online applications are being built to make tax reporting automatic when transactions are conducted,[32] and to automate business tax payments.[33] One can imagine automating small-business accounting in the same way. Where necessary, authorities can set data standards that make it possible to require competing platforms to make themselves interoperable, getting away from the monopolistic winner-takes-all structure. Governments can even develop their own platforms on an open interface basis. For example, the Norwegian government has developed Entur, a national route planner app that integrates all existing transport planning information in a single interface that allows travel planning and ticket purchases anywhere in the country.[34]

All the policies set out in this chapter have one thing in common: they increase competition. They do so by understanding that it is necessary to restore a balance of power that allows workers to move between employers and businesses to compete on the merits of what they have to offer. Otherwise, disempowered workers and small businesses cannot challenge and compete with the most powerful actors. The overarching principle is that *protective* policies can also be *pro-competitive* policies, and vice versa. Getting these protections right—so that they favour those at risk of precarity or market exclusion, rather than those who dominate them—can also improve productivity and benefit the whole economy.

8

Macroeconomic Policy for the Left Behind

The remedy for the boom is not a higher rate of interest but a lower rate of interest! For that may enable the so-called boom to last. The right remedy for the trade cycle is not to be found in abolishing booms and thus keeping us permanently in a semi-slump; but in abolishing slumps and thus keeping us permanently in a quasi-boom.

—JOHN MAYNARD KEYNES, 1936[1]

The end of belonging in Western economies started many decades ago. It was the product of deep, slow-moving forces— above all, technological change—and a permanent improvement will require equally long-term policies. But a programme for a new economics of belonging should start by ensuring that misguided short-term policies do not add to the chronic problems—a sort of Hippocratic do-no-harm oath for economic policy makers.

The most important short-term economic policies are those that affect the amount of spending in the whole economy, known as macroeconomic policies. The economy moves in cycles, where total desired spending can outrun the capacity to produce all the goods and services people seek to buy, causing the economy to "overheat," before giving way to a slump in spending where demand falls short of the economy's supply capacity. In those slumps, resources lie idle, with people unemployed and productive capital underused, unless macroeconomic policy can make up for the missing private demand.

Policy makers have two main tools of boosting aggregate demand when necessary. Fiscal policy adjusts budget deficits, which can create more demand through spending than is taken out of the private economy via taxes. Monetary policy adjusts the cost of borrowing, with lower interest rates encouraging consumers to spend and businesses to invest.

There are two reasons why good macroeconomic policy matters for an economy of belonging. One is that it is an essential support for the longer-term reforms needed to make the economy work for everyone. In the last two chapters, I have advocated policies to shift the economy towards more productive, higher-paid jobs and to rebalance power and risk in favour of the most vulnerable members of our societies. But as I have already mentioned, these policies are not enough on their own: they may put an end to some jobs that exist today without creating a big enough number of new, better ones. This is where macroeconomic policy comes in. To ensure that the labour market changes I have described really do bring everyone along with them, spending in the economy must grow robustly enough that there is demand for employers to create the new and more productive jobs in sufficient numbers.

There is a second reason why macroeconomic policy matters to the left behind, besides supporting policies to create better jobs. Poor macroeconomic policy can on its own directly undermine the economic social contract. The costs of mismanaged aggregate demand fall disproportionately on those on the margins of the economy, hurting the already left behind or adding new victims to their ranks. That is what happened after the downturn triggered by the global financial crisis of 2008.

As John Maynard Keynes insisted more than eighty years ago, macroeconomic policy must aim to make good economic times last as long as possible and, conversely, to end recessions as fast as can be done. For a short moment in April 2009, world leaders lived up to this standard. Assembled for a summit in London, they committed to a coordinated stimulus of their economies, using both government budgets and central bank policies to reverse the collapse in economic activity and get the global economy back to growth. They succeeded. By letting budget deficits soar, cutting official interest rates to lows never seen before, and "printing" (really electronically creating) central bank money to buy bonds in order to make financing cheaper for households and businesses, they turned around the deepest slump since the 1930s. By late 2009, the recovery was under way.

But no sooner had growth returned than the same countries, often under the very same leaders, abruptly changed tack. Governments that a year earlier had focused on ending the recession were now increasingly apprehensive about their bleeding budgets. Budget deficits touched 10 per cent of national income in the United States, Japan, and the UK; 11 per cent in Spain; and 7 per cent in France. Even frugal Germany's deficit exceeded 4.2 per cent in 2009. Now, this was neither unexpected nor inappropriate. Record deficits were the combined result of the worst downturn since the 1930s and the correct policy choice to restore collapsed growth with fiscal pump priming. If any-thing, they were too small to offset fully the contraction in private spending. But no matter: from Europe to the United States, defi-cit reduction became a prime objective for policy makers. The era of austerity had begun. But in shifting their focus from growth to public finances, they were taking the recovery for granted.

Something similar happened to monetary policy. In concert with the coordinated fiscal stimulus in 2009, central banks had cut interest rates to levels never seen before. In the United King-dom and the United States, monetary policy makers had also bought large amounts of financial securities in order to inject newly created money into the economy. But central bankers, too, were getting cold feet. Increasingly consumed with how to "normalise"—that is to say, tighten—credit conditions, they also took the recovery for granted. In 2011, the European Cen-tral Bank even moved to increase interest rates.

The result of this premature turn to caution has been, at best, a lost decade. The eurozone was the worst case of self-harm: fiscal and monetary tightening in 2011 stamped out the recovery and tipped the bloc into a second recession by 2012. In the United States, the economy continued to recover but unimpressively; it never fired on all cylinders.

At the time of writing, the share of Americans in work has barely caught up with where it was in 2007. Unemployment has returned to precrisis lows and below, but it took the United States eight years of steady growth to get there. Europe was slower: it took ten years to unwind the jump in the EU-wide joblessness rate at the start of the crisis. Within Europe, the eurozone took even longer; its worst-hit member countries have still not returned to their precrisis employment rates. As for the United Kingdom, while unemployment came down fast and the share of people working has reached record highs, wage growth recorded its worst decade since the Napoleonic Wars. None of these can be called healthy recoveries; they are more like dragged-out slumps.

These numbers tell stories about the economy in aggregate. But recessions are not evenhanded: cruelly, they hit the worst off the hardest. This is obscured if you only watch a downturn through the prism of aggregate measures, such as the overall unemployment rate or the national pace of output growth. Many people lose jobs in a recession, but not all people are affected the same. Those already on the margins of the labour market suffer much more than the average population when jobs disappear in a downturn—those with low education, the young, many minority or immigrant groups, and in general those we have come to call the left behind.

Figure 8.1 shows that these groups, who are unemployed at higher rates than the overall population even at the best of times, suffer more job losses at the start of a recession than the average worker and remain more likely to be unemployed for longer.[2] This "unemployment gap"—the difference in the rates at which marginalised groups and average workers are unemployed—widens when overall unemployment rises; in other words, unemployment rises faster for those already more likely to be unemployed. In the United States, for example, "when the unemployment rate of whites increases by 1 percentage point, the unemployment rates of African Americans and Hispanics rise by well more than 1 percentage point."[3] It is only when a recovery is well established that the unemployment gap begins to shrink, showing that the average unemployment rate is a poor guide to how difficult it is for marginalised groups to get back into work. Simply put, they are fired first and hired last—and to help them, the recovery must be squeezed for all it is worth and not be prematurely snuffed out.[4] And if

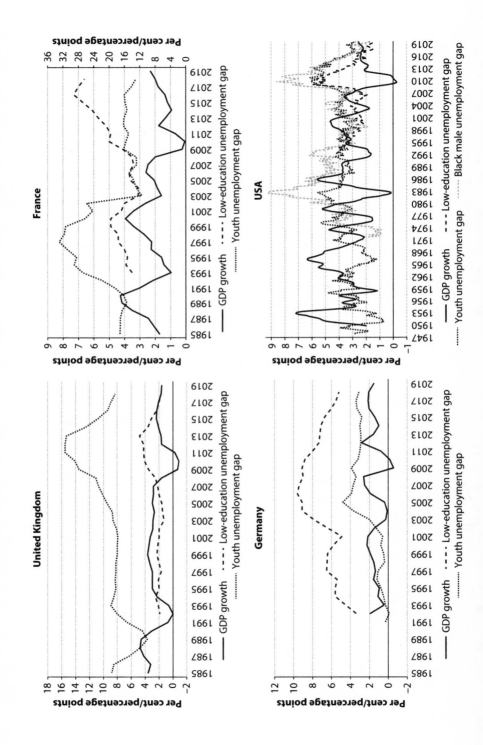

it is allowed to continue, those on the margins do benefit in the end; in the United Kingdom, for example, the tight labour market with record-high employment is making it easier for ex-prisoners to return to work.[5]

The unequal effects of a downturn in the economy are further compounded if a government responds by reining in budget deficits. Because these groups are likely to be most dependent on public support and the welfare state, it is obvious that austerity in the public finances also poses a much greater risk to them than to the average citizen. But that is only the beginning of the harms inflicted on the weakest groups by tight-fisted macroeconomic policies—harms that we know fuel the rejection of the liberal order.[6] It is important to understand that there are many other ways a recession or a stagnating economy affects marginal groups disproportionately—even in the absence of welfare budget cuts.

FIGURE 8.1. Real gross domestic product growth, annualised three-year moving averages, and unemployment gaps for four G7 economies. Annual data (quarterly for the US). Low-education gap is percentage-point difference between unemployment rate above age 24 for those with less than upper secondary education and for all education levels. Youth gap is percentage-point difference between unemployment rate for those aged 15–24 (20–24 in the US) and for those above age 24 (whole labour force in the US). Black male gap in the US is percentage-point difference between unemployment rate for black or African American men above age 19 and that for the whole labour force.

Sources: Europe: "GDP and Main Components (Output, Expenditure and Income)," Eurostat, last updated 2 January 2020, https://ec.europa.eu/eurostat/en/web /products-datasets/-/NAMA_10_GDP; and "Employment and Unemployment Statistics (Labour Force Survey)" (database), Eurostat, accessed 12 February 2020, https://ec.europa.eu/eurostat/web/lfs/data/database. United States: "Gross Domestic Product," US Bureau of Economic Analysis, last modified 17 May 2019, https://www.bea.gov/data/gdp/gross-domestic-product; and "Labor Force Statistics from the Current Population Survey—Unemployment," US Bureau of Labor Statistics, last modified 7 February 2020, https://www.bls.gov/cps /lfcharacteristics.htm#unemp.

Over the economic cycle, the people in these groups are out of work longer and in work for a shorter length of time than a typical worker. That hits their incomes directly, and by more than average earnings growth numbers would suggest. Staying longer outside the ranks of the employed also chips away at their employability in the future, and at their earning power once they manage to find work again. The longer someone is out of work, the harder it is to keep his or her skills up-to-date for future jobs. And we know that lack of work experience at the start of adult life casts a shadow decades into the future. Those who take longer to get into work in their twenties end up with lower earnings over their lifetimes, and this effect is stronger for those who already start out with fewer advantages in the labour market.[7] Longer recessions, in other words, plant the seeds of permanently greater inequality.

And not only greater inequality. It is bad enough that macroeconomic mismanagement makes for a more unfair division of the economic pie, but it also makes the pie smaller than it might be otherwise.

Many policy makers who steer macroeconomic policy are guided by a model of the economy in which business cycles are temporary fluctuations around a stable long-term trend. This view encourages central bankers to assume responsibility for minimising those swings—but to decide policy as if the long-term trend were given, and unaffected by their own moves to achieve short-term stabilisation. There is strong evidence, however, that temporary downturns can leave permanent scars on an economy's productivity in the long run. Despite what central bankers almost universally profess to believe, theory and experience suggest that short-term aggregate demand management does affect the underlying trend of the economy's productivity and the amount of wealth it can produce.

There are a number of reasons why this is the case. Investment is always the part of spending that falls most in a downturn—private investment because businesses are pessimistic about demand for what they sell and public investment because when governments want to limit soaring deficits, the easiest option is to postpone infrastructure and other projects. (Most Western governments have been investing significantly less after the crisis than they did before; some hardly spend enough to maintain the existing public capital stock.) But less investment in new capital means a less productive economy in the future, even after the downturn is over. Central banks that are slow to ease borrowing costs and governments that worry about their budgets contribute to this problem by keeping investment lower than it could be. Conversely, expanding budgetary spending (especially on public investment) and making financing cheaper can spark optimism about demand growth, which both is self-reinforcing (more spending leads to more hiring and higher incomes) and spurs businesses to invest in more capital to meet that anticipated demand.

In addition to new investment, businesses demonstrably respond to demand pressures by using more productively the resources they already have. Having more orders from customers than you can fill is the best possible encouragement to find ways to make more with the same inputs. This is why we generally see that productivity is "pro-cyclical"—it increases in upswings and falls in downturns.[8]

But the most important reason why a sustained level of demand pressure in the economy should be good for overall productivity is the same reason why it is good for equality: it draws the vulnerable and the left behind in from the margins of the economy. The waste of human potential I described in the previous two chapters, from people being stuck in low-productivity jobs or left with no employment at all, is quite conceivably the biggest avoidable drag on productivity in Western economies, and it therefore exacts a price in lost prosperity even on those who are doing well. To be clear, simply getting those on the margins into jobs is not enough (and may even drag average productivity down if the new jobs are poor ones); the point is to combine policies that together shift people from low-productivity jobs or no jobs at all into employment with higher or faster-rising productivity. Even those with few formal qualifications, for example, have been shown to be more productive when employed in companies that invest more in innovation.[9]

The costs of weak demand are, in other words, much greater than policy makers tend to admit. The aftermath of the global financial crisis is a glaring example, but a team of International Monetary Fund economists have established that this is the rule, rather than the exception.[10] Recoveries are rarely complete, in the sense that after a downturn, economic growth, on average, fails to catch up fully with the earlier trend—and this is especially true after financial crises.

But conversely, policy can make a positive difference, if it aims to keep demand pressures high. What Keynes called for so many decades ago is the same as what a minority of economists are calling for today under the label of a "high-pressure economy." This is an approach to macroeconomic policy that aims to keep aggregate demand at a high level at all times, and that stimulates it aggressively and persistently whenever a flagging desire to spend among households and businesses threatens to send the economy into reverse.

This is not what we have had in the West since the 1980s. The closest was in the 1990s, when Federal Reserve chair Alan Greenspan decided to ignore fears of overheating and presided over a productivity boom and demand growth that temporarily reversed the forces that were undermining the economy of belonging in the United States. That episode turned out to be an exception that confirmed standard policy practice. Even after the global financial crisis, macroeconomic policy was marred by nervousness about going too far.

This caution is a serious mistake. The same research that finds long-term losses from short-term demand weakness also establishes that greater macroeconomic stimulus can help to minimise the permanent loss of national income and productivity. Rather than worry about too much demand leading an economy to overheat, we should heed the evidence that after a downturn, economies can take significant stimulus in their stride. Productivity growth is usually particularly high in strong economic recoveries: in other words, pushing the economy to exceed its perceived speed limit helps to push the limit up.[11] And economies where policy makers have succeeded in making the short-term swings less violent by stimulating more aggressively in downturns are rewarded with higher long-term growth rates.[12]

What does all of this add up to? Every downturn delivers a particularly harsh series of blows for those already left behind by long-term trends. It creates permanent setbacks for those suffering a downturn at the start of their working lives. If policy makers can soften or shorten a downturn but fail to do so, they aggravate the suffering of the left behind and expand their numbers. And the resources available to help them—the economy's overall productive potential—are lower in the long run the deeper and more frequent the slumps. In short, the price of timidity in the short-term management of downturns is permanent damage to livelihoods, hitting those with the fewest advantages hardest.

A macroeconomic policy geared towards supporting an economy of belonging must aim for high-pressure demand conditions as the economy's normal state. That requires a change in the standard perspective guiding mainstream macroeconomic policy makers. This aims to minimise the short-term fluctuations in economic activity around what they see as the steady trend and uses the rate of inflation as a yardstick to measure whether they are doing so. In simplified terms, if prices rise faster than the target (2 per cent annual consumer inflation is the commonly targeted rate), economic growth is unsustainably fast and policy should be tightened; if inflation is lower, economic activity is considered below its potential and demand should be boosted by stronger stimulus.

Note two things about this conventional perspective: it is *symmetric*, and it takes the *average* of the economy to determine the right policy action. An alternative perspective, to institutionalise a high-pressure policy orientation, would be *asymmetric* and look at the *margins* of the economy.

An asymmetric take on cyclical policy would be more concerned about the harms of a recession than about overheating in a boom. The facts that bouts of unemployment and periods of subpar growth leave an economy permanently less productive and that productivity responds when demand stimulus may seem to run up against the economy's limit justify an explicit bias towards stimulus. They justify aiming for an economy where demand pressures are as much as possible kept just ahead of the economy's potential, in the expectation that this can prolong booms and shorten slumps, as Keynes encouraged in the 1930s.

Aiming for a high-pressure economy would also take the economy's performance at the margin rather than the average as the most relevant measure of whether the policy stance is right. That is because we know the demand pressure is high precisely when it reaches those most left behind by structural disadvantages. Demand is only sufficiently strong, in this perspective, when those most likely to be unemployed are finally pulled in from the sidelines of the labour market, when employers must improve wage and work conditions even for the least well paid in order to keep up with demand, and where their confidence in continued growth makes them put in the effort to make even the least skilled workers more productive.

Is this too good to be true? When a high-pressure economy has been tried, it has worked. In the United States in the 1990s, the Federal Reserve kept interest rates lower than a conventional analysis of the economy's capacity would have indicated. But instead of overheating, the economy's speed limit turned out to be higher—productivity growth increased (thanks in part to the revolution in information technology), and labour force participation reached an all-time high at the end of the 1990s.

Contrast this with the post-2008 recovery.[13] It took a decade to put as many prime working-age Americans (defined as those between twenty-five and fifty-four years old) back to work as had been employed right before the crisis—79.5 per cent of that age cohort. With higher demand pressure, there is no reason why that could not have been achieved much earlier, at the very least by 2013, when output had recovered past its pre-recession peak. Because of lack of demand, there were five or more entirely unnecessary years of underemployment, the burden of which was felt disproportionately by the young, the lower skilled, and others on the margin of the labour market. Macroeconomic policy caused a lost decade for the US economy—a missed opportunity to make the economy work for everyone.

It is impossible to justify the postcrisis macroeconomic policy in the West on the grounds that these outcomes were satisfactory, whether in the United States, as just illustrated, or in most other Western economies post-2010. Even on their own terms, central bankers must admit they have failed: across the

Western world, inflation rates have remained stubbornly below central banks' targets, let alone risen above them because of the economy overheating. One could argue, however, that macroeconomic *policy* reached its limits even if the *economy* did not. And during the West's slow recovery, it was widely believed that policy makers had done all they could because policy was powerless to boost aggregate demand any more than it already did.

While it was rarely put in those terms, this belief amounted to macroeconomic policy makers pleading impotence. Why did they think they had done all they could to speed up the recovery? The answer depends on whether we are talking about fiscal stimulus, achieved by increasing government spending or cutting taxes, or monetary stimulus, which central banks carry out by cutting official interest rates or otherwise injecting newly minted money into the economy.

On the fiscal side, the argument has been that more deficit spending would drive governments closer to bankruptcy, an alleged constraint going by the name of "fiscal space." That concept, a staple of macroeconomic policy discussions from Washington to Brussels, is supposed to capture how far a government can go in using budget deficits to stimulate demand without public finances becoming unsustainable. If debts spiral out of control or markets refuse to lend the government money except at prohibitive interest rates, it may seem sensible to worry that expanding deficits makes this risk worse. That, at any rate, was the main argument behind the universal swing to austerity in 2010–11, in the United States, in the United Kingdom, and across the eurozone—including in countries, such as Germany, where it was absurd to say their public finances were in jeopardy.

No doubt the argument was at times vicarious, advanced by those (especially in the United Kingdom and the United

States) who saw an opportunity to shrink the state and those (especially in the eurozone) who worried that indebted governments would require help from other countries' taxpayers. But more importantly, the argument is flawed. While deficits funded from public borrowing add to the nominal amount of public debt, deficit expansion in a depressed economy adds to growth, increasing the national income from which the debt has to be paid—even increasing it permanently, for the reasons just outlined. Fiscal austerity in a downturn, far from being necessary to bring public debt under control, makes a debt problem worse; and deficit-funded fiscal stimulus, far from exceeding limited "fiscal space," improves a depressed economy's ability to service its debts (and this positive arithmetic is amplified the larger the debt burden at the outset).

This realisation gradually imposed itself on the policy-making establishment. In 2012, the centre-left economists Bradford DeLong and Lawrence Summers published an article showing that in a depressed economy where interest rates will not be reduced further—the situation in much of the eurozone, and, indeed, most of the Western world—a fiscal stimulus could pay for itself by creating enough additional growth that the extra tax revenues more than covered the original deficit expansion.[14] The following year, the International Monetary Fund's chief economist, Olivier Blanchard, found that the fund had significantly underestimated the effect of fiscal policy on growth in depressed European economies.[15] By now it had been demonstrated beyond doubt that austerity in the eurozone worsened rather than lightened the public debt burden.[16] In 2019, Blanchard, an elite member of mainstream academic economics, used his presidential address to the American Economic Association to consecrate the new orthodoxy that when interest rates are low, "public debt may have no fiscal cost."[17]

What all this means is that the notion of "fiscal space" borders on incoherence. If fiscal stimulus in a recession *improves* public finances, then deficit expansion creates the fiscal space it needs. The constraint used to excuse fiscal inaction—or worse—after the Great Recession turns out to have largely existed only in policy makers' own minds.

There is one exception. Where governments find themselves unable to borrow the money for deficit spending in their budgets, the limits of "fiscal space" are real. This happened to Greece and other countries hit by the eurozone debt crisis of 2010–12. Meanwhile, on the monetary side, the claim has been that once interest rates come close to zero—often dubbed the "zero lower bound"—central banks run out of ammunition to boost demand. In both cases, the excuse for letting economy-wide spending collapse is nevertheless weaker than it may seem. The reasons for this, however, belong to a much broader theme, which is how the West's financial system has worked against the economy of belonging, and what policies are required to change this. Those are questions I turn to in the next chapter.

The plea of macroeconomic policy impotence is also rooted in part in historical experience. Demand stimulus had been used to try to revive prosperity in the face of the deep forces that were tearing at the economic social contract, with policy makers deploying public deficit spending in the 1980s and cheap credit in the 2000s. By the time of the global financial crisis, this seemed to have brought nothing but an overhang of high government debt in many European countries, and a bubble of private debt ready to burst on both sides of the Atlantic.

Those episodes should not, however, be seen in isolation from other policy choices. In the previous two chapters, I described how Western economies could be shifted towards a model of high-productivity and secure work—with the caveat that for those policies really to enable such an economy of belonging, macroeconomic policy must also do its job of sustaining high demand growth. Conversely, in the absence of those structural policies to change the labour market, demand boost may not do much on its own. That explains why the results of the 1980s fiscal stimulus and the 2000s credit stimulus were so ephemeral. But it also shows that they are no argument against a high-pressure economy, provided other policies of economic belonging are also in place.

Notwithstanding an avoidably slow recovery, most Western economies are now approaching full employment or have already passed it. But it would be wrong to think that this renders macroeconomic policy irrelevant in pursuit of the bigger goal of rebuilding an economy of belonging. Another downturn will come sooner or later—at the time of this writing, pessimism is again in the air—and cyclical swings are an inevitable part of market economies.

The argument of this chapter has been that the policy mistakes from the last recession were not one-offs. Instead, they reflect a macroeconomic policy mind-set that systematically underplays the ability of policy makers to run the economy at a "hotter" pace over time, fulfilling Keynes's call for keeping us permanently in a quasi-boom, and thereby alleviating, if not eliminating, the harms stagnation causes the left behind and marginalised groups. This mind-set is a learned helplessness camouflaged as responsibility, and there is every reason to think it will produce mistakes again. The first step towards rebuilding an economy of belonging, therefore, is to change a macroeconomic policy regime that threatens it at every downturn.

9

A Smarter Financial System

When the anticonsumerist magazine *Adbusters* issued a call to "occupy Wall Street" in 2011, the scale and speed of the response took everyone by surprise—including perhaps the Occupiers themselves. Anticapitalist activists and their sympathisers flooded the streets, starting in Zuccotti Park in Manhattan and spreading quickly to St Paul's Cathedral in London, next to the London Stock Exchange, and across the world. But the real surprise is that this did not happen sooner. Anger with the banks and the mess they had caused had been boiling for three years. Even the US House of Representatives, not normally an anti–Wall Street body, had attempted to impose a 90 per cent tax rate on bonuses at bailed-out financial companies.

The Occupy Wall Street movement did not have the political impact that its global scale and the media attention it commanded might have led one to expect.[1] Its criticisms of financiers and the financial system have been appropriated by populists who include them in their general denunciations of Western liberalism. Beyond them, however, those criticisms have not been adopted more broadly. But they should, for restoring an economy of belonging requires deep reforms of the financial sector.

There are three main charges against finance. One is that it is destabilising: it creates booms and busts, and as the previous chapter explained, such swings inflict the most pain on the most vulnerable. The second is that it chronically distorts the economy, and the distortions create gains for a few at the top while undermining broad-based prosperity. And the third is that by its global nature, finance wriggles free of any discipline national governments may try to impose on it. In this chapter I want to show that the first two charges are well justified—but also set out a range of policy responses national policy makers should resort to in response. If they do, they can remedy much of what is wrong on the first two counts, proving that the third worry need not require going back on economic openness.

Start with the first charge: instability. Finance is indeed inherently destabilising. The main reason is that the banks' creation of credit is self-reinforcing. (While banks' activities are the most straightforward to describe, other parts of the financial system—such as the packaging of mortgages into tradeable securities in the run-up to the global financial crisis—can create similar self-reinforcing dynamics.) Lending booms bid up the financial value of assets, which therefore look like safer security for loans. Since this seemingly improves both the business case for lending and the safety of banks' balance sheets, credit growth intensifies the incentives for more lending. This fuels the demand for goods and services, partly directly because of the easy access to loans, partly indirectly because of optimistic expectations of continued strong growth. This anticipation encourages businesses to hire, invest, and expand;

and it encourages people to spend as houses and other assets go up in price, making them feel richer. For as long as this goes on, every person's exuberant spending is justified by the exuberant spending of everybody else.

But this depends on individual expectations that together do not add up: even if credit-powered exuberance pushes growth higher for a while, it is not enough to make everyone as wealthy as they think they will become. At some point, this cannot go on any longer. When people adjust their expectations down, the bubble bursts, and all the mechanisms just mentioned go into reverse. Consumers hold back spending; businesses cut investment and let employees go. Asset prices fall, and people feel poorer or, even worse, are trapped by "underwater" debt, such as mortgages on which they owe more than their houses are now worth. Such debt can be crippling. Not only does it prevent people from moving in search of better job prospects, but they may also find it harder to service the debt, especially if their incomes are suddenly lower than they originally thought they would be. And it dooms entrepreneurial spirits who could have been successful if past debt accumulation did not wreck their chances of getting any new credit. All these things—the upswing and the downturn—happened in the United States around the 2008 crisis.

But arguably the most damaging effect of a bursting credit bubble is what it does to the financial system that inflated the bubble to start with. As demand growth falters and asset prices fall, loans made in the boom suddenly look less profitable and more risky. Out of self-preservation, the priority of lenders is to reduce their exposure and stop making new loans altogether—even to profitable ventures. When Spain and Italy fell into banking crises after the 2008–9 downturn, a common complaint was that even exporting businesses, whose prospects were relatively rosy, struggled to expand because they could not obtain the necessary credit to do so.

Banking regulations designed to keep banks safe have too often amplified these self-reinforcing spirals. That is because in a boom, high asset values make banks look safe, so they are permitted to expand further. Then in the bust, banks look endangered, so the rules require them to "deleverage" or scale down their loans according to their ability to absorb losses without going bankrupt.

What this means is that finance worsens the problems I described in chapter 8. The self-reinforcing nature of (especially) banking, unless carefully regulated, intensifies the economy's cycles and makes downturns deeper and more protracted. History shows that a rapid increase in bank credit is a telltale sign of a looming crisis, that economic slumps are worse in areas that have seen particularly fast credit buildup, and that recoveries from a recession caused by a financial bust are slower than from ordinary business-cycle downturns.[2] Since we know downturns hurt the left behind and the vulnerable more than the average person, financial cycles are a chronic danger to strong economies of belonging.

Financial instability also makes it harder for governments to act forcefully to maintain the high-pressure economy I called for in the previous chapter. When a credit boom leaves a trail of underwater debtors or "zombie" companies that spend most of their revenue on servicing debt, even a solid government stimulus may struggle to spur increased spending and investment in those parts of the economy: the debt overhang constrains the private sector's ability to respond to stimulus.[3] But worse, a debt overhang may constrain governments too. A downturn inevitably increases budget deficits, partly for the good reason that a fiscal stimulus is the right policy in a downturn, and often for the more dubious reason that governments take responsibility for private debts by bailing them out. As I explained in the previous chapter, unsustainable public debt (or lack of "fiscal space") is usually a bad reason for restraining fiscal stimulus in a downturn, but there are cases in which there is no choice. Greece in 2009, like several other eurozone countries in the years that followed, found that its big public debt overhang scared away the markets so that it could not borrow money for its huge deficits without help from other governments.[4]

Instability, however, is only one of the ways in which excessive finance undermines an economy of belonging. Beyond worsening cyclical ups and downs, a badly regulated financial sector also chronically steers the economy in the wrong direction. "Financialisation," the increasing size and influence of the financial sector on decision-making in other parts of the economy, has arguably struck at least three blows to the postwar economy of belonging: the falling share of wages in national income, the widening gaps between regions, and the slowdown in overall productivity growth.

Here is why. One harmful effect of financial sophistication is to increase the ability of the managers and financiers who control the allocation of capital to extract economic value for themselves. Much of the increase in financial activity has had that function. That includes practices such as using stock market options to engineer payouts for top executives out of all proportion to the value they create;[5] using financial engineering to break apart or merge companies, which on the whole does not increase productivity but generates fees for investment banks; or individualising savings that used to be implicit and collective, such as pensions provision or student funding. Similarly, the number of intermediaries in the financial chain between savers and borrowers has multiplied while there has been a general increase in financial trading—for which financiers are paid by volume, rather than for creating any underlying economic value. In addition, growing levels of credit favours those who already own assets because it helps them borrow to accumulate even more—leading, for example, to a concentration of house ownership and putting it out of reach for those with little or no wealth. The consequences of these changes are manifest in how the division of national income has shifted in most countries. The financial sector's share and that of individuals at the very top have gone up; the share paid out in wages has gone down. The distribution of wealth has become more unequal everywhere.

This capture of economic value by the financial and managerial sectors and by the asset-rich, moreover, does not play out equally across the land. There is a case, put forcefully by Nicholas Shaxson,[6] that an outsize banking sector may be a prime cause of regional divergence because it facilitates financial engineering that draws money from around a country into the cities that house financial centres. Many Western countries saw a spike in regional inequality in the 1980s. This reflected the move towards financial liberalisation across the Western world in that decade, which created a burst of income flowing to financial centres in places with incomes already above national averages.

But even where Shaxson's charge does not fully apply— divergence happens in many countries without serious financialisation—a general shift of income towards capital owners increases the income and wealth gap between regions even if it does not benefit the financial sector itself. That is simply because the asset-rich tend to be concentrated in more affluent places. And banking may make things worse. Just as credit creation (and destruction) is self-reinforcing over *time*, unequal provision of credit between different *places* is self-reinforcing, too. Profit-maximising banks will pour more lending into sectors or places that already have plenty of it (because that is where asset values are high), and stay away from those in the grip of a credit drought (where they are low).[7]

Finally, an overgrown financial sector allocates resources to the wrong things. Rather than funding the business activities that promise most productivity growth, it, too, often funds activities that offer physical security for loans—above all, real estate and construction.[8] In contrast, the sectors of the future—especially knowledge-intensive ones with only intangible assets—get less funding than they need.[9] This is a feature of credit, and above all bank credit, because such loans commonly require the borrower to offer security that the promised payment terms are upheld. Noncredit financing—such as equity or other forms of direct or indirect ownership—does not promise a predefined return that needs to be secured. Instead, investors get a return that depends on the investments' profitability, as well as retaining a risk of loss if the investment is unsuccessful. Once we realise that loans with fixed payment terms are not well suited to productivity-boosting but risky investments, it should come as no surprise that beyond certain levels, more debt in an economy reduces growth—again, especially bank debt—whereas this is not the case with more stock market funding.[10]

So there we have it. The financial sector has been allowed to grow into something that increases the inequality between people and regions, and reduces the economy's overall ability to create prosperity. And while the activists of Occupy Wall Street would no doubt agree, these conclusions have in recent years also been endorsed at the pinnacles of the financial policy establishment: the International Monetary Fund, the OECD, and the Bank for International Settlements. In his presidential address to the American Finance Association—the heart of financial economics' intellectual orthodoxy—the economist Luigi Zingales summed it up like this in 2015: "There is no theoretical reason or empirical evidence to support the notion that all the growth of the financial sector in the last 40 years has been beneficial to society."[11]

What, then, must we do to make it so? In the pages that follow, I set out the principles for how an economics of belonging must regulate finance, but before that, I want to underline one point. All the problems of excess financialisation that I have noted thus far arise even in the absence of any financial *globalisation*. To think that they could largely have been avoided if only national borders were more closed to capital flows is to underestimate the effect of deregulatory policies at the purely domestic level. Conversely, I contend that the solutions outlined shortly can remedy a lot of finance's ill effects without giving up on financial openness. Indeed, they would make cross-border finance itself safer (in part because we could expect them to make international capital flows smaller, not by putting obstacles in their way but because the motivations for sending money across borders would be weaker). I develop this argument further in chapter 12.

Wean the economy off credit financing. The most radical goal of a financial economics of belonging is to protect against the harms of credit by weaning the economy off debt financing. As I pointed out earlier, credit (or debt, depending on your perspective), and especially bank credit, is a particularly noxious form of finance, both in its instability and in the way it erodes economic growth by directing capital to activities with low productivity potential. Debt has also at times pacified the left behind by offering apparent improvements in consumption that are in the end unsustainable, at the cost of eventually leaving some trapped with greater debt burdens than they had been led to expect.[12]

This trap is all the more insidious as it blunts the tools policy makers have to relaunch the growth that would make the debt burden more easily bearable. Overindebted people spend any income increases on reducing their debts faster rather than consumption that boosts demand in the economy. Overindebted companies spend their revenues servicing their obligations rather than investing in expansion or productivity. Overstretched banks reduce their balance sheets to lower their bankruptcy risk. And overindebted governments feel unable to engage in aggressive deficit spending. In all cases, a surfeit of debt slows down the impulses of growth, which makes reducing debt all the harder. This is the "debt deflation" dynamic first identified in the 1930s and then reintroduced by observers of the Japanese economy after its financial crash in the early 1990s.[13]

An economy of belonging needs to avoid this trap if it can, and find a way out if it cannot. The solution is twofold. First, steer the economy away from funding its spending with debt in favour of other forms of finance such as equity. Second, transform debt itself so that it behaves more like equity.

What would the first outcome look like? It would see companies finance themselves much more with share capital— where investors hold a stake in the company and are rewarded (or not) depending on how profitable the business is, rather than according to predefined interest and repayment terms as is the case with loans. But not just companies. For individuals,

too, we would see more equity-like financing arrangements—
for example, for house purchases, where the "creditor" would
receive a share of the price appreciation of the house when it
was resold (and lose if the price fell). Equity-like financial contracts could be devised for much more inventive purposes—
for example, education and training "loans" whose repayment
would depend on how much they boost the "borrower's" earnings. Such financing would make it less risky for individuals to
invest in physical capital or their own skills and remove the
danger of debt traps.[14] Even governments could fund themselves more by issuing "sovereign equity" whose payments
would vary with the growth of the economy, in contrast with
the typical sovereign debt that governments issue today.[15] In
all cases, the advantage is that in a downturn, financial claims
would simply lose value—like falling stock prices—instead of
burdening debtors with preagreed payment commitments.
Unpayable debts would no longer hold the economy back from
the activities that restart growth, such as moving for new and
better jobs, shifting from unsuccessful to successful products,
and funding promising business initiatives, nor would they prevent public deficit spending to spur demand.

There are many policies that could promote such a shift
from debt to equity financing. Most tax systems let corporations deduct interest payments to creditors but not dividends
to equity investors; if that were switched around, it would shift
incentives. Many countries let homebuyers deduct mortgage
interest from their taxable income; personal taxes should be
designed to favour equity-type financing instead. Financial regulations, too, should shift so that financial providers—whether
banks or other financial companies—are rewarded by regulators for providing equity-type financing instead of conventional
loans.

Governments, of course, can simply choose to issue equity-like financing instruments and be willing to pay the higher price investors may require. They can also offer such products for individuals and businesses—for example, in the place of existing government student loans schemes or start-up loans—or "sponsor" them by proposing standard contracts or templates for the private financial industry to offer. If a move away from debt increases growth, as the economic evidence suggests it will, the initially higher costs of unfamiliar financial products should pay for themselves.

A final, radical policy to promote the necessary shift would be to introduce an official form of electronic money.[16] Today, what we treat as "money" to make payments and keep savings in a safe place is rarely physical cash backed by the government. Instead, it is claims on private banks in the form of deposit accounts. But the ability of banks to offer a product that fulfils the function of money is part and parcel of their ability to create credit at will. Most deposit money is in fact a by-product of lending: when a bank issues a loan, it does so by writing up the amount in the borrowers' account.[17] But central banks could get in on this game. Allowing everyone to have "sovereign" money in electronic form—through accounts with the central bank, or electronic tokens in official "wallets" that would circulate like cash—would force private banks' business models to change. They would find it harder to hold on to deposits—why choose a private bank when you can have the safety of the central bank?—and would have to consider alternative forms of funding, which would be either more equity-like or easier to write down than deposits.[18]

Even with such incentives, much financing would still come in the form of debt, including bank debt. But not all debt is equal, and here we come to the second approach to weaning the economy off debt financing, which is to regulate away not debt itself but its most dangerous features. It is possible to give debt contracts the most important characteristic of equity, which is the requirement that when there is not enough money to repay, the investor bears the loss. By making debts easy to restructure, the traps outlined earlier can be avoided. This is the principle behind bankruptcy legislation: it is better for everyone that when debts are unpayable, they are written off—even for the creditor, who will receive a reduced amount but with certainty, rather than a protracted time of uncertain waiting that only prevents the debtor from recovering. A greater expectation that lenders will have to accept losses when loans turn out badly may discourage investors from offering credit-based financing in the first place—and that would reinforce policies aiming to shift finance from a debt-based to an equity-based model.

In an economy of belonging, therefore, debt restructuring has to be applied more aggressively and more widely than it is in any Western country today. Not just business but personal debt write-downs should enjoy uncomplicated procedures, rather than the long-winded judicial walk of shame personal bankruptcy involves in some countries. Above all, government debt should be made easier to restructure, too, as should bank debt. Many steps have been made in this direction since the global financial crisis, especially in Europe. Eurozone governments now include restructuring clauses in their sovereign bonds, which lower the bar for getting creditors to agree to postpone or reduce payments when trouble hits. And the European Union has introduced rules that in principle prohibit taxpayer bailouts of failing banks unless investors are first forced to accept a write-down of their claims (a so-called bail-in).[19] As I explain shortly, both of these make for more effective macroeconomic policy. But the experience so far with these technical improvements reveals a massive cultural and political allergy to bankruptcy, write-downs, and debt restructuring. Even when the tools are there, policy makers resist using them. A shift from a debt-based to an equity-based and restructuring-friendly economy will take a big change in mind-sets. Realising that an excessive respect for debt and debt contracts is inimical to an economy of belonging is a first step towards such a change.

Rein in the extremes of the credit cycle. This is not to say there is *no* place for credit or debt in an economy of belonging. Conventional bank loans or corporate bonds may often be a suitable form of financing if they are less dominant in the economy overall. But even in an economy that is less vulnerable because the role of credit is smaller, the built-in instability still has to be addressed. Governments everywhere must do more than they have done to make the credit cycle less pronounced.

This is not straightforward, since credit in modern economies is created by the private banking system, and how much private banks choose to lend is only partially under the control of government authorities. One reason for this, but only a partial reason, is indeed globalisation; private borrowers can always look for a lender based abroad, and domestic banks can expand credit across borders rather than at home. But the more important reason is that domestic private credit creation is much less regulated than in the immediate postwar decades. That this domestic deregulation worsened financial instability is clear from the banking crises that roiled the United States and northern Europe in the 1980s and early 1990s. The global financial crisis itself owes much to the US decision in 1999 to give financial derivatives an exemption from *domestic* regulation.

What has been deregulated can, however, be reregulated. That does not mean returning to the strictures of the 1950s, but it does entail finding new constraints on credit that fit today's economy. After 2008, many jurisdictions began to do just that. Most important are the so-called macroprudential regulations. These restrain or loosen banks' ability to lend depending on how risky financial conditions are (hence "prudential") in the economy at large (hence "macro," as opposed to "microprudential" regulation, which tries to ensure the safety of individual institutions). The belated adoption of macroprudential regulations shows that much of the financial excess in the pre-2008 era happened not because governments were powerless to control financial conditions but because they did not make enough effort to do so earlier. Political leaders who want to rebuild the economic social contract of the Western order must prevent such negligence in the future. In addition, governments should take three important further steps.

The first is to deploy macroprudential rules more forcefully. The most likely way that our new financial regulations may fail to do their job in the future is not that politicians remove them altogether because of naivety or pressure from the finance industry (though the risk of this is significant and it should be resisted) but that those in charge of the rules apply them too weakly. While regulators everywhere require banks to have much bigger financial reserves as a cushion against losses than before the crisis, they have rarely gone far enough.[20]

The second is to avoid allowing global capital to escape the discipline of macroprudential rules by crossing borders. Suppose a country restricts mortgage lending to a lower multiple of income, or tells banks to put more of their own capital against risky loans, in order to slow credit growth. If borrowers can simply borrow from a bank in another country, this will not work—credit will keep growing, and domestic banks will complain that they are being unfairly treated to boot.[21]

The solution is to tie financial regulation to the domestic advantages even foreign capital cannot do without. In the case of a mortgage, a foreign lender still needs the domestic legal system to repossess a house whose owner has defaulted on the mortgage, for example. Authorities can make the right to repossess conditional on having complied with the relevant macroprudential rules, regardless of where the lender is based. All contracts that require enforcement by domestic authorities create this sort of opportunity to make enforcement conditional on prior compliance, even when that compliance is extraterritorial.

In doing this, financial regulators would be relearning a forgotten lesson from the Bretton Woods era. What is usually remembered from the monetary-financial history of the 1950s and 1960s are the international features of the system: fixed exchange rates and controls on capital mobility across national borders. It is less well known that domestic credit controls were used actively to manage credit conditions, especially to separate credit growth from the level of interest rates, which were sensitive to global conditions even then.[22] This is possible in a world of capital mobility, too; indeed, macroprudential rules on credit growth could discourage destabilising cross-border capital flows, in effect substituting for limits on financial openness.[23]

The third step is to use credit policy to address regional inequality. Deregulation has not just unleashed wild swings in the credit cycle; it has also intensified the uneven access to credit in different places. In chapter 11, I return to the problem of how to reverse widening regional divergence, including through financial reform. This will involve policies to boost credit growth responsibly in places where the banking system has failed, perhaps through a reinvention of the old institution of the community bank, updated for the twenty-first century.

Make finance work in support of good macroeconomic policy. The reforms set out here help address the obstacles to a high-pressure economy—how does a central bank stimulate growth when interest rates are near zero, and how does a government run a deficit if markets will not buy its bonds (see the previous chapter)?

Central bankers began expressing their fear of running out of effective strategies as soon as interest rates were cut to near zero in 2009 in most big economies. They then turned to buying large amounts of financial assets in the markets with freshly (electronically) printed money. The goal was to bring down the private costs of borrowing and increase liquidity in the financial market even though it was thought the normal central bank interest rate had been taken as low as it could go.

There is no doubt central bankers were in uncharted territory. Never since the invention of central banks had official interest rates been so low. But for that very reason, the notion that there was a "zero lower bound" on interest rates was an entirely theoretical construct: nobody had ever tried to make rates go below zero. The theoretical argument for thinking this could not be done was plausible enough. Since physical money effectively pays a zero interest rate (cash keeps the same nominal value forever), taking rates negative might simply make savers convert all their deposits into cash. That would mean further monetary stimulus would have no effect, as all new central bank money would be immediately swapped for cash and rates would stay at zero. This theoretical situation is called a "liquidity trap."

But it turned out that central banks were not "trapped" at zero at all. This became clear when the Riksbank—Sweden's central bank—was the first to introduce a negative interest rate in 2009. Switzerland, Japan, and eventually the European Central Bank itself followed suit. No matter the theory, it turns out that cutting interest rates below zero in practice looks very similar to cutting them when they are positive. It makes borrowing conditions cheaper, and nothing too special happens at the zero mark. Admittedly, there are signs that private banks do not like imposing negative rates on their customers—and so they may not match central banks' rate cutting as fast as they have tended to do in normal times—but they are increasingly beginning to do so.[24] Similarly, the theoretical worry about a "zero lower bound" has shifted to new worries about a supposed "effective" lower bound somewhere below zero. At some point, so the argument goes, the interest rate would hit a "reversal" level where low rates hurt banks' profits so much that they reduce rather than expand lending.[25] The answer to this is the same as to the supposed zero lower bound: when stimulus is required, do not let theoretical concerns stop you until you see real evidence that you have cut interest rates so far that it is doing actual harm.

As it is, no central bank has yet tried to go very far below zero: the lowest the Riksbank's deposit rate ever reached was −1.25 per cent. There was no sign of flight into cash there, or in any of the other economies where central banks have broken through zero. Nor have shrunken bank profits led to reduced lending. If a central bank kept cutting, there might be a lower bound or reversal rate *somewhere*, but it is clear that it is not zero, and no central bank has ever come up against it. If this did happen, however, the official e-money that I suggested earlier would help. If people held their money in something like central bank deposits, the central bank could introduce negative rates on these in a way it cannot do on cash. It could, moreover, penalise conversions of e-money into physical cash so that the negative rate could not be avoided.

There are other, less radical measures central banks could have taken to speed up the slow postcrisis recovery. They could have expanded asset-purchase programmes further. Alternatively, instead of using such programmes to influence indirectly the cost of long-term financing in the market, they could have targeted long-term interest rates outright (conventionally, central banks only steer short-term rates directly). A long-term interest target would have given central banks a more immediate handle on the rates businesses and households actually face to finance their investments. Only one major central bank has tried—in 2016, the Bank of Japan announced it would keep the ten-year rate on government bonds close to zero—and has had no difficulty achieving the desired control. Finally, central banks could in extremis create more demand by "printing" money to distribute directly into people's pockets. This policy—known as "helicopter money"—has never been tried for the simple reason that it is so radical. But for a central bank determined to boost demand in a deeply depressed economy, the option is always available.

To sum up: rather than running out of strategies, central banks have engaged in a sort of learned helplessness. Rebuilding an economy of belonging requires them to unlearn it.

On the fiscal side, too, the financial market reforms set out in the previous pages help remove one perceived obstacle to a high-pressure macroeconomic policy, the lack of "fiscal space." When Greece and the other countries on the eurozone's periphery were hit by the sovereign debt crisis of 2010–12 and needed to fund large budget deficits, they were simply unable to borrow money in the private market to pay for them. As members of the euro, they could not direct their own central banks to finance their budgets either. Instead they agreed to be helped with official loans from their eurozone partner countries. As is now incontrovertible, the conditions attached to these loans made the downturn worse than it needed to be.[26]

But in Greece and elsewhere, an alternative existed: radically writing down the existing debts of governments and banks, so that taxpayers would not be on the hook for those past mistakes. As I have explained at length in another book,[27] this would have dramatically reduced the scale of the financial rescues needed. That is because the bulk of the financing needs did not involve paying for ongoing budget deficits but servicing old debts. Take Greece: the country received more than €200 billion in three successive rescue loans. But only about 10 per cent of that ever went to cover government deficits. The rest was used to pay off old government and bank debts so as to avoid imposing losses on the creditors.

Greece and other countries in the same situation could instead have written down the claims of bondholders. (In the end, Greece did this in 2012, but it was too little and too late.) A much smaller rescue loan could then have financed much larger deficits to sustain aggregate demand and avoid the deepest-ever depression in peacetime, with Greece's national income falling by more than 20 per cent. A deep enough restructuring would have brought even private investors back faster, reducing the likely need for any official rescue loan at all. Bond investors do not stay away *after* sovereign defaults; on the contrary, they stay away if they think one might happen to them because the debt is still unsustainably large. A proper restructuring would have returned market financing for deficit spending much faster. A more restructuring-friendly financial system, in short, makes a high-pressure economy easier to achieve.

In sum, the domestic deregulation of finance from the 1980s on went too far; and the resulting "financialisation" has brought instability, shifted incomes, held back productivity growth, and put obstacles in the way of good macroeconomic policy—all in ways that disproportionately hurt the less well off. While simply unwinding four decades of deregulation is neither plausible nor desirable, there is a strong case for *new* regulation fit for the modern economy. This chapter has proposed a range of them, some radical but all eminently feasible, and an economy that saw them implemented would not just make finance safer but also make financial *globalisation* less risky.

10

A Tax Policy for the Left Behind

The previous chapters have described how economic transformations and policy failures changed market economies that once included everyone into ones that split populations apart. Market mechanisms that create good jobs and prosperity for some, but bad jobs and precarity for left-behind groups, have undermined the West's social contract. We must now turn to the power of the state that could most obviously have counteracted these mechanisms: the tax system. In all Western countries, government authorities lay claim to anything from about one-third to one-half of the economy's total resources. Whom they choose to levy their funding from can make a big difference to how fairly prosperity is spread across the population, as well as the productivity from which that prosperity must spring.

But most countries have failed to use their tax systems to remedy the downsides of economic change. This is demonstrated by a few key facts. As chapters 2 and 4 described, the portion of national income going to paying workers' wages in most countries has fallen in the last four decades.[1] Labour earnings themselves have become more unequal, stretching out the gap between the thriving and the striving.[2] While the biggest changes in the distribution of income happened in the 1980s and have somewhat stabilised (at more unequal levels) since then, the very highest earners kept pulling away from the rest throughout the 2000s boom. Most dramatically of all, we have seen a shocking and continuing concentration of wealth (as opposed to income).[3] Even if *income* inequality has stopped increasing on most measures, the fact that it is higher than in the postwar decades means that it helps to concentrate ever more *wealth* in fewer hands every year (Figure 10.1).

This could well be made worse by the technological disruptions still to come: the likely waves of automation about to wash over sectors such as retail and road transport. If large numbers of jobs are made superfluous, with value creation concentrated in business models short on workers and long on robots or other labour-saving technology, this could reinforce the distributive effects of the earlier labour shedding in manufacturing.

Western countries' tax systems have not adapted to these changes. When one group increases its share of the economic pie, one might expect the government's take of their rewards to increase commensurately—and more than commensurately if it aims to counter the underlying economic forces. Yet despite the increased share in national income of capital earnings and of wealth, their share of taxes paid has not followed suit. If anything, tax reforms since the 1980s have added to the underlying distributional changes (Figure 10.2). While income inequality has gone up, income tax systems have become less progressive insofar as the marginal rates on the highest incomes have been significantly reduced. In most countries, corporation tax has

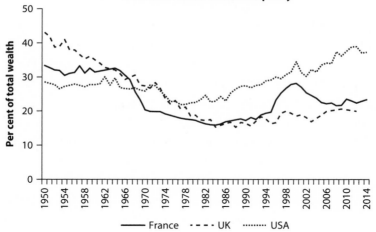

FIGURE 10.1. Top 1 per cent share of total net personal wealth.
Source: World Inequality Database, via https://ourworldindata.org/grapher/top-1
-share-of-net-personal-wealth-wid-2018.

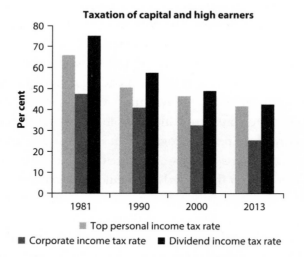

FIGURE 10.2. Statutory tax rates on personal income (top marginal rate), corporate
income, and dividend income, OECD average.
Source: OECD, "FOCUS on Top Incomes and Taxation in OECD Countries:
Was the Crisis a Game Changer?," OECD Directorate for Employment, Labour
and Social Affairs, May 2014, https://www.oecd.org/social/OECD2014
-FocusOnTopIncomes.pdf.

also been lowered. While there is an argument that this may have benefitted workers because higher posttax profits have allowed higher wages than otherwise, it is above all a boost to those who make income from capital—certainly that is what business lobbying for corporation tax cuts would indicate.

The standard "progressive" response to increased inequality is to call for higher taxes on income. Certainly Western economies could operate perfectly adequately with top marginal income tax rates closer to where they were in the postwar decades. But we should be sceptical that *much* more progressive income tax regimes will do a lot of good, as German economist Marcel Fratzscher has pointed out in his critique of German inequality.[4] He argues that if market incomes are distributed very unequally, the rates of income tax needed to compensate for this inequality would be so high, and have to kick in at such moderate income levels, that they risk becoming punitive enough to cause real damage to the willingness to work or invest in skills and productivity.

While highly progressive income tax systems worked well in economies whose pretax income distributions were much more egalitarian than today, a new economics of belonging needs to think about tax fairness differently. There are three serious reforms that together could make a significant redistributive shift—taking the burden off the left behind and placing it on those with the broadest shoulders—without harming incentives for productivity and broad-based growth. Indeed, each of these three reforms would actually improve those incentives if done smartly, thereby boosting the economy's overall productivity relative to business as usual and growing the pie that the tax system divides up. Potentially, in other words, they could secure that elusive prize for economic policy, a "free lunch."

The three reforms are, first, to tax all wealth directly; second, to do much more to stop the evasion and avoidance of taxes on capital; and third, to tax activities that have bad side effects on society—above all, environmental pollution—but in ways that benefit rather than hurt the left behind. This chapter explains how all three are in the gift of national governments, irrespective of globalisation.

Net wealth taxes. I have mentioned how the concentration of wealth has intensified over the past decades. The total amount of wealth in Western societies (the value of everything their private and public sectors own) has also grown much faster than their annual national incomes (the value of all new production in a year). In the mid-1970s, rich countries' total national wealth amounted to about two and a half to three and a half times their national income. This national wealth-to-income ratio has nearly doubled to between four and six in most countries today, even as the ownership of that wealth has become much more concentrated. If governments were at all interested in using tax systems to respond to the shifts in the market distribution of prosperity that has happened since 1970, their top priority would have been to increase the amount taken through net wealth taxes.

Net wealth taxes are annual levies assessed as a percentage rate on taxpayers' total *net* worth—the value of all their assets, with a deduction for all their debts. Such taxes are unusual, however, and more unusual than they used to be. In the early 1990s, a dozen or so rich countries still had taxes on net wealth. Most have abolished them since then or are phasing them out. Today only three still have full-fledged net wealth taxes: Switzerland, Norway, and Spain. (In addition, the Netherlands and Belgium have limited versions.)

At the time of writing, net wealth taxes are nevertheless experiencing a renaissance because of the Democratic primary race of the 2020 US presidential election. Democratic contender Senator Elizabeth Warren made a net wealth tax a flagship policy of her campaign. She has proposed that Americans with more than $50 million in net worth pay an annual 2 per cent tax on the amount of their net wealth above this threshold, while billionaires would pay an extra 1 per cent on their wealth above their first billion. Her rival on the left, Bernie Sanders, followed her with a net wealth tax proposal of his own.

This rekindled interest is unusual. The lack of familiarity with net wealth taxes and their abandonment in many countries make them a hard sell. But I will argue here that they are a central part of the tax reforms needed for a new economy of belonging.

In contrast with net wealth taxes, there is one type of levy on wealth that is exceedingly familiar. Virtually every country imposes *property* taxes—taxes on real estate such as land and buildings—typically assessed as an annual percentage levy on a stipulated property value. To understand the virtues of net wealth taxes, it is useful to first understand the flaws of real property taxes. Unlike net wealth taxes, property taxes do not consider tax wealth held in the form of non–real estate assets (financial wealth, business stakes, luxury items such as boats, or collectibles such as artwork), even though the wealthier someone is, the lower the share of their wealth they are likely to hold in real property. Even for real estate, property taxes often use unrealistic tax values (in the United Kingdom, they reflect the housing market as of 1991). And they are assessed on *gross* property values, ignoring any debt incurred to buy the property.

As attempts to tax wealth, such taxes are extraordinarily badly designed because they fail to make the wealthiest pay most. Consider this hypothetical example: Under a standard property tax, somebody buying a £500,000 home with a £450,000 mortgage—whose net wealth is therefore just £50,000—is typically assessed on the gross value on the property. That means they will pay more in tax on their very modest wealth than someone who is debt-free and has £500,000 sitting in their bank account—whose net wealth is therefore ten times greater—because that wealth is not placed in property.

Such a system puts greater obstacles in the way of the lower-middle class to increase their wealth through saving and investing (since the single biggest investment such people make tends to be in a house) than it does for the very richest people. In short, it makes it likelier that if you are left behind, you will stay behind. An initial lack of wealth easily excludes people from any chance of accumulating it at all—like young working people who could easily service a mortgage from their income but do not have the deposit needed to secure a loan to buy a house. This situation is neither efficient nor fair.

A fundamental principle of tax fairness is that those with the broadest shoulders should bear the greatest burden of taxation. Virtually every country applies this principle to how it taxes incomes, albeit often imperfectly. But it is at least as natural to define people's ability to pay tax by the magnitude of their stock of net wealth as by their income flow. Two people can have similar incomes, but one who has significant wealth can clearly afford a larger tax bill than one who has little or no wealth. So the same ethical principle that justifies progressive income taxes justifies levying a progressive annual tax on people's wealth. People seem to agree with this: US polling has shown strong support for Warren's tax proposal, for example.[5]

Why, then, did net wealth taxes go out of fashion in the first place? As late as the early 1990s, twelve OECD countries imposed them—mostly on personal wealth, but in some cases on the net wealth of corporations rather than their owners. Net wealth taxes have, however, been abolished almost everywhere; even in Spain and Norway, the revenue raised from them has stagnated. Only in Switzerland has net wealth taxation as a share of national income been rising—though only to about 1 per cent. The other countries that have them raise even less. The low revenue from net wealth taxes was one motivation for countries to stop levying them. Another is that existing or past taxes have been riddled with loopholes, with one or another asset class exempted or granted discounted valuations, resulting in much effort being put into attempting to reclassify assets in order to pay less under the rules.

Existing net wealth taxes have usually raised little revenue because rates have been low—hardly any other countries have applied the rates at the level proposed by the Warren and Sanders campaigns. On the other hand, they have typically applied net wealth taxes from much lower thresholds.[6] Net wealth tax revenues similar to Switzerland's are arguably achievable with a higher rate from higher thresholds, as in the Warren plan.[7] But there is reason to think that putting a net wealth tax at the centre of a strategy to shift the tax burden from labour to capital, and onto those who have done best from the economic changes since the 1970s, could raise much more than this. To do so, however, it would have to combine a high rate with a low threshold, as well as eliminating all loopholes.

To be specific, suppose a net wealth tax applies only above the amount of net wealth that puts someone in the richest 10 per cent of families, so that 90 per cent of the population does not pay it at all. In most large Western economies, wealth is concentrated in such a way that the taxable portion of private wealth then amounts to some two to two and a half times annual national income. This is a large tax base, and if a net wealth tax with a rate of 2 per cent per year were levied efficiently on the entire base, it could raise 4–5 per cent of national income.[8] Those are huge amounts—one-tenth to one-fifth of Western governments' total tax revenue—that could be used to lower other taxes or finance public spending. For comparison, it would equal or even exceed what many Western governments spend on education, or on public capital investment. Most ambitiously, such revenues could fund reforms of welfare systems and labour markets to make them work for the left behind, as proposed in chapters 6 and 7.

But the arguments for a net wealth tax go beyond just the promise to raise revenue, or to keep taxation of capital in line with the growth of capital itself. This could, after all, be done by increasing other, more common levies on capital, such as taxes on dividend income or capital gains. A net wealth tax has an added advantage: it is the least harmful way to tax capital because it is likely to encourage greater productivity. That is because a net wealth tax creates unique incentives for *how* savings are invested—bearing in mind that net wealth taxes are levied without reference to actual income from the wealth that is taxed. A fortune of a million attracts the same tax payment whether it takes the form of a high-return business or piece of infrastructure, or a luxury item that loses value over time. That means net wealth taxes effectively penalise low-return investments and reward high-return ones. Capitalists with low returns finds their net wealth tax eating up most of their meagre profit in tax, whereas more successful entrepreneurs, whose investments produce much larger returns, have more left over after the net wealth tax is paid. This is a big contrast to standard profit taxes, which are bigger the greater the return on the capital that is invested.[9] Indeed, it has been estimated that just replacing existing US taxes on capital with a net wealth tax raising the same revenue would boost national income by nearly 10 per cent.[10] It is in this sense that I have said net wealth taxes are the handmaiden of a productive capitalism.[11]

Some may worry that a tax on net wealth discourages saving. But the most obvious effect of a *progressive* net wealth tax on savings is to spread capital ownership more broadly across the population (because large fortunes are taxed more than small ones), which itself should be good for a cohesive economy. And Switzerland shows there is little reason to fear that a wealth tax hurts overall wealth accumulation: the country has one of the highest savings rates of all rich economies.[12] More importantly, the productivity argument suggests that even if a significant wealth tax did reduce the overall amount of capital in an economy, that capital would be more productively deployed. And allocating more capital to high-productivity investments will make productive capital accumulate faster than otherwise. That, in turn, means the economy's overall productivity will grow at a more rapid pace. By raising the rate of productivity growth overall, a net wealth tax is a method of taxing capital that grows the economic pie even as it redistributes.

There is good reason, in fact, to think that when countries have not found it worth their while to keep a net wealth tax in place, it was because it was not big enough. The productivity effects of a net wealth tax are not perceptible if the rate is too low, and if it brings in little revenue as well, it is both easy to give into lobbying to create loopholes and reasonable to judge that a complicated tax is not worth the administrative burden. A net wealth tax of the ambition I have set out here, however, would certainly be worth the administration costs, could measurably improve the productivity of investments, and would be more resistant to lobbying—because public treasuries would find it much more costly to carve out loopholes for favoured interests.

Fixing corporate taxation. Besides taxing wealth directly, the taxation of capital *income* also needs to be made fairer and more efficient. One of the biggest single taxes on capital is corporation tax: levies on the profits of companies. It makes up roughly 10 per cent of rich countries' government revenues. The system for levying this important tax remains largely stuck in the 1970s. Its base—corporate profit—is defined by reference to legal entities and their physical presence. In a world of multinational corporate structures, cross-border supply chains, and increasingly intangible economic value, this does a poor job of pinning down where profits are really made, and therefore which government should tax them. Companies can easily arrange their accounts to make profits show up in the places with the lowest tax rates.

The economists Thomas Wright and Gabriel Zucman have shown that US multinationals saw their effective foreign profit tax rate fall from about 35 per cent as late as 1990 to about 20 per cent in 2015.[13] Some of this was because other countries cut their headline rates of corporation tax. But at least half the fall is because more profit was accounted for *as if* it arose in the places with the lowest taxes. According to Wright and Zucman, "[US multinational] profits booked in tax havens have surged, from 20% of all foreign profits in the first half of the 1990s to 50% in recent years."[14]

US businesses are particularly egregious, but such "profit shifting" is a global phenomenon. In another study, Zucman and colleagues estimated that 40 per cent of the global profits of the world's multinationals is shifted into tax havens every year.[15] The biggest beneficiaries are US companies; the biggest losers are those European Union countries that are not themselves tax havens. When the Green Party group in the European Parliament wanted to look into how Europe taxes multinationals, they found a huge mismatch between nominal tax rates and the taxes companies actually paid. On average across the European Union, multinationals paid about 15 per cent of their profits in tax, as against the 23 per cent they would have paid according to nominal rates.[16]

These problems are not necessarily due to illegal tax evasion. In fact, much of it is perfectly legal tax avoidance, and even intentional on the part of policy makers—both from tax havens that use low tax rates to induce companies to "book" their profits there, and from big economies that allow their corporations to do so. For example, Wright and Zucman as well as other scholars attribute the move of US multinationals' accounting profits to tax havens to the so-called check-the-box regulation by which some foreign subsidiaries of US companies can escape America's corporate tax net by using legal entities that exploit inconsistencies between different jurisdictions.[17] As another example, Donald Trump's 2017 tax law rewarded past multinational profit shifting by hundreds of billions of dollars.[18] Because of such policies, more than one-third of the world's cross-border investment probably consists of "phantom investment," capital moved solely to make use of accounting rules that reduce tax.[19] These examples show that capital's ability to avoid taxation reflects choices made by national governments. If we want a tax system fit for an economy of belonging, these flaws must be repaired, because they hurt the left behind in at least three ways.

The first is simply the shortfall in capital owners' tax burden compared with the shift in wealth and income patterns since the 1970s. This is particularly grave for capital employed in international economic activity, and it aggravates the forty-year erosion of the West's social contract.

A second and more insidious effect is that tax avoidance by multinationals discriminates against more place-bound companies. A retail shop or local taxi company cannot minimise its tax liability by arranging its international accounts the way Amazon or Uber can. Instead of a level playing field, current business tax rules tilt the marketplace against local economic activity, in particular in those left-behind places far from where large multinationals and their shareholders like to allocate their profits. This unequal treatment adds insult to injury by taking unfair advantage of the left behind.

Third, such an unequal playing field is not just unfair but also bad for productivity. Privileged tax treatment shields those who enjoy it from competition and the imperative to be as productive as possible. This is true even if some of the most famous multinationals are hyperproductive creators of trailblazing digital technology. Conversely, the creation of what is effectively a greater tax burden on domestic and local businesses risks their being out-competed even when they are more productive than their rivals. Flawed corporate taxation therefore makes Western economies poorer than they need to be. That, in turn, means fewer economic resources to address the economic problems from which the left behind suffer disproportionately.

There are two misconceptions to avoid here. This is not just a problem in the digital economy. Several European countries have recently moved to impose special taxes on the big internet tech companies, arguing that Big Tech is a particular offender in avoiding profit taxes through profit shifting. France, for example, has introduced its *taxe GAFA* (named for Google, Amazon, Facebook, and Apple), a levy on the national turnover of big IT multinationals. But the techniques used to engineer away tax liabilities are just as available for entirely "physical" activities. A case in point is Starbucks, whose coffee is as tangible as anything. The company used to reduce taxable profit in the United Kingdom to almost nothing, despite billions in coffee sales, by having the UK operation pay royalties for the Starbucks brand to a Dutch subsidiary.[20] So by asserting that the profit relates to a brand or intellectual property, and moving the "address" of such intangible values to tax havens, multinationals are allowed to avoid corporate taxes even on products that decidedly predate the internet era. The digital giants, in their turn, deal in many physical activities: the Amazon and Uber examples should remind us that retail deliveries and taxi rides are as locally physical as they always were.

The other misconception is that this problem is an inevitable downside of globalisation. True, cross-border supply chains and capital mobility facilitate profit shifting. But they do not force governments to allow this to happen. Too often, governments refrain from unilateral actions that could address the problem, such as disallowing accounting techniques that enable profit shifting or even just monitoring and enforcing the rules. Sometimes governments even have actively legislated to encourage tax avoidance. As the foregoing examples show, much of the tax avoidance taking place today is the result of unilateral choices in national tax treatment. In contrast, the French and other governments have demonstrated that it is perfectly possible for determined national authorities to pull the profits a multinational makes in their territories into the tax net.

Ending the undertaxing of multinationals need not, in other words, require any radical proposals—certainly nothing like the radicalism of substantial wealth taxes—as long as the will is there. Even unilaterally tightening up and enforcing national tax rules could go a long way. A comprehensive solution to profit shifting does, however, require international collaboration. That is because the basic principle that taxability follows legal entities is codified in a network of bilateral tax treaties first developed in the 1970s. These were intended to prevent double taxation of incomes from cross-border economic activity. In practice, they have often facilitated double nontaxation instead. Unilaterally withdrawing from taxation treaties would be confrontational, and costly for any one country to undertake on its own; a negotiated reform would be far preferable. That should take the form of an agreed formula for allocating the tax base—the global profits of multinationals—among the countries in which they operate, based on measures of value creation such as productive capital, employment, and sales. Such a formula would replace the current practice of accounting for profits on the basis of where a company's various legal entities are notionally resident.

That would take some hard political work, but much of this is happening already. At the time of writing, staff at the OECD multilateral economic institution are developing proposals for a new way to define national taxing rights to multinational profits and a global minimum corporate tax rate.[21] Even the International Monetary Fund has pointed to a formula approach, as described earlier.[22] In the meantime, there is much national governments can do unilaterally, which would increase the incentive for others to be collaborative.[23]

The reward for reform is sizeable. Without profit shifting, Zucman found, corporate tax revenues would be 18–28 per cent greater in the largest European economies (14 per cent greater in the United States), or about 0.5 per cent worth of national income.[24] This is the amount that could be added to government budgets at prevailing corporate tax rates, with no loss and probably a gain to productivity. It is more, for example, than the UK government's entire annual spending on capital investments in health care (for example, building and maintaining hospitals) today. And the true tax-collecting potential is even greater than this. If countries have been cutting tax rates *because* of profit shifting—to discourage it or, worse, to get in on the game of stealing other countries' tax bases—then an end to profit shifting would facilitate higher rates.

Taxing "bads": tax-and-dividends for a just carbon transition. While both wealth taxation and multinational profit taxation are attempts at addressing the undertaxation of capital, the third prong of a tax policy for the left behind addresses a very different challenge. Capital is not the only undertaxed economic resource; another is carbon, given the possibly existential threat of global climate change. It costs much less for producers or consumers to emit carbon than it would if the contribution to climate change risk were included. This risk is potentially catastrophic, and it is inevitable that economic policy will increasingly be constrained by this fact. That entails one very concrete policy implication, well explained by the climate economist William Nordhaus in his 2018 Nobel Prize lecture: "To be effective, the policies have to raise the price of CO_2, and by doing that, correct the externality of the marketplace. If you are going to be effective, you have to raise the price. Putting a price on our activities is the only way to get billions of people now and in the future, millions of firms, thousands of governments, to take steps if we are going to move in the direction we want." Nordhaus thinks the global carbon price today is at best one-tenth of what it needs to be. A \$91/tonne carbon tax would be needed to keep temperature rises below 3 degrees beyond preindustrial levels, and as much as \$225/tonne to stay below 2 degrees.[25]

Such taxes would be a direct blow at the left behind, who, in the short run at least, bear the lion's share of higher carbon prices. Carbon use roughly follows consumption overall, so the richer you are, the bigger your carbon footprint—but taxing that footprint can hurt the left behind more. This is in part because those with a lower income spend a larger *share* of it on essential energy and transport costs. It is in part because cities are more energy efficient than the less densely populated left-behind areas where car use is unavoidable and public transport poor. Finally, it is partly because those in precarious economic situations cannot easily afford to adapt to economic incentives for less carbon-intensive behaviour (by paying more for energy-efficient cars and appliances, say).

Imperative as it is to raise the price of carbon, it therefore looks like a recipe for worsening the culture wars over not just climate policy but Western politics overall. Mishandled deindustrialisation has already undermined entire ways of life in many Western countries. The changes now required to address climate change threaten to do the same all over again to the very same communities, while satisfying concerns held most vocally by the urban middle classes. An economy of belonging must therefore address the challenge of climate change (if only because the "belonging" must embrace future generations too) while at the same time lessening the exclusion of the left behind—and in particular the exclusion of left-behind places. This dilemma is acute in tax policy since any adequate climate strategy will end up adopting a meaningful carbon tax, and carbon taxes are, by themselves, regressive. A solution is needed that can undo the regressiveness of a carbon tax without removing its incentive for carbon reduction.

Such a solution exists. It has been gathering support among US policy makers across political dividing lines, and support is quickly picking up across western Europe. In the United States it goes by the name of "carbon fee and dividend," and economists have coined the term "carbon cheque," but the idea is the same: to impose a meaningful carbon tax on all emission sources, from which the entire revenue would be immediately redistributed as a "dividend" to the population on a flat per capita basis, rather than go into the general government budget. James Hansen, a founding father of climate science, proposed it first.[26] Canada is trying to implement it; official economic advisers in France and Germany are advocating it.[27]

This would create a permanent direct cash stream into everyone's pocket. Anyone who uses less than average amounts of carbon would receive more in payments than they lost in higher prices—protecting the most vulnerable while rewarding anyone who reduces their carbon footprint. The cash stream would give struggling groups the wherewithal to respond to such incentives in ways that work for them—by upgrading to more energy-efficient equipment, say. It would also at a stroke create a constituency in favour of increasing environmental taxes further (and this idea could be extended to other environmental problems than carbon emissions). If that constituency were large enough, it would overcome the culture war.

There is every reason to think that it would be large enough, and that the left behind would benefit substantially. The tax revenue from even modest carbon taxes would be substantial. The US Treasury has modelled a \$49/tonne carbon tax, significantly less than what an ambitious climate change policy will require but calculated to raise about 1 per cent of US national income.[28] At the \$91/tonne or higher rates modelled by Nordhaus, that revenue would be commensurately higher: Hansen's own costing of a \$115/tonne tax puts it at nearly 3 per cent of national income.[29]

Such amounts would give governments huge room for manoeuvre to restore the economic pillar of our broken social contracts. A per capita dividend in such amounts would make a real difference to the livelihoods of low-income families. The US Treasury estimates that its stipulated $49/tonne tax would cover a $538/year payment to each American resident, or more than $2,000/year for a family of four. Even taking into account the higher prices of fuels and other carbon-intensive goods, this would leave lower-income Americans significantly better off from the combined policy, as Figure 10.3 shows. The poorest tenth of the population would see their living standards go up by almost 10 per cent, the US Treasury study finds. A large majority would benefit: the dividend would be greater than the higher cost of living caused by the carbon tax for everyone but the 30 per cent highest earners. Similarly, a study by France's official economic analysis bureau found that a "carbon cheque" that is differentiated by type of region (whether rural or urban) can be designed so that it makes virtually everyone in the bottom half of the income distribution better off even after paying higher carbon taxes on fuel and energy.[30]

It will not escape readers that a carbon fee and dividend, almost by accident, encompasses a universal basic income/negative income tax. While not motivated by any of the arguments for basic income I discussed in chapter 7, an ambitious carbon tax of 2–3 per cent of national income can still serve those objectives to a significant degree (and less money would have to be found elsewhere for a full-fledged universal basic income/negative income tax). A similarly beneficial coincidence can be found in the other two tax reforms proposed here. A net wealth tax works to improve productivity and help the asset-poor even as it raises substantial resources to pay for other policies to help the left behind (including cutting other taxes). And fixing the

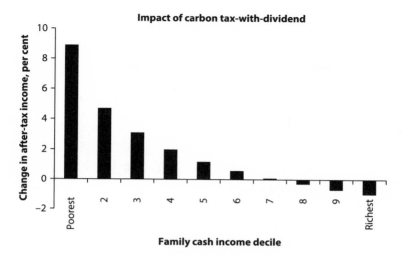

FIGURE 10.3. Estimated distributional effects of a $49/tonne US carbon tax rebated as per-capita dividend, in percentage change of after-tax income, by decile of family cash income.
Source: "Methodology for Analyzing a Carbon Tax," US Department of the Treasury Office of Tax Analysis Working Paper 115, January 2017, https://www .treasury.gov/resource-center/tax-policy/tax-analysis/Documents/WP-115.pdf.

corporate tax system levels the playing field for smaller and more local, place-bound businesses, while also enabling costlier choices for public policy. Together the three reforms have good direct effects while raising revenues potentially of 7–9 per cent of national income when put together—an enormous room for manoeuvre for a government that wants to put restored belonging at the heart of its policies.

11

Whose GDP?

British academic Anand Menon has spent the last four years travelling the length and breadth of the United Kingdom holding events designed to increase public understanding and debate of the implications of Brexit. "One incident at a town hall event sticks in my mind," Menon relates. "A couple of colleagues and I were in Newcastle, in the northeast, discussing the fact that the vast majority of economists agreed that Brexit would lead to an economic slowdown. A two percent drop in the United Kingdom's GDP [gross domestic product], I said, would dwarf any savings the country would generate from curtailing its contribution to the EU budget. 'That's your bloody GDP,' came the shouted response, 'not ours.'"[1]

Menon's anecdote captures two important facts. One is about subjective perception: many people across the Western world feel, like the lady in Newcastle, that the expert and governing classes do not speak for them—not just that they do not have their interests at heart but that they do not know how they live. The other is about factual reality: a national statistic, such as GDP, is composed of ever more divergent experiences for different parts of the population. It has increasingly become true that there really is "one GDP for us and another GDP for them." I already touched on this in chapter 8, where I showed how the national average measures of the economy's health used to guide macroeconomic policy obscure the fact that some people systematically lag behind in upswings and are the first to be hit in downturns. But one dimension of this divergence—between different parts of the same country—is not just a matter of cyclical swings. It has become a permanent and worsening feature of Western economies.

During the postwar economy of belonging, entire regions of Western nations benefitted from increasing prosperity. Not only that: poorer places grew faster and were catching up with the most prosperous areas, typically the countries' capital regions and other big cities. The fall in *individual* income inequality in the postwar decades went along with a fast-paced narrowing of *regional* disparities in productivity and income. But the economic transformation of the past forty years has shifted the engine of value creation from a territorially spread-out system of labour-intensive industrial production to more concentrated activity of knowledge-based and high-tech services. Regional convergence has long since stalled or gone in the reverse.

The pattern is particularly visible in the United States. As Figure 11.1 makes clear, something changed around 1980. Before then, output per capita grew consistently faster in poorer areas than in richer ones. But in the ensuing decades, this correlation disappeared. Poorer places were no longer catching up with richer ones; indeed some of the already richest states and localities—places like California and New York—pulled ahead of the pack.[2]

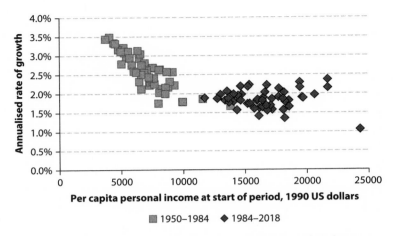

FIGURE 11.1. Annualised growth rate of per capita personal income plotted against its level at the start of the period, for all US states and the District of Columbia. Constant 1990 dollars, adjusted by the national Personal Consumption Expenditures price index.
Source: "Personal Income by State," US Bureau of Economic Analysis, last modified 18 December 2019, https://www.bea.gov/data/income-saving/personal -income-by-state.

And we can look in more detail at how precisely the convergence stopped. In the heyday of Western growth, the greater prosperity of the cities showed up in wages that were higher than in smaller towns and the countryside for all skill levels. More recently, this "city premium" in low-skill wages has largely disappeared—indeed, it can be worse than that because of high urban housing costs. Low-skilled people no longer have the opportunity to better their condition by moving to the big city. Meanwhile, high-skill incomes have soared ahead in the big cities—but not elsewhere. This means two things: inequality between high-skill and low-skill pay within big cities is high, as is the inequality in high-skill pay in the big cities compared with elsewhere. In other words, the reward for high skill outside the big cities has fallen behind.[3]

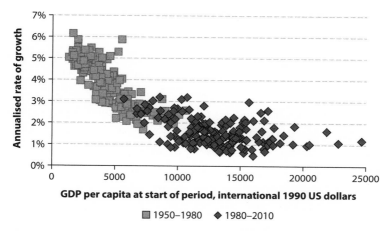

FIGURE 11.2. Annualised growth rate of per capita gross domestic product plotted against its level at the start of the period, for 173 subnational regions of 16 west European countries. International 1990 US dollars.
Source: Joan Rosés and Nikolaus Wolf, eds., *The Economic Development of Europe's Regions: A Quantitative History since 1900,* New York: Routledge, 2018.

The data is grainier for Europe, but there, too, similar changes have taken place. A cross-country team of researchers have painstakingly reconstructed GDP numbers for subnational regions in western Europe going back a century, to be able to look at the regional distribution of productivity and income over the long term.[4] They found a similar pattern to that in the United States: up until about 1980, regional productivity differences were narrowing. But since then, different parts of western European countries have seen diverging fortunes (Figure 11.2). Capital regions, which were typically already the most prosperous, have grown the most. Meanwhile, many other regions, especially those previously reliant on manufacturing jobs, have fallen behind—or further behind.

The case of postcommunist central and eastern Europe is more intricate: a look at the European continent as a whole since the 1980s will show that many poor eastern regions have been catching up spectacularly with the richer West as they entered the orbit of the European Union's economy and system of rules. But there, too, the impact has varied greatly from place to place, with capital regions benefitting disproportionately and pulling far ahead of the more remote places.

It is in these left-behind places that the revolt against the Western liberal order has been strongest. Andrés Rodríguez-Pose, an economic geographer, calls it "the revenge of the places that don't matter."[5] Such places can now be found in most countries in the West, and the most down-at-heel regions almost invariably support antisystem parties more strongly than places of prosperity. Areas devastated by industrial decline were strongholds for both Brexit and the Trump vote. The far-right Alternative for Germany and the hard-left Linke are strongest in the former East Germany, whose productive base shriveled with the end of the Soviet control and which remains significantly poorer than the West. The Italian Mezzogiorno, chronically poor and ill governed compared with the north of the country, put its stock in the antisystem leftish Five Star Movement and has recently swung to the increasingly xenophobic and anti-European League party. In the postindustrial North and rural South of France, both struggling regions, voters have thrown their lot in with the far-right movement of the Le Pen family, as well as hard-left parties such as La France Insoumise (France Unbowed), and the *gilets jaunes* protest movement originated mostly in small towns in decline. In eastern Europe, too, the parties most opposed to the European Union's liberal, rules-based way of doing things disproportionately find their voters in a countryside that, while growing, has fallen behind the big cities.

This is more than a coincidence; it is not just that individuals with reason to oppose the Western order happen to be clustered in the same places. As Rodríguez-Pose emphasises, "In the Brexit vote and in the elections of Donald Trump and Emmanuel Macron, there is little evidence that interpersonal inequality played a decisive role. Populism was not most popular among the poorest, but instead in a combination of poor regions and areas that had suffered long periods of decline. The places that don't matter, not the 'people that don't matter,' have reacted. Interpersonal inequality still matters, but the challenge to the system has come from neglected territorial inequalities."[6]

That is not so surprising once we take a hard look at what some of these places have become. My colleague at the *Financial Times*, Sarah O'Connor, wrote a much-read portrait of Blackpool, once a prime seaside holiday spot for factory workers, now a place where "you find people on the outside of the economy looking in":

> Blackpool exports healthy skilled people and imports the unskilled, the unemployed and the unwell. As people overlooked by the modern economy wash up in a place that has also been left behind, the result is a quietly unfolding health crisis. More than a tenth of the town's working-age inhabitants live on state benefits paid to those deemed too sick to work. Antidepressant prescription rates are among the highest in the country. Life expectancy, already the lowest in England, has recently started to fall. Doctors in places such as this have a private diagnosis for what ails some of their patients: "Shit Life Syndrome."[7]

Two important characteristics mark Blackpool and other left-behind places. One is a self-reinforcing downward spiral: an initial economic hit is amplified when those with the best chances of economic success leave, while those who struggle in the new economy are attracted by lower housing costs.[8] The other is that the decline manifests itself not just in incomes but also in broken communities. In Blackpool, this is seen in high rates of antidepressant use. In down-at-heel communities in the United States, it plays out as an epidemic of "deaths of despair"—lives lost to drug poisoning, suicide, or alcohol-related disease. This epidemic "spread from the [US] Southwest, where it was centered in 2000, first to Appalachia, Florida, and the West Coast by the mid-2000s, and is now countrywide," economists Anne Case and Angus Deaton have found. It has been causing so many deaths every year that, uniquely among rich countries, mortality among middle-aged people with little formal education has stopped its secular decline and is instead rising.[9]

Another colleague, *Financial Times* columnist Simon Kuper, has observed that much of Europe's put-upon white working class has only the ties of communities left, after economic transformations destroyed their livelihoods and the protections and services previously offered by the national state have eroded away.[10] If their local community unravels, too, it is not surprising if many reject the prevailing order. After all, the prevailing order has given up on them.

What does this mean for policy? One hardheaded economic perspective would be to say that when the economy changes so as to make previously thriving places economically unviable, the best option is to help people move away and relocate to the new centres of economic activity. But it is too cruel—and also politically self-defeating—to tell people that they must choose between prosperity and community. Besides, Blackpool provides a stark illustration of the fact that urging people to relocate and give up on the place they come from typically means relocating those with the greatest opportunities and abandoning the rest. In practice, "managed decline" just dumps more of the burden of decline onto the worst off. Except perhaps in the most extreme cases, an economics of belonging must do much better than that.

A politically and morally acceptable strategy to address regional disparity needs to be at the same time sensible and sensitive. It must recognise the deep forces driving divergence, while finding ways for those in left-behind places—especially those tied to them most strongly—to adapt to economic change without demanding that they sacrifice community. That means equipping both individuals *and* places with the means to thrive in the new economy. Any alternative to the counsel of despair of simply managing the decline of left-behind places must have as an express objective to sustain places across national territories as good places to live, and as productive places to work and produce. That means making policy at least in part "place-sensitive" and not just "spatially blind."[11] Because of the self-perpetuating forces set in motion by our economies' structural change, it is a mistake to think that helping individuals will suffice to help places, too.

But which place-sensitive policies? The answer is not obvious, partly because the challenges are themselves complex and require a combination of policies; partly because the range of policies that have been tried is so large as to constitute an embarrassment of riches for a well-intended policy maker. To develop a policy *strategy* from a ragbag of policies, it helps to define three very different ways of thinking about what to do with left-behind regions.[12] Let us call them the three strategies of *reversal, connectivity*, and *attraction*.

1. The reversal strategy. The first is a strategy of *reversal*. This would consist of policy interventions that aim to undo the effects of the technological and market change by offsetting or compensating for the cost disadvantage left-behind places face in the new economy. It is essentially a strategy of subsidy or targeted tax cuts to tilt the playing field between types of places back to where it used to be. Crudely put, if factories in a midsize town are becoming uncompetitive because structural changes increasingly advantage factories elsewhere (closer to markets, say, or within supply chains with lower barriers to just-in-time production techniques), then the policy is to put enough public money into such businesses to allow them to compete anyway. The stark image of defeat when a local industry or steel plant has to close in communities highly dependent on such economic cornerstones means there is often strong political pressure for such policies. That is why attempts at reversal (or less generously, at turning back the clock) are the most traditional type of industrial policy, which governments spend significant sums on.

The strategy is not always doomed. European investment subsidies in declining areas have been shown in one study to raise capital investment and employment above what they would otherwise be in existing manufacturing plants—but only for small companies. The subsidies did not change the behaviour of big manufacturers that received them, however, nor did they boost the emergence of new firms. And beyond the increase in capital, overall productivity (the effectiveness with which that new capital was used) was unchanged.[13] Many studies show that tax cuts for business activity in left-behind places do little to boost their performance or create jobs, and what benefits they bring only come at an exorbitant price.[14] It is very unclear that business tax cuts stimulate investments in the right kinds of capital that would not have happened anyway.

While the reversal strategy can sometimes reduce the pain of economic change, it cannot succeed as a general approach. That is because the aim of keeping alive already-established economic activity that has come under pressure is predicated on resisting change rather than adapting to it. That risks holding back long-term productivity growth and making adjustment harder when it finally cannot be postponed anymore—which always happens in the end since the cost disadvantage of obsolete productive structures increases over time.

If subsidies are partially financed by local governments, they can sometimes have an even worse effect than doing nothing. When local governments compete for investment from large companies, it can lead to a race to the bottom that aggravates the extraction of value from the local community to company owners situated elsewhere, and shrink the funds available for local public goods, including those that offer the greatest promise for increasing productivity in the area.[15] The scramble for the privilege to host a new Amazon headquarters was a case in point: 238 cities competed for the dubious honour, often promising the company big subsidies.[16] The race made some of the world's top economists so worried that they signed a petition calling for a "non-aggression pact" between the competing towns.[17]

Finally, the reversal strategy also goes squarely against the principle of protecting workers rather than jobs and easing the job-to-job mobility that is instrumental in creating higher-productivity and ultimately better-paid employment (as discussed in chapter 6).[18]

2. The connectivity strategy. The second is a strategy of *connectivity*. Its goal is to remedy the way left-behind areas find themselves disconnected from centres of economic activity and to allow them to become part of successful agglomerations. These are policies to prevent *geographical* distance from becoming *economic* distance that makes it costly to engage in joint economic activity. It is clear that for some left-behind areas, isolation is a main cause of their lack of value-creating activities, and making them better connected might allow them to succeed as satellites to already-thriving economic centres. This primarily involves building infrastructure of hard and soft kinds—transport and broadband connections, but also the social, educational, and psychological ability to "connect" with activities in the centre.

Paradoxically, the digital revolution should have made it easier for remote areas to remain connected. In principle, coding can be done as well in Kentucky as in California. But the broad definition of connectivity is crucial.[19] Without the "software" of economic connectivity—the education, skills, and social aptitude to participate in the most modern economic activities—reducing "hard" distance may achieve little. Extending the area from which poorly paid workers can commute into cities to do low-productivity service work (or providing such work remotely, for example through call centres) does nothing to restore a sense of economic belonging. A striking illustration of how physical distance overlaps with psychological and social distance is that even in the era of ubiquitous social networks, people's networks of online "friends" thins out fast with how far away they live.[20] This matters for access to a knowledge economy where high-value services rely on cognitively and socially specific communication.

These reservations notwithstanding, the connectivity strategy can work. The OECD has shown that in the past decade, rural areas situated geographically near cities have been catching up, defying the trend of regional divergence since the 1980s. And it has better prospects than the reversal strategy:

infrastructure and skills upgrading have measurably positive effects on productivity.[21]

But this strategy also cannot alone restore nationwide economies of belonging. Sometimes, my colleague Chris Giles has cautioned, "we can build infrastructure, but this is not sufficient to overcome locational disadvantage."[22] Economic distance is not the only reason for decline; some activities become obsolete no matter how well connected they are to economic centres. And connections can make things worse. The commuting case just mentioned is one example; another is that greater social connectivity could make it easier for the most skilled to leave declining areas altogether—making things even worse for those who stay behind, as the fate of Blackpool illustrates.

3. The attraction strategy. Where it does not solve problems on its own, however, connectivity can still provide necessary support for the third and hardest strategy, which is the one a true economics of belonging must pursue. This is the strategy of *attraction*—the ambitious goal of making places that have depended on declining activities leapfrog towards becoming centres of high value-added creation in their own right. Achieving this is very hard; it will require a lot of things to be done right simultaneously. In a nutshell, it requires simultaneously building up several sorts of capital in places where all of them have become depleted.

The fundamental kind of capital is, of course, *human* capital. Declining regions do not suffer from low skill levels by chance. The problem is dynamic: they lose the people with good opportunities and attract those without them. As we have seen, regional differences are strongly driven by the gap in rewards to high-skilled workers between thriving and struggling places. The human reality behind that economic statistic is that many highly able individuals find they need to leave their communities to fulfil their potential. A key policy goal, therefore, must be to turn *places of decline* into *poles of attraction* that can draw in skilled people adept at plugging into today's fast-growing, high-value sectors. Central to the strategy of attraction is to create, retain, and attract highly productive human capital in areas that are currently losing it—or in more human terms, build places where enough skilled and highly educated workers want to live and can find rewarding work.

This requires two things: more capital of every *other* sort, and a robust enough level of local purchasing power to sustain the sort of services that makes a place nice to live in and is a central part of the draw of living in successful cities.

Struggling places need *physical* capital for the digital, transport, and other connectivity infrastructure I mentioned earlier—both to be productive and to be attractive. This is not limited to infrastructure investment to reduce physical and economic distance to economic centres (which is the only focus of the connectivity strategy). Left-behind areas also need capital that reduces physical and economic distances *within* them. For example, poor transport links in rural and suburban areas of the United States have caught the Federal Reserve's attention as a barrier to matching workers with jobs in a productive way.[23] A further type of necessary physical capital is in the form of public goods that increase the appeal of a place in terms of the services and social connectedness—think libraries and arts institutions—that typically suffer from underfunding when the local economy fails.

Another type of capital needed in a putative pole of attraction is *financial* capital. Even catching up in skill levels and connectedness is of little use if businesses lack the financial capital to avail themselves of the better opportunities. But part of the vicious cycle bedevilling left-behind places is that credit creation is self-reinforcing.[24] Economic decline makes lending less attractive to banks, and their withdrawal of credit aggravates the decline. In the United States, the financial crisis deepened a credit drought that was hitting smaller places particularly hard. Small community banks, which were a mainstay of local business lending, had already been disappearing, while many larger banks stopped issuing small business loans after the crisis.[25] In Europe, the eurozone crisis saw a dramatic flight of finance from the hardest-hit crisis countries, which meant even solid businesses struggled to expand. (As discussed in chapter 9, even when easily available, bank lending is a dangerous form of finance. In places where debt and credit rise particularly fast, a turn in economic fortunes can destroy creditworthiness while trapping people in debt that prevents them from moving for work or starting new businesses.)

When these forms of capital are depleted, it is harder to attract human capital, too; and when human capital flees, these other types of investments tend to dry up.

Similarly, when local purchasing power is weak, the services that keep a community connected and contented wither—and those who can, have greater reason to leave. So the second thing that a strategy of attraction must achieve is a robust level of aggregate demand *locally*, so that there is a market both for new activities to replace those in decline—typically service jobs replacing factory work—and for the sort of services and amenities that often attract the high skilled to the big cities: a range of local shops, eateries, entertainment, arts and culture, and craft manufacture and repair. And of course these matter to those who never left as well. A big reason why left-behind communities feel forgotten is that they often are physically neglected. A striking finding of a study of what voters in Britain's most deprived areas want after Brexit is that one of their main concerns was "high streets blighted by empty shops," and that a priority would be to have the sort of shops available in more affluent areas.[26] The foundations of social connectedness can be strikingly modest: one French mayor introduced a pop-up bread shop in the town hall when his village lost its only bakery.[27] *Gilets jaunes* protests were three times likelier to break out in places whose last convenience shop had closed than in other French communities.[28]

We should see in these self-reinforcing problems not just despair but also the contours of a solution: a potential virtuous cycle. Physical and financial capital are much easier to attract where the concentration of human capital is also high—in part because the human capital makes the other forms of capital more valuable. Higher spending is easier to sustain when higher-earning people are more attracted to living in the community.

What policies can realise the strategy of attraction, and achieve this reaccumulation of capital and purchasing power in the left-behind areas? The first part of the answer—and the reason why this chapter comes towards the end of the book—is that many of the policies I have set out in earlier chapters would do a lot of the work in a strategy of attraction, even if they were not presented as explicitly directed towards left-behind *places*.

Consider the policies to discourage low-productivity labour in chapter 6, high minimum wages combined with spending on skills and easing job switches. These help ensure that when old activities become obsolete, the newer jobs that replace them will be good ones, provided of course the demand is there to create them. The high-pressure macroeconomic policy advocated in chapter 8 would do just that, by ensuring that the tap of aggregate demand stimulus was not turned off before the effect was felt in left-behind regions. Universal basic income, as recommended in chapter 7, would support local aggregate demand as well, thereby making it more viable to maintain an attractive range of services locally. This is illustrated by the unique basic income–like system of Alaska's "permanent dividend" from oil revenues, which seems to boost not just retail and leisure services but health and personal care services as well. Universal basic income and the other "empowerment" polices from chapter 7 would also increase the share of value creation retained in the local community rather than transferred to investors or suppliers elsewhere, thereby supporting local demand indirectly as well. The financial reforms set out in chapter 9 would improve access to financial capital if new "mission banks" were set up to remedy local credit droughts (see below), and reduce the risk of damaging credit bubbles and ensuing debt traps by promoting alternative forms of finance to conventional bank loans. And the tax reforms from chapter 10 would counteract some of the market mechanisms that push value towards the leading cities. All of these polices combined would by themselves go a long way towards making forgotten places feel they matter again.

But going a long way is not going far enough. A strategy of attraction must, in addition to those general approaches, identify and pursue explicitly place-specific policies—that is to say, those targeted at particular places identified as most threatened by economic change. Such policies are by their nature hard to specify in general terms. But we can learn from where they have been implemented successfully. Consider the economist Timothy Bartik's case study[29] of Grand Rapids, Michigan. This is a region that relies more on manufacturing than the US average, so one would expect it to have been badly hit by the large drop in US factory jobs since the 1980s. It did indeed suffer outsize job losses in the early years of the 2000s. But it rebuilt and grew manufacturing employment before and after the worst periods of decline much better than the national average. Between 1990 and 2015, the United States as a whole lost about 30 per cent of its factory jobs. In contrast, Grand Rapids had added 9 per cent to its factory payroll at the end of those twenty-five years.

How did Grand Rapids escape the fate of other manufacturing-heavy places? Bartik documents similar policies in Grand Rapids and the other (rare) turnarounds in US manufacturing communities (whether success is defined as outperforming the national trend in factory jobs or, in contrast, achieving strong nonmanufacturing growth that more than makes up for shrinking industry). In Grand Rapids, this included the following. On skills, better-than-average funding of job-training programmes was complemented with policies to increase skill levels from early childhood and to attract academic institutions (a medical school) and the high-skilled workforce that comes with them. On productivity, significant funding was put into manufacturing extension services, and related businesses were helped to work together to overcome common challenges to expansion—for example, through the West Michigan Medical Device Consortium, which is aimed at helping local manufacturers shift into producing supplies for the medical device industry. As examples of what this achieved, a car-part maker began producing orthopaedic devices, and a wrappings supplier moved into medical packaging. On infrastructure, extensive investments were made in downtown Grand Rapids.

Not every last place in economic decline can be turned around. It is key for a strategy of attraction to identify the places across the national territory with the greatest potential to become local poles of attraction, and which can also benefit their surrounding areas. Learning from case studies and the economic research allows us to define the most promising general place-specific policy package for such places. It has five branches.

First, squeeze every opportunity to boost local productivity to the limit. There is a lot of low-hanging fruit. Targeted *business extension services* that help lift local business to best practice and aid adaptation into the most profitable new sectors make a big difference.

Second, *customise* job training programmes for the local economy and create *general* policies to increase local skill levels overall. The Kentucky "coal to code" project, which successfully teaches coding to laid-off miners, shows what is possible.[30] But job training must be understood broadly to include aiding the cultural adaptation to more cognitive or more caring-oriented jobs than those that disappear. Even manufacturing and mining are now dependent on high-level cognitive service–style work (engineering, programming, and other problem-solving activities).

In addition to training, there is much to be gained from simply making the process by which workers and jobs are matched the best it can be. Consider Germany, whose rising regional pay gap owes much to the fact that smaller places are worse at matching the right people to the right jobs. Economists have found that simply by improving the matching of employers and workers to the level found in big cities—for example, through better transport infrastructure and more efficient job search facilities—lagging towns would go a long way towards catching up with leading centres.[31]

Common to these first two policy branches is that they cost relatively little—certainly compared with the productivity improvements they achieve—and can therefore escape difficult budget trade-offs.

That may be less true for the third policy branch, which is to prioritise public spending on the *infrastructure and other forms of capital* described earlier—that is to say, devote extra public money to investments in particular areas. That means devoting the money needed for good roads, public transport, broadband connectivity, and the like, as well as adequate public services in areas of health, culture, and other "social" infrastructure. There is no way around the need for government resources for these things.

But there are also further ways to mobilise private capital that need not cost the public purse much. As one example, with just a small equity stake, authorities can set up or sponsor special-purpose financial institutions with a mission to provide business financing in specific credit-starved communities (even a minimal one-stop-shop service helping small businesses navigate all available financing and grant opportunities could be useful). The goal would be to reinvent the old institution of the community bank—a credit-creating institution with a noncommercial (or not exclusively commercial) charter committing it to provide credit to an underserved area. It would, however, have to be updated for the twenty-first century. In line with the policies I proposed for financial reform in chapter 9, such institutions may be chartered with a view to providing noncredit forms of financing. They could also be set up to favour the sort of activities that traditional lending is biased against (see chapter 9), and target, for example, knowledge-intensive start-ups with intangible assets that normal bank lending struggles to use as collateral.[32]

Another example is to use planning laws to lower business costs—for example, by improving the use of land—or increase population density. The UK think tank the Centre for Cities argues, based on successes in the Netherlands and Germany, that making a region thrive depends on increasing the density of its cities to deepen the available pool of knowledge workers available and "make it easier for people and organisations to share information and come up with new ideas."[33]

Fourth, a necessary ingredient for a critical mass of knowledge workers is a *critical mass of knowledge-intensive jobs*. Governments can (in many places, if not everywhere) provide that critical mass by supporting research environments of a certain size. These could be highly research-intensive private institutions, but more obviously they could be research universities (as opposed to educational institutions focused only on teaching), as the economic blogger Noah Smith has strongly advocated as a means of regional regeneration in the United States.[34] The evidence supports such calls: research universities create striking economic benefits for the regions they are situated in by increasing the share of high-skilled workers who increase the productivity of local businesses.[35]

Fifth, and perhaps counterintuitively, aim to *globalise* the left-behind places. Exporting is linked to productivity—more productive companies are more likely to export, but producing for export markets also helps productivity because of the greater scale it makes possible. Some of the greatest productivity boosts for left-behind places should therefore come from nurturing their export potentials. This means dedicating some of the business services mentioned earlier to improving the performance of local exporters, and to help new or existing companies that do not yet export over the obstacles to their doing so.[36]

This last point returns us to the backlash against the Western social order and, above all, its pillar of economic openness. As this chapter shows, there is reason to hope that a considered policy for left-behind places can turn many of them around, allowing them to manage and ultimately thrive on economic transformation to the point of turning economic openness to their advantage. What holds for a regional policy of attraction is also true more broadly. Economic openness is not just compatible with a domestic economics of belonging; with the right policies, more globalisation can make it stronger. The next chapter explains how.

PART III

The Way Forward

12

Globalisation with a Human Face

Bliss was it in that dawn to be alive,
But to be young was very heaven!
—WILLIAM WORDSWORTH

William Wordsworth's admiring verses about the 1789 French Revolution still reverberated exactly two hundred years after he wrote them, during another world-historical event. For those—like me—who came of age around 1989, those lines could just as well have been written about the fall of the Berlin Wall, the collapse of communism, and the return to the West of the half of Europe that had been locked up behind the Iron Curtain for forty years.

At the time it was possible to dream of a new world, where the three pillars of the Western liberal order would be adopted by all countries and borders between nations would gradually fade away. Democracy and free expression for all; Western living standards everywhere; and the ability to work, travel, and love unconstrained by borders. This is what globalisation meant for much of my generation, above all those who had earlier been denied the opportunities enjoyed in the West. It was a beautiful dream and one those with our lives ahead of us could delight in more than anyone.

That dream has now turned into a nightmare—or that is what many want to make us believe. The political leaders and strategists who are now working to undo the Western liberal order altogether are doing their best to depict the globalisation that followed 1989 as a great betrayal. Even many of their opponents accept their premise that globalisation has "gone too far" and that this is the main reason why the West's foundational values are under threat in its own heartlands.

One reason for writing this book has been to try to salvage the dream from 1989. I have already argued that the economic hardships suffered by the left behind have other, more significant causes than economic openness, and that the West's economies of belonging withered as the consequence not of globalisation but of technological change and more or less wilful *domestic* policy mismanagement. In this chapter I want to go further than simply arguing that globalisation is innocent of the charges placed against it. I will defend a stronger claim: that with the sort of policies I have set out, economic openness is not just not a threat but in fact a positive contribution to the domestic economy of belonging. With the right domestic policies in place, we can confidently pursue more—but better—globalisation.

Historically, it is a mistake to think of a trade-off between international openness and domestic economic cohesion. Instead, the two tend to go together. The Nordic countries, widely seen as doing the best job of bringing along those left behind by economic change, have also long been among the most open economies in the West. In fact, it is arguably *because* they are so open that their social contracts underpinned economies of belonging and still sustain them more than many other countries. Public understanding that trade brings prosperity, but that global fluctuations can hit hard and unpredictably, has increased support for large welfare states.[1]

My point in this chapter is that this relationship also works the other way around. If the domestic policies take good care of everyone, globalisation will also remain broadly politically acceptable. To see how this might work, look at the history of Norway in this century.

Norway is not a member of the European Union, but it has tied itself to most of the EU's economic rules and regulations through an economic and political partnership known as the European Economic Area. That makes the country a participant in a European legal order that is about as deep an effort at globalisation as any seen in history through peaceful means. The reward for Norway is that this small but highly trade-dependent nation gets all its products and services automatically authorised for sale in a market with a hundredfold more people than itself, and its citizens have the same rights to live and work around Europe as those of full EU member states. The price is that whenever EU rules change, Norway must change its own rules accordingly, without any say in what the rules should be. So when ten formerly communist countries from central and eastern Europe joined the EU in 2004, millions of workers from low-paid countries could freely come to seek work in Norway under the bloc's "free movement" rules.

And come they did. In the years 2004–18, some 250,000 Poles, Balts, and other East Europeans came to Norway, adding 0.3 per cent to the population on average every year.[2] This was one of the highest rates of work immigration from the EU's new member states to any West European nation. In particular, it was higher, for the country's size, than in the United Kingdom, where East European immigration and EU free movement became an extremely controversial argument for the Leave campaign in the 2016 referendum on EU membership. In Norway, in contrast, public opinion towards immigration hardly shifted at all, despite grumbles about the EU's free movement rules in the most affected sectors. If anything, *more* people thought immigrants should have the same rights as Norwegians to work in 2018 than in 2004.[3]

Why did Norwegians continue to embrace this aspect of globalisation when Britons—who also have a long history of economic openness and a much stronger tradition of embracing immigration than Norway—did not? Not because high immigration left jobs and wages unaffected: Norwegian wages did grow somewhat more slowly for the jobs most commonly filled by immigrants than elsewhere in the economy. Instead, the obvious answer is that Norway has sustained a stronger economy of belonging than Britain. Three things, in particular, have been important. First, Norway maintained a high-pressure economy through stimulative government spending (large accumulated savings from oil production made this easier), in complete contrast to Britain's austerity drive from 2010. Second, it legislated to put in place effective wage floors for jobs in the most exposed sectors, such as those of cleaners and builders, despite not having a general minimum wage. And third, a well-trained workforce and a smooth job market facilitated job switching, so many native workers in the exposed sectors moved into better jobs. On top of this, the efforts of the new immigrant workers of course added to Norway's rate of economic activity and boosted national income in myriad ways: more building work carried out; more nursing, caring, and domestic help provided; and a greater expansion of leisure services than Norwegians would otherwise have enjoyed.[4]

This illustrates an important fact about the economics of belonging: it can turn globalisation itself into something that works for more people. Even if it deals with problems that are technological and domestic in origin, in other words, a restored economics of belonging makes for better globalisation, too. Without raising barriers for products, people, or money flows across national borders, the best domestic policies reduce the risk that they harm the left behind, and may in *practice*, if not by design, end up diminishing cross-border flows—in particular those liable to do more harm than good. This is true for each of the three dimensions of globalisation I examined in chapter 5, and here is why.

How a domestic economy of belonging makes globalisation safer. In chapter 5, I showed that globalisation has been blamed for too many of the problems of left-behind groups, real as they are. Relative to technological change and the economic transformations it has caused, trade and migration explain at best a small fraction of the disappearance of good jobs and rising inequality. Still, we cannot simply dismiss those who really have been hurt by freer trade, whose costs, while modest in total, have been concentrated on particular groups and communities. The same can be said for migration. The best evidence is that the negative effects of low-skilled immigration are very small. But here, too, we should not deny the modest negative effects that do exist. The most thorough studies indicate that it puts *some* downward pressure on wages in the lowest-paid jobs—reinforcing the effect of technological change. Native workers often end up benefitting anyway because they move into other, better-paid professions, but even this can be experienced (especially by those who fail to make this move) as having had one's job, or the status it used to grant, taken away by newcomers. When the local population grows fast, moreover, public services can deteriorate if funding does not keep pace. When such population pressures come from immigration, short-changed host communities may blame the newcomers for it. And beyond the economic, there is a psychological impact of immigration— some feel a genuine loss of community when suddenly many of their neighbours no longer have the same roots as they.[5]

The economics of belonging I have set out in the preceding chapters is designed to make sure nobody is left behind by the technological transformations the Western economies have undergone for the last four decades. The effects of those transformations resemble the effects trade liberalisation and low-skilled immigration can sometimes have on those most exposed to them. After all, this similarity is why it is so easy to blame it all on globalisation. Conversely, this means policies that mitigate the downsides of technological change can also take the sting out of both trade liberalisation and low-skilled immigration.

Let us therefore survey the policies advocated in the preceding chapters and assess how they modify the perceived negative effects of economic openness. Particularly important is the "high-pressure" macroeconomic approach (chapter 8), combined with policies to help people move to better jobs (chapters 6 and 7). An aggressive macroeconomic policy (especially when directed towards productivity-boosting investment) can help increase the number of higher-paid and more productive jobs, even when companies adopt technologies that economise on low-skilled labour. The same policy would also benefit lower-paid native workers who are displaced not by machines but by import competition or immigrant workers coming into low-paid jobs. Combined with high minimum wages and job-switching help, a high-pressure macroeconomic stance that boosts demand for skilled work would make it much easier for native workers to move up the job scale to better and higher-paid jobs—because it would spur businesses to expand the number of such jobs to be filled.

A side effect of our "car wash" policy of encouraging businesses to use cheap labour less by making it costlier for them to do so may even be to lower immigration rates. This is not because of restrictions on anyone who wants to come and work but because, if the driver of low-skilled immigration is the growth of businesses that use low-productivity labour intensively, then a policy aimed to discourage such business models would damp that expansion and hence the demand for immigrant workers. It is likely, for example, that if the United Kingdom had had higher minimum wages and stricter labour rules and enforcement after 2004, the scale of immigration from eastern Europe would have been smaller. The immigrants who would have come anyway would have earned more and would therefore have both spent more locally and paid more in taxes—in turn supporting both high-pressure demand and public service funding. This would have happened without tighter immigration rules—that is, no *less* globalisation. Instead, we could have seen a *better* globalisation, and therefore a more popular one.

Another suite of policies were those focusing on helping *places* specially affected by economic change (chapter 11). Again, since the downsides of new technology often hit regions disproportionately vulnerable to trade or low-skilled immigration, the policies that help with the former can also help with the latter. High-pressure demand policy should be complemented by smart policies to direct the higher aggregate demand to the places most in need of it. It is obvious that this should include public funds keeping pace with local population growth (indeed, whether from immigration or not) to sustain the amount and quality of public services. Schools, hospitals, and roads should all be planned and funded while taking the most reliable short-term population projections into account. In the case of trade, geographically targeted high-pressure demand and the specific regional policies from the last chapter can help restore the fortunes of the places particularly exposed to import competition.

What about financial globalisation? In previous chapters, I mentioned a number of ways in which globally mobile capital can be harmful. One is allowing corporations to escape the national tax net by "placing" their profits in low-tax jurisdictions, and encouraging governments to shift taxes onto workers instead. The other is that when capital crosses borders, so can the financial instability it brings. Global investors' ability to flood a country with money can create dangerous credit booms, and their right to pull capital out on a whim can cripple a government's autonomy to act in its citizens' best interests. A "sudden stop" is economists' term for when an inward flood of easy money not only dries up but is suddenly reversed. Such a balance-of-payments crisis can paralyse an economy that has relied on foreign money to finance trade deficits and investments in excess of domestic savings. An abrupt adjustment to live within one's means is invariably painful—much more so when financial claims built up during good times also have to be paid back.

As with trade and immigration, the consequences of financial globalisation could be tamed by policy proposals set out earlier in the book, even though these are primarily designed to remedy negative effects on the domestic economy. On tax avoidance, chapter 10 discussed at length how to use the full powers of national governments to tax corporations the same regardless of whether they are domestic or global. Here I just repeat that national governments have a lot of unexploited power to tax the profits from business carried out in their countries and do not need to treat companies housed abroad more lightly than those at home. Simply making national corporate tax systems fit for purpose will remove a good deal of the incentives for intricate corporate structures that shift taxable profits into tax havens.

Another domestically oriented policy that can make financial globalisation safer is to move the financial system away from debt and towards other forms of financing that leave more risk with the investor. As I explained in chapter 9, this means treating bank loans and bond purchases less favourably while encouraging equity-type financing (where the investors' return depends on how profitable the project is, rather than being fixed in advance) or direct investment (where investors put money into building new capital that they own directly). A variation on this would be to change the way the legal system treats debt so that it is much easier to write down—effectively making it behave like equity or direct investment when things go badly.

We know that this can blunt the dangers of financial globalisation because we have historical examples of how it has done so. The story of Greece is well known: huge money inflows from other euro countries created a boom in the early 2000s and produced a crippling debt crisis in 2009 when the inflows stopped and the government could not raise funds to cover a huge deficit, let alone pay back existing loans as they became due. But just next door and much less well known, Bulgaria was *more* dependent on foreign financing than Greece in the boom (in terms of both the annual inflows and the accumulated claims of foreign investors). It, too, faced a "sudden stop" of foreign finance in 2008. And yet by 2015, Greece was still in crisis, while Bulgaria had not just recovered but grown its economy by another 10 per cent, after a sharp but short dip in 2009. Why did Bulgaria do so much better when it was even more exposed than Greece? Because Bulgaria's external financing came in the form of foreign direct investment, whereas Greece's was entirely in the form of debt.[6]

When foreign debt investors turn tail, the debt still has to be serviced. That put the squeeze on the Greek economy. But when investors' claims cannot be pulled out, as with equity or direct investment as in Bulgaria, the two principal harms from a balance-of-payments crisis are limited. First, past financing will not have to be paid back; the claims will instead be written down or lose their value. The foreign investors, not the receiving country, will take the loss or wait for the value to recover. Second, new financing will paradoxically be *easier* to attract because fresh investors need not worry that their funds will be spent on bailing out earlier ones. Together, these mean the necessary economic adjustment from a balance-of-payments crisis is smaller, and economic growth restarts sooner. In fact, if cross-border investors expect to be the ones shouldering any losses, they may also direct their money more cautiously in the first place, so that investments are more productive and excessive booms are less likely.

Neither of these policies puts any limits on capital crossing borders. They are not in that sense contrary to globalisation. They may, however, have the practical effect of making it less profitable to shift capital around at quite the scale and the speed we have seen. Again, we see that we can have *better* economic openness with no *less* openness—in this case through policies that keep financial borders just as open but reduce the risks of harm.

All of these policies of economic belonging are entirely within national policy makers' hands. None makes it harder for goods and services, people, or money to cross national borders, or for workers, consumers, or businesses in different countries to interact with one another. Along all three dimensions, then, better domestic policy is capable of taking the worst sting out of globalisation while maintaining, even enhancing, the benefits. Saying "globalisation has gone too far" and needs to be ratcheted back to preserve the domestic economy of belonging presents us with a false choice.

How to globalise even better. But it is of course false to say globalisation is *never* a constraint on a government's room for manoeuvre. Just as no man is an island, no country is entirely isolated from the world. Countries that are economically linked influence one another in ways that create some new opportunities but may limit others. The deeper the integration, the greater the interdependence.

So while I have been at pains to stress just how much more national policy makers can do for those of their own who have been left behind, I do not deny that the form globalisation happens to take matters enormously. Therefore, the rules of the global economy, too, must be written to put as few obstacles as possible in the way of strong economies of belonging within nations. Above all, that means that we should pursue economic integration across national borders in ways that allow countries to act on their collective preferences and values—otherwise, antiglobalisers will be right to want to "take back control."

The brute fact of international economics is that different countries have different preferences for how goods and services are produced, expressed in laws, regulations, and culture. Often these are deeply held moral or cultural values, arrived at through the resolution of long historical conflicts. Trade, immigration, and cross-border finance bring these national values into tension with one another because they raise the question of whose rules should predominate. The antiglobalising answer is to reduce economic interdependence so that each country can straightforwardly decide how things are done within its borders and—supposedly—not worry about what happens beyond them. This is the answer logically suggested by the "globalisation trilemma" posited by Dani Rodrik, as strong a friend of the liberal order as any (see chapter 5).

But there are two other answers, both of which are more compatible with an economics of belonging that is also open to the world. The first is to keep borders open but without compromising on the rules for selling goods and services or providing labour or capital *within* each national economy—provided these rules express real national preferences for the shape of how we buy from, sell to, work for, and finance one another, and are not a roundabout way of discriminating against foreigners. The second, which I leave for the next section, is to globalise our politics at the same time as our economies.

The first point means that we should not confuse globalisation with deregulation. In trade, we should not think lowering import barriers requires lowering the standards that governments demand of the goods and services for sale in their jurisdiction. In the debate over Britain's future outside the EU, a big question is whether it will allow agricultural imports from new trading partners that do not comply with the EU's standards. The totemic case is chicken meat washed in chlorine, which in the United States is a tolerated practice to remove bacterial contamination at the end of the production process. In contrast,

EU and therefore pre-Brexit UK rules require strict hygienic outcomes at each production stage. Britons will have to decide for themselves whether to accept such chicken meat in their shops. The point here is simply to understand that if they decide not to, this will not constitute a refusal to globalise—so long as chicken farmers in the United States and other countries are allowed to sell meat into UK markets that *does* comply with whatever standards the United Kingdom applies.

The general principle is that economic openness, the third pillar of the Western social order, consists in allowing foreigners to participate in one's national economy on the same terms as one's own people. It does *not* require accepting cross-border transactions under standards one would not accept at home. To think that it does is to confuse globalisation with deregulation. That confusion has often been created—by the statist left to oppose globalisation, and by the deregulatory right to advocate it—but it is a mistake.

Properly understood, this principle also justifies writing social and environmental clauses into free trade agreements. This is the way EU trade policy has been moving in recent years. Its proposed free trade agreement with Mercosur (the South American trading bloc that includes Brazil) contains innovative commitments to combat climate change. At the time of this writing, however, ratification is in jeopardy because of doubts that the agreement holds Brazil strongly enough to these commitments, in particular regarding the preservation of the Amazonian rain forest. The same free trade agreement provides for duty-free access to the EU for eggs from the Mercosur countries only insofar as they are produced according to EU animal welfare standards. Canada, too, has moved in this direction, pushing for higher labour standards in the renegotiated North American Free Trade Agreement with the United States and Mexico, for example. It is simply a misconception to say that such conditions are barriers to *trade*; they are rather an expression of the collective preferences of what the prospective importing nations want to *consume*, whether traded internationally or not (in this case, whether they want to consume goods produced in ways that contribute to climate change, violate animal welfare, or are produced by low-paid labour).

In the most extreme instance, this principle could justify what at first glance seems like plain protectionism: tariffs or other constraints on offending imports. But just as trade liberalisation should not be seen as *requiring* a country to import goods it collectively does not want—there is nothing "liberalising" about that—it also should not be seen as requiring a country to facilitate the shift elsewhere of practices it finds intolerable at home. A good example is the fast-changing world of Big Data and how governments are imposing privacy rules on how companies handle and use data collected from users. If those governments impose the same restrictions on cross-border *trade* in their citizens' data, that is not a refusal to liberalise trade (at least if they do allow data trade with countries that have similar restrictions in their own rules). It is simply a refusal to open up loopholes in the law under the cover of trade. The same can be said for so-called carbon border taxes—tariffs imposed on imports from countries that do not make producers pay as much for their carbon emissions as domestic producers do. These are not barriers to trade as much as measures to prevent domestic laws from being undermined. Again, globalisation should not be confused with deregulation when the former is used to camouflage the latter.

This reasoning extends to other dimensions of globalisation. In the case of immigration, openness need not allow immigration to undermine established labour standards at home.

This is usually a matter of enforcing more strongly the laws that already exist, since immigrants may be more at the mercy of unscrupulous employers than native workers. But when those standards themselves result from social conventions or an institutionalised balance of power, it may require new legislative or policy actions to compensate for a weakening of traditional norms and institutions. A case in point is the tightening of EU rules on "posted workers"—those working outside the country where they are formally employed—to make host-country rules kick in sooner and more comprehensively. Another example is when Norway resorted to administrative extensions of collective bargaining outcomes in sectors with a lot of migrant workers. This established sectoral minimum wages in all but name in a country where this was traditionally left to collective bargaining.

In finance, too, it is possible to regulate in such a way that capital flows from other countries do not escape the strictures imposed on domestic capital, without putting barriers in the way of cross-border money. I have already explained the room for national policy manoeuvre in taxation (chapter 10) and "macroprudential" regulation of financial services (chapter 9).[7] When a bank is situated beyond your country's border but has the right—thanks to financial globalisation—to lend to your country's citizens, how do you make such regulations work? The answer is to enforce it on the borrowing side—for example, by making it illegal to borrow more than specified amounts in specified circumstances, where those circumstances can include whether the foreign lenders satisfy regulatory requirements. Or it can be to otherwise use regulations and taxes to penalise borrowing and encourage safer forms of financing such as equity and direct investment. While a foreign bank may be outside the jurisdiction of a national regulator, it will still require the help of domestic authorities to, say, seize the security collateral from a delinquent borrower who is not servicing his or her loan. That help can be made conditional on the foreign lender having complied with domestic policy choices and not allowed the domestic borrower to circumvent them.

All these examples have something in common. They do nothing to bar access to foreign sellers, service providers, workers, or investors. That is to say, they are not discriminatory and put no limits on economic interactions across borders (other than the limits put on the same interactions inside national borders). Instead, they use national powers so that the law that binds domestically also applies to transactions with foreigners. The consequence *could* of course be that it becomes less attractive to sell, work, and lend across borders. But there would be nothing antiglobalising about such an outcome. It would simply reflect that some cross-border economic flows were a response not to globalisation but to deregulation, or more specifically the circumvention of regulations needed to uphold a domestic economy of belonging.

Globalising the economics of belonging. There is one final way of upholding a domestic economy of belonging while encouraging more international openness. This is for several countries to agree on a common set of rules and remove economic borders accordingly between those that join the agreement. This is how the European Union works—the deepest voluntary project of globalisation the world has ever seen. The common rules on goods and services production that EU member states decide jointly mean that, uniquely in the world, they have no border controls on goods that flow between them, and in principle no limits on cross-border services trade. Most of them also have done away with passport controls for people crossing borders.

If countries are close enough in their values that they can come to such agreements, they can also globalise more, and reap the benefits in greater productivity, without undermining their own economies of belonging. The existence of the EU ought to lay to rest the idea that globalisation and regulation need to be traded off against one another. Its approach to economic globalisation, based as it is on more common rules, admittedly leaves less room for national ones. But the point here is that the more extensive common rules do not undermine differing local or national values; on the contrary, they reflect values held in common.

European countries have enough of a fellowship of values to have gone much further down this route than any other part of the world. Such a fellowship is utopian elsewhere—except in specific areas. Taxation is a timely example. In the 1960s and 1970s, countries signed a network of bilateral tax treaties that restricted their ability to tax companies based elsewhere. At the time, when economic activity largely required a physical presence, this was a set of agreements that tied governments' hands somewhat, but in a way intended to free them to tax more effectively without putting obstacles in the way of cross-border business through double taxation. By now, this system is beyond obsolete and has badly undermined national economies of belonging (see chapter 10). But that is because of what these particular rules specifically prescribe, not a necessary consequence of the mere existence of international rules. If the work currently under way to reform multinational corporate taxation is successful, it will serve as a renewed example of how binding international rules can at the same time promote economic globalisation *and* enhance national governments' ability to pursue a domestic economy of belonging if they so wish.

To align the political values of different nations, whether in the broad sense that the European project seeks or in a specific area such as cross-border corporate tax reform, is not a mere technical policy challenge. Successfully melding openness and domestic satisfaction requires statecraft. But statecraft deployed to restore the Western social order—by making globalisation compatible with, even supportive of, an economy of belonging at home—is statecraft well spent.

13

Beyond Left and Right

I started this book by asking readers to cast their eyes back to 1933. In a world where hope was thin on the ground, Franklin Roosevelt rekindled faith in rising prosperity for everyone with a policy programme full of what he called "bold, persistent experimentation." In an example soon to be followed by many others, Roosevelt's administration put economic radicalism in the service of defending political centrism and liberalism. I have argued we can do the same today and have set out why and how I think it can be done. The argument developed in this book amounts to an unabashed defence of liberal centrism, which explicitly seeks to disarm the illiberal fringe movements that have been on the rise throughout the West. One might even say that it sets out to make liberalism great again.

When such an argument is focused mainly on economics, it owes an answer to those who ask: What about the politics? In fact, there are two questions to answer. The first looks back. If my diagnosis is right, how did the liberal centre let it come to this in the first place? The end of belonging happened on the centrists' watch everywhere, so why did centrist politicians fail so badly? The second question looks to the future: Is the radical economics of belonging I have proposed politically realistic? After so many mistakes, can liberal centrist parties be expected to adopt, let alone implement, such a programme?

The early chapters hinted at some answers to the first question. The survey in part 1 of the economic forces that ended the postwar economy of belonging highlighted both the lack of adequate policy responses to the transformations undergone by Western economies and, in many places, a political shift towards policies that made matters even worse. The most seductive explanation for why governments let these problems happen is the wave of centre-right support that washed over the West in the 1980s. That was above all the Reagan and Thatcher revolution, a carefully prepared (and often well-funded) intellectual and political crusade to discredit New Deal liberalism and postwar social democracy. But the ideas these politicians brought with them into power in the United States and the United Kingdom also enjoyed far-reaching influence in many other countries, including those where centre-right parties were not as electorally successful. A programme of deregulation, lower tax rates, and looser state control of the postwar social democratic economy was implemented in many countries over the following decades. Many social democratic parties were among the liberalisers.

The rightward shift in the United States and the United Kingdom can be partly attributed to the policy makers and analysts who laid the intellectual groundwork for Reagan's and Thatcher's programmes and had long popularised and defended them in the public square, as well as the patient money invested in think tanks and fellowships to produce public intellectuals who could advance and defend a deregulatory agenda. But this cannot explain the fact that virtually all of the West shifted politically at the same time. A bigger reason, even in the United States and the United Kingdom, is that electorates were ready for change, because it had become obvious that some modernisation of the postwar economic system was needed. In the 1970s, oil shocks and monetary chaos brought stagnation and inflation spikes to most Western countries, just as the number of factory jobs peaked. This created an appetite for reform in electorates that rewarded politicians willing to provide it.

That, together with the fall of communism in 1989, which eliminated the only serious alternative to capitalism, also explains why the centre-left—or the third way, as the crop of young politicians coming to power in the 1990s liked to think of their revamped parties—embraced or at least did not reverse the liberalising reforms. Leftist parties reforming themselves in the 1990s took on board much of the deregulation and tax cutting that had been controversially pushed through by centre-right parties in the 1980s. Sometimes they doubled down on the 1980s reforms—witness the German labour reforms in the early 2000s (mentioned in chapter 4), which made work more precarious and caused wage stagnation for many, passed and put in place under Gerhard Schröder, a Social Democratic Party leader. In general, the "third way" centre-left was prepared to let free markets work much like its centre-right rivals, but using the fruits of growth to increase redistribution or spend more on public services.

In this way, both the centre-right and the centre-left either left unchecked or spurred on the underlying dynamics of divergence and inequality in the economy, which were beginning to take effect but escaped serious attention. In other words, both sides of the political centre neglected the deeper changes under way while fighting elections over competing policies that made little difference to the bigger problems. Why was this? The main answer, I think, lies in the specific nature of the economic changes themselves. The divergence I have described— between central and peripheral regions, and between those with "new" and "old" skills—created two political difficulties for established political parties, difficulties that they have still not managed to overcome.

The first difficulty is that the problems of the left behind are easily obscured by the success of those who thrive in the new economy and benefit most from economic openness. These "winners" are, I should add, much more likely to work in party politics, policy making, or the media. That contributes to intellectual capture—an impaired ability to see the problems that afflict the left behind, paired with an embrace of theories and economic "narratives" that justify the benefits enjoyed by the winners (such as the third way's focus on meritocracy). This sort of blind spot seems to have been at work when policymaking elites almost unanimously pursued macroeconomic policies (excessive fiscal austerity and insufficient monetary stimulus) that had bad consequences for the economy as a whole and devastating ones for those on its margins (chapter 8). The same intellectual capture can be seen in the benign neglect (or active cheerleading) of dangerous financial expansion in the early 2000s, or the fear of restructuring failing banks after the crisis (chapters 4 and 9).

The second political difficulty is that with divergence in terms of economic success came divergence in the real material interests of groups that were rapidly growing apart. That made traditional electoral coalitions harder to straddle. This has been a particularly acute problem for centre-left parties, which have struggled to stitch together policy programmes that appeal to both the liberal knowledge workers in cities and what remains of the more traditional working class. But in many European countries, the traditional centre-right has also struggled in a party landscape that continues to fragment. One might think that seeing a once-powerful voter coalition fragment would make a party that used to rely on it all the more alert to the underlying problem. But the more immediate consequence has been to make parties incapable of identifying policies that can both reverse the divergence between their traditional supporting groups and retain the votes of all of them—especially when we add in the psychological and intellectual blind spots divergence itself has caused.

The contention of this book is that a programme like the one I have set out can overcome this dilemma. Most of the argument has focused on solutions to an economic system that has been driving people apart. But the economics of belonging could also be the basis for a new political programme that could rebuild a winning coalition for centrist parties, here and now.

Which centrist parties? Is this a programme for the centre-left or for the centre-right? Both the diagnosis and the prescriptions I have offered may strike many readers as having a distinctly left-of-centre feel to them. The programme does, after all, aim to resolve a problem—the end of belonging—that is associated with the decline of post–Second World War social democracy. And throughout the book, my focus on the rise in inequality and a concern with the ill effects it has brought may look like something that belongs squarely on the left of the political centre.

The intention, however, is not to reconstruct the same institutions and policies that sustained the previous era of economic belonging. These would no longer be fit for purpose given how the economy, technology, society, and the world of work have themselves changed. Indeed, the electoral support for the West's rightward political shift in the 1980s came about in part because postwar social democracy's ways of doing things was already seen as obsolete.

And it takes only a moment's reflection to see that many aspects of the twenty-first-century economics of belonging I advocate are not traditionally left wing. To start with, it does not put much stock in state ownership (with narrow exceptions, such as being open to government-sponsored internet platforms as a form of digital public infrastructure, mentioned in chapter 7). It also is not fundamentally wedded to a given size of the state—in particular not to a *bigger* state—as a share of national income. While sufficient public funds must be committed to the basic foundations of an economy of belonging— such as education and skills training, active labour market policies, and infrastructure—this does not preclude reducing spending on other things so as to keep overall public spending unchanged. Whether pursuing a coherent economics of belonging means a bigger state will really differ from country to country. Japan and Iceland, for example, have public spending at about 40 per cent of national economy, suggesting an economy of belonging does not need Scandinavian or French levels of state expenditure. Those rich countries with the smallest state share of the economy may need their public sector to expand to establish a successful programme of economic belonging. But those with the biggest share may find such a programme affordable even while *reducing* the government's overall economic imprint.[1]

I have also defended an agnostic attitude to unions. The essential economic functions they fulfilled in the postwar economy need to be restored and sustained, but this can often be achieved in other ways more effectively than by simply re-creating unions or strengthening those that are weak or dysfunctional. Furthermore, while inequality has been at the heart of the analysis, mere redistribution has not. Certainly, the tax reforms in chapter 10 and the universal basic income (UBI)/negative income tax (NIT) proposal in chapter 7 would have redistributive effects. But much more important is to create markets that deliver good opportunities for all, so that there is less need to redistribute in the first place. And this in turn is only achieved by promoting what we might call *equality of productivity*, or policies that boost the productivity of those on the margin, so that higher earning power will follow in free but well-regulated markets.

All these points illustrate that while certainly compatible with centre-left politics, the economics of belonging is not a social democratic throwback. There are many elements of it that would sit equally comfortably with a centre-right party. The net wealth tax, for example, is a proposal not for higher taxation but for different taxation. As I explained in chapter 10, it should be seen as a capitalist-friendly tax, because it rewards those who make the most of their capital and punishes those who manage their wealth badly. That is especially true if it replaces other, more commonly used taxes on capital, such as dividend or capital gains taxes. A progressive net wealth tax also promotes more widespread wealth holdings—one might even say it encourages a "property-owning democracy." That is surely something a centre-right party could embrace with gusto.

UBI/NIT, too, has long been supported on the right. Milton Friedman and his followers understood how means-tested welfare benefits could disempower recipients and create low-income traps because of the exorbitant effective marginal tax rates borne by lower-middle earners who face the withdrawal of their benefits if they achieve higher pay. As chapter 7 explained, a UBI/NIT system would dramatically lower these rates and could therefore be marketed as a tax cut. The pro-competition policies of the economics of belonging should also sit easily with a centre-right political outlook, as should the overall defence of globalisation and economic openness from the last chapter.

Creating an economics of belonging will, however, require the state to play an important and active role in intelligently steering the economy. That does not mean the detailed central planning of the former communist countries, nor, as discussed earlier, does it mean a very *big* state. But it does presuppose a conscious directing of resources—to such things as human capital and regional productivity—and a willingness to coordinate private-sector behaviour in ways that support this focus.

This would not fit a right-wing party professing a radically libertarian or laissez-faire economic philosophy. Then again, my economics of belonging would hardly be more acceptable to a left-wing party with an outright Marxist ideology. But the centrist parties that commanded Western politics in the 1990s and early 2000s should not find it difficult to embrace. The value of "belonging" itself sits comfortably with all parts of the political centre. Traditional centre-right conservative parties and traditional social democratic parties alike can find a space for belonging in their political vocabularies—and more importantly, their political programmes—and so, of course, can traditional liberal parties.

While some specific elements of the economics of belonging I have proposed may seem closer to particular centre-right or centre-left parties readers may have in mind, there is nothing that could not be endorsed in full by a principled politician of either camp. The key, however, is to adopt them in combination as a total policy package, making up a comprehensive programme of government. A centrist economics of belonging must be radical in its scope and scale for two reasons.

The first is that the different policies complement and reinforce one another, and are therefore less likely to produce their desired effects if implemented in isolation. For example, higher wage floors and better workplace rules will only improve productivity without lowering employment if a high-pressure economy encourages businesses to hire and there is good provision of education and retraining opportunities. A high-pressure economy can in turn only safely be pursued if the financial system is more stable. And none of these things will reliably help the left behind without redirecting the tax system and regional policy in their favour. Tax or regional policies, meanwhile, will not do as much as they could in the absence of high demand pressure and incentives to increase productivity.

The other reason is that a piecemeal approach is much easier for vested interests to block. Pick any particular policy to promote an economy of belonging: even if implementing it would do some good, there will always be some group that will want to mobilise to frustrate it, while the beneficiaries—almost by definition—are those who are too disempowered to make their voices heard. A comprehensive large-scale programme has two advantages: it multiplies the fronts on which opponents of reform have to fight, and it increases the opportunity for mobilising support from and on behalf of those who would benefit from it.

The political viability of a policy programme depends on it delivering on its promises. So for the reasons just mentioned, a centrist party faces better political prospects with a radically ambitious economic policy than with an incremental approach. At the time of this writing, such grand narratives are starting to emerge in Western politics. One, which started on the left but in Europe has gained currency on the centre-right as well, is the "green new deal" or the "European green deal"—an attempt to package a number of reformist economic policies around the goal of addressing climate change. (If this book has not paid much attention to that challenge, it is because the end of belonging is a big enough problem on its own, and the policies

I recommend would have been needed even in the absence of the climate threat. If addressing the latter can help mobilise support for the former, so much the better.) Emmanuel Macron's rhetoric of "a Europe that protects" has been more modestly deployed in a similar way, combining liberalising labour market reform in France with pushing for a tightening of "posted workers" rules at the European level (see chapter 12). And while it remains to be seen whether Boris Johnson's government elected in December 2019 will keep its promises, the rhetoric of "levelling up" the country seems at least to have created political room on the right for a big shift towards regional investment and other interventionist measures to reconfigure the UK economy.

I mention these examples simply as illustrations of how the political support for an economics of belonging could be built. They show that centrist parties, whether long established or more recent, are able to come up with grand narratives under which a comprehensive policy programme can be successfully presented to voters. Not only can they do this, but they must do it if the populists are not to be the only ones to make the left behind feel that they are being listened to. Centrist parties, those who want to defend the Western social contract, must also listen, but not just that: they must paint a convincing vision of a restored economy of belonging, and offer a comprehensive and radical programme for getting there. Only by matching talk with action can they hope to win back the left behind *and* prove to those who have been the winners of the last decades of economic change that radical reform is in their own long-term interest.

For that is the truth that defenders of the liberal order must hold on to and not allow to be forgotten. As I set out at the beginning of the book, the threat to the Western social contract comes from the crumbling of its economic pillar, which has fuelled a rebellion against the pillars of liberal politics and international openness. Those who most oppose this rebellion are very often those who have benefitted handsomely from the end of economic belonging—it is, after all, not *they* who no longer belong. But let me be clear: they have benefitted insofar as the entire liberal order has not yet crumbled with its economic pillar. What happens to them if it does? That is the question well-off liberal centrists must ask themselves. They cannot safely enjoy the political and international pillars of the postwar Western order if the economic pillar is not repaired. If they are genuine in their support for liberal politics and a globalised world, they will need to see them defended even at some cost to themselves. Some of them will, perhaps, be able to see some of their own favourable economic situation as the luck of the draw, and that restoring belonging and hope to those who have lost them is in the gift of those who retain them. One may hope in turn that realising this stops them from instinctively opposing those policies proposed here that might hurt their short-term material interests.

In the preceding chapters I have tried to draw connections to show how the political situation many of us fear today grew from economic changes over the lifetimes (or longer) of those who hold this book in their hands. Better understanding how the world is connected can sometimes spur us to be motivated by something more than our own narrow self-interest, in the knowledge that in the longer term, our deepest interests are bound up with those others who live very different lives from ours. That knowledge is the foundation for a fair and liberal society, and it has rarely been more urgently needed than today.

NOTES

Chapter 1. The End of Belonging

1. Indeed, the economist and inequality scholar Branko Milanovic classifies China's "political capitalism" as a subvariant of a globally dominant capitalist system in his account of a global economy where capitalism is now unchallenged. Milanovic, *Capitalism, Alone: The Future of the System That Rules the World*, Cambridge, MA: Belknap Press of Harvard University Press, 2019.

Chapter 2. Who Are the Left Behind?

1. Clifford Krauss, "Texas Oil Fields Rebound from Price Lull, but Jobs Are Left Behind," *New York Times*, 19 February 2017, https://www.nytimes.com/2017/02/19/business/energy-environment/oil-jobs-technology.html.

2. "The Trials of Life in Tilbury," *Economist*, 16 August 2014, https://www.economist.com/britain/2014/08/16/the-trials-of-life-in-tilbury.

3. The characteristic elephant shape of the chart has been challenged; see Chris Giles and Shawn Donnan, "Globalisation 'Not to Blame' for Income Woes, Study Says," *Financial Times*, 13 September 2016, https://www.ft.com/content/93f2d4ba-7901-11e6-97ae-647294649b28; and Dylan Matthews, "The Global Top 1 Percent Earned Twice as Much as the Bottom 50 Percent in Recent Years," Vox, 2 February 2018, https://www.vox.com/policy-and-politics/2018/2/2/16868838/elephant-graph-chart-global-inequality-economic-growth. But some of the criticism has been misplaced. That is especially true of "refutations" of the claim that the elephant chart proves globalisation caused the relative stagnation of the rich-country "lower middle"—a claim the creators of the chart did not make. Indeed, this chapter and later ones explain how the "low base of the trunk" should be attributed to labour-saving technological change and misguided domestic policies, even if the "high back," or the strong income growth of the emerging poor-country middle class, clearly is related to those countries' inclusion in global manufacturing supply chains. The empirical criticisms are also weaker than they may seem at first glance. Adjusting the comparison of income groups over time to be more "like-for-like" and looking more closely at which countries contribute most to the characteristic shape end up buttressing the original interpretation of the data: that the global middle and the very richest enjoyed very high income growth while those in the lower part of rich-country income distributions suffered relative stagnation.

See Martin Sandbu, "The Charting of Inequality Deserves Greater Scrutiny," *Financial Times*, 13 September 2016, https://www.ft.com/content/9d6f9c3c-799a-11e6-a0c6 -39e2633162d5; and Martin Sandbu, "Shooting an Elephant," *Financial Times*, 14 September 2019, https://www.ft.com/content/6465d860-79c3-11e6-97ae-647294649b28.

4. Cyrille Schwellnus, Andreas Kappeler, and Pierre-Alain Pionnier, "Decoupling of Wages from Productivity: Macro-level Facts" (OECD Economics Department Working Paper 1373, Organisation for Economic Co-operation and Development, 24 January 2017), https://www.oecd.org/social/labour/Decoupling-of-wages-from -productivity-Macro-level-facts.pdf.

5. See Mai Chi Dao, Mitali Das, Zsoka Koczan, and Weicheng Lian, "Drivers of Declining Labor Share of Income," *IMFBlog*, 12 April 2017, https://blogs.imf.org/2017 /04/12/drivers-of-declining-labor-share-of-income/; and Mai Chi Dao, Mitali Das, Zsoka Koczan, and Weicheng Lian, "The Hollowing Out of Middle-Skilled Labor Share of Income," *IMFBlog*, 14 April 2017, https://blogs.imf.org/2017/04/14/the -hollowing-out-of-middle-skilled-labor-share-of-income/. Outside the United States, this advantage for capital owners often came through the increased share of housing rents in national income. See Germán Gutiérrez and Sophie Piton, "Revisiting the Global Decline of the (Non-housing) Labor Share" (Staff Working Paper No. 811, Bank of England, 19 July 2019), https://www.bankofengland.co.uk/working-paper/2019 /revisiting-the-global-decline-of-the-non-housing-labor-share.

6. International Monetary Fund, World Bank, and World Trade Organisation, *Making Trade an Engine of Growth for All: The Case for Trade and for Policies to Facilitate Adjustment*, 10 April 2017, https://www.imf.org/en/Publications/Policy-Papers /Issues/2017/04/08/making-trade-an-engine-of-growth-for-all.

7. Mark Muro and Siddharth Kulkarni, "Voter Anger Explained—in One Chart," Brookings, 15 March 2016, https://www.brookings.edu/blog/the-avenue/2016/03/15 /voter-anger-explained-in-one-chart/.

8. This is the sort of pure ideas-based efficiency (economists call it "total factor productivity") that Paul Romer received the 2018 economics Nobel Prize for analysing. For the amazing story of how the shipping container transformed trade, see Tim Harford, "50 Things That Made the Modern Economy: The Simple Steel Box That Transformed Global Trade," BBC World Service, 9 January 2017, https://www.bbc .co.uk/news/business-38305512.

9. Martin Sandbu, "How Blue-Collar Aristocracy Was Laid Low," *Financial Times*, 19 November 2018, https://www.ft.com/content/b336e428-e8e5-11e8-a34c -663b3f553b35.

10. Krauss, "Texas Oil Fields."

11. Martin Sandbu, "Place and Prosperity," *Financial Times*, 16 December 2016, https://www.ft.com/content/63f71020-c21f-11e6-9bca-2b93a6856354.

12. Robert Frank and Philip Cook, "Winner-Take-All Markets," *Studies in Microeconomics* 1, no. 2 (December 2013): 131–54, https://doi.org/10.1177/2321022213501254.

13. Jason Furman, "Forms and Sources of Inequality in the United States," VoxEU, 17 March 2016, https://voxeu.org/article/forms-and-sources-inequality-united-states.

14. Ben Ansell and David Adler, "Brexit and the Politics of Housing in Britain," *Political Quarterly* 90, no. 52 (April 2019): 105–16, https://doi.org/10.1111/1467-923X.12621.

15. Raven Molloy, Christopher L. Smith, and Abigail Wozniak, "Internal Migration in the United States," *Journal of Economic Perspectives* 25, no. 3 (2011): 173–96, https://doi.org/10.1257/jep.25.3.173. Britons, too, move less often between parts of the country for work than they used to; see Sarah O'Connor, "Fewer People Move between UK Regions for Work," *Financial Times*, 15 August 2017, https://www.ft.com /content/c66b127c-80ee-11e7-a4ce-15b2513cb3ff.

16. "Trials of Life in Tilbury."

17. Alan Gerber, Gregory Huber, David Doherty, Conor Dowling, and Shang Ha, "Personality and Political Attitudes: Relationships across Issue Domains and Political Contexts," *American Political Science Review* 104, no. 1 (February 2010): 111–33, https://pdfs.semanticscholar.org/f6f2/7543241293daa6e3cd415a3737f493b816d1.pdf; Harry Garretsen, Janka I. Stoker, Dimitrios Soudis, Ron Martin, and Jason Rentfrow, "Brexit and the Relevance of Regional Personality Traits: More Psychological Openness Could Have Swung the Regional Vote," VoxEU, 25 February 2018, https://voxeu .org/article/more-openness-could-have-swung-regional-brexit-vote.

18. Daniel Cox and Robert Jones, "Still Live Near Your Hometown? If You're White, You're More Likely to Support Trump: PRRI/The Atlantic Survey," Public Religion Research Institute, 10 June 2016, https://www.prri.org/research/prri-atlantic-oct-6 -poll-politics-election-clinton-trump/.

19. "Employment by Major Industry Sector," Bureau of Labor Statistics, last modified 4 September 2019, https://www.bls.gov/emp/tables/employment-by-major -industry-sector.htm.

20. See Nicolas Lamp, "How Should We Think about the Winners and Losers from Globalization? Three Narratives and Their Implications for the Redesign of International Economic Agreements" (Queen's University Legal Research Paper No. 2018-102, Kingston, Ontario, December 2018), https://papers.ssrn.com/sol3/papers.cfm ?abstract_id=3290590.

21. Martin Sandbu, "Shackled to the 1950s," *Financial Times*, 19 January 2017, https://www.ft.com/content/6dad0560-de36-11e6-9d7c-be108f1c1dce.

22. For example, about 10 per cent of childcare and preschool staff in Norway are men; in the United Kingdom and the United States, the number is around 3 per cent. In nursing, however, the three countries' share of men is similar at about 10 per cent. And the Nordic societies, while excelling at female work participation, often fall short compared with other countries in terms of the number of women in high private-sector positions. See "Employed Persons by Detailed Occupation, Sex, Race, and Hispanic or Latino Ethnicity," Bureau of Labor Statistics, last modified 18 January 2019, https://www.bls.gov/cps/cpsaat11.htm; "Calls for More Men to Work in the Early Years," Gov.uk, 24 April 2019, https://www.gov.uk/government/news/calls-for -more-men-to-work-in-the-early-years, https://epi.org.uk/publications-and-research /the-early-years-workforce-in-england/; and "Ansatte i barnehage og skole," Statistics Norway, updated 3 July 2019, https://www.ssb.no/utdanning/statistikker/utdansatte.

23. Anne Case and Angus Deaton, *Mortality and Morbidity in the 21st Century*, Brookings Papers on Economic Activity, 2017, https://www.brookings.edu/bpea -articles/mortality-and-morbidity-in-the-21st-century/.

24. Andrew Gregory, "Deaths Jump Fivefold as Doctors Dole Out Opioids 'like Smarties,'" *Times* (UK), 25 August 2019, https://www.thetimes.co.uk/edition/news /deaths-jump-fivefold-as-doctors-dole-out-opioids-like-smarties-kmcm7nbh5.

Chapter 3. Culture versus Economics

1. Matthew Goodwin and Roger Eatwell, *National Populism: The Revolt against Liberal Democracy*, Harmondsworth, UK: Penguin, 2018.

2. I am talking here about the overall support for pro- and anti-integrationist forces across the EU as a whole. Of course anti-European populists advanced in some countries from 2014 to 2019—notably Italy—but they lost support in others. See Nicolas Véron, "European Parliament Election Results: The Long View," Bruegel, 29 May 2019, http://www.bruegel.org/2019/05/european-parliament-election-results -the-long-view.

3. This also fits the academic research that shows financial crises tend to be followed by a rise in support for right-wing populism and extremism. See Manuel Funke, Moritz Schularick, and Christoph Trebesch, "Going to Extremes: Politics after Financial Crises, 1870–2014," *European Economic Review* 88 (September 2016): 227–60, https://doi.org/10.1016/j.euroecorev.2016.03.006.

4. K. K. Rebecca Lai and Allison McCann, "Exit Polls: How Voting Blocs Have Shifted from the '80s to Now," *New York Times*, 7 November 2018, https://www .nytimes.com/interactive/2018/11/07/us/elections/house-exit-polls-analysis.html.

5. Danny Dorling, "Brexit and Britain's Radical Right," *Political Insight* 9, no. 4 (2018): 16–18, https://doi.org/10.1177/2041905818815197.

6. "Unemployment Statistics," Eurostat, last updated October 2019, https://ec .europa.eu/eurostat/statistics-explained/index.php?title=Unemployment_statistics.

7. Ronald Inglehart and Pippa Norris, "Trump, Brexit, and the Rise of Populism: Economic Have-Nots and Cultural Backlash" (Harvard Kennedy School Working Paper RWP16-026, July 2016), http://dx.doi.org/10.2139/ssrn.2818659.

8. Pippa Norris, "It's Not Just Trump. Authoritarian Populism Is Rising across the West. Here's Why," *Monkey Cage* (blog), *Washington Post*, 11 March 2016, https:// www.washingtonpost.com/news/monkey-cage/wp/2016/03/11/its-not-just-trump -authoritarian-populism-is-rising-across-the-west-heres-why/.

9. Ernesto Dal Bó, Frederico Finan, Olle Folke, Torsten Persson, and Johanna Rickne, "Economic Losers and Political Winners: Sweden's Radical Right," February 2019, 2, http://perseus.iies.su.se/~tpers/papers/CompleteDraft190301.pdf.

10. Dal Bó et al., 2.

11. Lai and McCann, "Exit Polls."

12. Thiemo Fetzer, "Did Austerity Cause Brexit?," *American Economic Review* 109, no. 11 (November 2019): 3849–86, https://doi.org/10.1257/aer.20181164. See also

Sascha Becker, Thiemo Fetzer, and Dennis Novy, "The Fundamental Factors behind the Brexit Vote," VoxEU, 31 October 2016, https://voxeu.org/article/fundamental-factors -behind-brexit-vote, where the authors establish many of the patterns described in this chapter.

13. Jed Kolko, "Trump Was Stronger Where the Economy Is Weaker," FiveThirtyEight, 10 November 2016, https://fivethirtyeight.com/features/trump-was-stronger -where-the-economy-is-weaker/.

14. Delphine Strauss, "Squeezed Middle Faces Growing Risk of Poverty," *Financial Times*, 15 June 2018, https://www.ft.com/content/13fe209e-707f-11e8-852d -d8b934ff5ffa.

15. Christian Dustmann, Barry Eichengreen, Sebastian Otten, André Sapir, Guido Tabellini, and Gylfi Zoega, "Populism and Trust in Europe," VoxEU, 23 August 2017, https://voxeu.org/article/populism-and-trust-europe.

16. Cameron Ballard-Rosa, Amalie Jensen, and Kenneth Scheve, "Economic Decline, Social Identity, and Authoritarian Values in the United States," March 2019, http://web.stanford.edu/group/scheve-research/cgi-bin/wordpress/wp-content /uploads/2019/03/AuthorUS_Mar-19.pdf; Cameron Ballard-Rosa, Mashail Malik, Stephanie Rickard, and Kenneth Scheve, "The Economic Origins of Authoritarian Values: Evidence from Local Trade Shocks in the United Kingdom," 7 March 2019, https://web.stanford.edu/group/scheve-research/cgi-bin/wordpress/wp-content /uploads/2019/03/The_Economic_Origins_of_Authoritarian_Values__March2019 .pdf; Catherine De Vries, Margit Tavits, and Hector Solaz, "Economic Hardship, Rightwing Authoritarianism & the Demand for Socially Conservative Policies," 13 July 2017, https://catherinedevries.eu/EconomicGrievancesRiseAuthoritarianism2.pdf.

17. Robert Sapolsky, "How Economic Inequality Inflicts Real Biological Harm," *Scientific American*, 1 November 2018, https://www.scientificamerican.com/article /how-economic-inequality-inflicts-real-biological-harm/.

18. Angus Deaton, "Relative Deprivation, Inequality, and Mortality" (NBER Working Paper No. 8099, National Bureau of Economic Research, Cambridge, MA, January 2001), https://www.nber.org/papers/w8099.

19. Fiona Kiernan, "The Great Recession and Mental Health: The Effect of Income Loss on the Psychological Health of Young Mothers" (UCD Geary Institute Working Paper 2018/21, University College Dublin, 9 October 2018), http://www.ucd.ie/geary /static/publications/workingpapers/gearywp201821.pdf.

20. Immo Fritsche, Eva Jonas, Catharina Ablasser, Magdalena Beyer, Johannes Kuban, Anna-Marie Manger, and Marlene Schultz, "The Power of We: Evidence for Group-Based Control," *Journal of Experimental Social Psychology* 49, no. 1 (January 2013): 19–32, https://doi.org/10.1016/j.jesp.2012.07.014; Hemant Kakkar and Niro Sivanathan, "Appeal of a Dominant Leader over a Prestige Leader," *Proceedings of the National Academy of Sciences* 114, no. 26 (June 2017): 6734–39, https://doi.org /10.1073/pnas.1617711114.

21. Emma Onraet, Kristof Dhont, and Alain Van Hiel, "The Relationships between Internal and External Threats and Right-Wing Attitudes: A Three-Wave Longitudinal

Study," *Personality and Social Psychology Bulletin* 40, no. 6 (2014): 712–25, https://doi .org/10.1177/0146167214524256.

22. Miguel Carreras, Yasemin Irepoglu Carreras, and Shau 1 Bowler, "Long-Term Economic Distress, Cultural Backlash, and Support for Brexit," *Comparative Political Studies* 52, no. 9 (2019): 1396–424, https://doi.org/10.1177/0010414019830714, summarised in Miguel Carreras, Yasemin Irepoglu Carreras, and Shaun Bowler, "It Is the Interplay between Economic Factors and Individual Attitudes That Explains Brexit," LSE British Politics and Policy blog, London School of Economics and Political Science, 7 May 2019, https://blogs.lse.ac.uk/politicsandpolicy/economics-and-culture-brexit/.

Chapter 4. Half a Century of Policy Mistakes

1. Robert Solow, "The Future of Work: Why Wages Aren't Keeping Up," *Pacific Standard*, 11 August 2015, https://psmag.com/economics/the-future-of-work-why -wages-arent-keeping-up. Also see Nelson Lichtenstein, *Walter Reuther: The Most Dangerous Man in Detroit*, Urbana: University of Illinois Press, 1997, chap. 14.

2. Susan Pedersen, "One-Man Ministry," review of *Bread for All: The Origins of the Welfare State*, by Chris Renwick, *London Review of Books* 40, no. 3 (2018): 3–6, https://www.lrb.co.uk/v40/n03/susan-pedersen/one-man-ministry.

3. Solow, "Future of Work."

4. Esteban Ortiz-Ospina and Max Roser, "Taxation," Our World in Data, 2019, https://ourworldindata.org/taxation.

5. Joseph McCartin, "The Strike That Busted Unions," *New York Times*, 2 August 2011, https://www.nytimes.com/2011/08/03/opinion/reagan-vs-patco-the -strike-that-busted-unions.html.

6. Florence Jaumotte and Carolina Osorio Buitron, "Union Power and Inequality," VoxEU, 22 October 2015, https://voxeu.org/article/union-power-and-inequality. This study suggests the effect is causal.

7. Robert Moffitt and Sisi Zhang, "Income Volatility and the PSID: Past Research and New Results" (NBER Working Paper No. 24390, National Bureau of Economic Research, Cambridge, MA, March 2018), https://www.nber.org/papers/w24390; Robert Moffitt and Sisi Zhang, "Income Volatility and the PSID: Past Research and New Results," *AEA Papers and Proceedings* 108 (2018): 277–80, https://doi.org/10 .1257/pandp.20181048; Noah Smith, "America Is Poorer Than It Thinks," Bloomberg Opinion, 26 November 2018, https://www.bloomberg.com/opinion/articles/2018-11 -26/poverty-in-america-greater-than-statistics-indicate; Daniel Tomlinson, *Irregular Payments: Assessing the Breadth and Depth of Month to Month Earnings Volatility*, Resolution Foundation, 15 November 2018, https://www.resolutionfoundation.org /publications/irregular-payments/.

8. Martin Sandbu, "The Rise of the Precariat," *Financial Times*, 6 August 2015, https://www.ft.com/content/d42ddef4-3c1b-11e5-8613-07d16aad2152.

9. Sarah O'Connor, "The New World of Work: Recovery Driven by Rise in Temp Jobs," *Financial Times*, 4 August 2015, https://www.ft.com/content/b2171222-31e4 -11e5-8873-775ba7c2ea3d.

10. Marcel Fratzscher, "A German Debate over the Future of Europe Is Long Over-
due," *Financial Times*, 28 February 2017, https://www.ft.com/content/54d0ed6e-fda7
-11e6-8d8e-a5e3738f9ae4.

11. Timm Bönke, Matthias Giesecke, and Holger Lüthen, "The Dynamics of Earnings in Germany: Evidence from Social Security Records" (Deutsches Institut für
Wirtschaftsforschung Working Paper 1514, Berlin, October 2015), https://www.diw
.de/documents/publikationen/73/diw_01.c.517674.de/dp1514.pdf.

12. Sandbu, "Rise of the Precariat"; Tom Krebs and Martin Scheffel, "German
Labour Reforms: Unpopular Success," VoxEU, 20 September 2013, http://www.voxeu
.org/article/german-labour-reforms-unpopular-success.

13. Martin Sandbu, "'Verteilungskampf,' by Marcel Fratzscher," review, *Financial Times*, 25 July 2016, https://www.ft.com/content/9cded0ee-0afa-11e6-b0f1
-61f222853ff3.

14. Jacob Hacker, *The Great Risk Shift: The New Economic Insecurity and the Decline
of the American Dream*, Oxford: Oxford University Press, 2008.

15. See Martin Sandbu, "Europe's Social Model Is Still Doing Its Job," *Financial Times*, 9 May 2019, https://www.ft.com/content/f5acd758-722f-11e9-bbfb
-5c68069fbd15; and Thomas Blanchet, Lucas Chancel, and Amory Gethin, "How
Unequal Is Europe? Evidence from Distributional National Accounts" (WID.world
Working Paper No. 2019/6, World Inequality Lab, 2019), https://wid.world/document
/bcg2019-full-paper/.

16. For example, Enrico Berkes, Ugo Panizza, and Jean-Louis Arcand, "Too Much
Finance?" (International Monetary Fund Working Paper No. 12/161, 1 June 2012),
https://www.imf.org/en/Publications/WP/Issues/2016/12/31/Too-Much-Finance
-26011. See further references in the longer treatment of these findings in chapter 9.

17. "Banks? No, Thanks!," *Economist*, 11 October 2014, https://www.economist
.com/business/2014/10/11/banks-no-thanks.

18. Bank of England data series LPQVYBF, European Central Bank statistical
data warehouse series BSI.M.U2.N.A.T00.A.1.Z5.0000.Z01.E, US Federal Reserve
data release H.8, retrieved from FRED, Federal Reserve Bank of St. Louis, 2 December 2019, https://fred.stlouisfed.org/graph/?g=oJkO.

19. Rajan's speech and the discussion that ensued are available on the conference
website: "The Greenspan Era: Lessons for the Future," Federal Reserve Bank of Kansas
City, 2005, https://www.kansascityfed.org/publications/research/escp/symposiums
/escp-2005.

20. Raghuram Rajan, *Fault Lines: How Hidden Fractures Still Threaten the World
Economy*, Princeton, NJ: Princeton University Press, 2010.

21. Geoff Tily, "17-Year Wage Squeeze the Worst in Two Hundred Years," Trade
Unions Congress blog, 11 May 2018, https://www.tuc.org.uk/blogs/17-year-wage
-squeeze-worst-two-hundred-years.

22. On stenographers, see Chris Summers, "Is Stenography a Dying Art?," BBC
News, 27 April 2011, https://www.bbc.co.uk/news/magazine-13035979. More gener-
ally, see Richard Baldwin, *The Globotics Upheaval: Globalization, Robotics, and the
Future of Work*, Oxford: Oxford University Press, 2019.

23. Daron Acemoglu, Philippe Aghion, and Giovanni Violante, "Deunionization, Technical Change and Inequality," *Carnegie-Rochester Conference Series on Public Policy* 55 (2001): 229–64, https://economics.mit.edu/files/5691.

24. See Sarah O'Connor, "How to Manage the Gig Economy's Growing Global Jobs Market," *Financial Times*, 30 October 2018, http://www.ft.com/content/5fe8991e -dc2a-11e8-8f50-cbae5495d92b, and Baldwin, *Globotics Upheaval*.

25. Andy Bounds, "Rise of Robots Will Deepen Britain's North-South Economic Divide," *Financial Times*, 29 January 2018, https://www.ft.com/content/0bf93ddc -02a9-11e8-9650-9c0ad2d7c5b5; Martin Sandbu, "All Economics Is Local," *Financial Times*, 31 January 2018, https://www.ft.com/content/8efe4cd8-0509-11e8-9650 -9c0ad2d7c5b5; Mark Muro, Jacob Whiton, and Robert Maxim, "Automation Perpetuates the Red-Blue Divide," Brookings Institution, 19 March 2019, https://www .brookings.edu/blog/the-avenue/2019/03/25/automation-perpetuates-the-red-blue -divide/.

Chapter 5. Scapegoating Globalisation

1. Dani Rodrik, *Has Globalization Gone Too Far?*, Washington, DC: Institute for International Economics, 1997.

2. Dani Rodrik, "Barbarians, Barbarians Everywhere," Dani Rodrik's weblog, 9 May 2019, https://rodrik.typepad.com/dani_rodriks_weblog/2007/05/are_there _barba.html.

3. Adrian Wood, "The 1990s Trade and Wages Debate in Retrospect," VoxEU, 25 April 2018, https://voxeu.org/article/revisiting-1990s-debate-globalisation.

4. Martin Sandbu, "Donald Trump's Love of Manufacturing Is Misguided," *Financial Times*, 14 February 2017, https://www.ft.com/content/f0a3e89c-f2ab-11e6-8758 -687615182la6; Martin Sandbu, "The Failing Policies of Factory Fetishism," *Financial Times*, 15 February 2017, https://www.ft.com/content/2744b37e-f36d-11e6-8758 -687615182la6.

5. Martin Sandbu, "In Some Places, Factory Jobs Are Plentiful," *Financial Times*, 16 May 2018, https://www.ft.com/content/d7c3c8e6-5827-11e8-b8b2-d6ceb45fa9d0. The data behind the chart are due to Adrian Wood.

6. Wood, "1990s Trade and Wages Debate."

7. Daron Acemoglu, David Autor, David Dorn, Gordon Hanson, and Brendan Price, "Import Competition and the Great US Employment Sag of the 2000s," *Journal of Labor Economics* 34, no. S1 (2016): 141–98, https://ideas.repec.org/a/ucp/jlabec /doi10.1086-682384.html; David Autor, David Dorn, and Gordon Hanson, "The China Shock: Learning from Labor Market Adjustment to Large Changes in Trade" (NBER Working Paper No. 21906, National Bureau of Economic Research, Cambridge, MA, January 2016), https://www.nber.org/papers/w21906; David Autor, David Dorn, and Gordon Hanson, "The China Syndrome: Local Labor Market Effects of Import Competition in the United States," *American Economic Review* 103, no. 6 (2013): 2121–68, https://doi.org/10.1257/aer.103.6.2121. See also Martin Sandbu, "Trading Down,"

Financial Times, 20 May 2016, https://www.ft.com/content/02a07038-1dbe-11e6
-a7bc-ee846770ec15.

8. In Norway, for example, the China shock, measured in the same way, was only
half as strong as in the United States—of the factory jobs that disappeared in the past
decades, only one-tenth of the decline in industrial jobs can be accounted for by Chinese import competition. See Ragnhild Balsvik, Sissel Jensen, and Kjell Salvanes,
"Made in China, Sold in Norway: Local Labor Market Effects of an Import Shock" (IZA
Discussion Paper 8324, Institute for the Study of Labor, Bonn, Germany, July 2014),
http://repec.iza.org/dp8324.pdf. A study that applies the same methodology to France
finds that "Chinese import competition explains about 13 percent of the decline in
the French manufacturing sector employment over the period 2001–2007." Clément
Malgouyres, "The Impact of Chinese Import Competition on the Local Structure of
Employment and Wages: Evidence from France," *Journal of Regional Science* 57, no. 3
(June 2017): 422, https://doi.org/10.1111/jors.12303.

9. Specifically, import competition from all countries eliminated between 2 million and 3.6 million US factory jobs over the 1995–2011 period, but export growth due
to trade liberalisation created another 2 million new ones. That makes for a net effect
of between 0 and 1.6 million jobs lost. See Robert C. Feenstra and Akira Sasahara,
"The 'China Shock,' Exports and U.S. Employment: A Global Input-Output Analysis" (NBER Working Paper No. 24022, National Bureau of Economic Research, Cambridge, MA, November 2017), https://www.nber.org/papers/w24022; and Martin
Sandbu, "Do Not Forget the Winners from Freer Trade," *Financial Times*, 23 January 2018, https://www.ft.com/content/4f03a838-0024-11e8-9650-9c0ad2d7c5b5.

10. See Wolfgang Dauth, Sebastian Findeisen, and Jens Südekum, "Sectoral
Employment Trends in Germany: The Effect of Globalisation on Their Micro Anat-
omy," VoxEU, 26 January 2017, https://voxeu.org/article/globalisation-and-sectoral
-employment-trends-germany.

11. Bradford DeLong, "NAFTA and Other Trade Deals Have Not Gutted American
Manufacturing—Period," Vox, 24 January 2017, https://www.vox.com/the-big-idea
/2017/1/24/14363148/trade-deals-nafta-wto-china-job-loss-trump.

12. See Robert D. Atkinson, "Which Nations Really Lead in Industrial Robot
Adoption?," Information Technology and Innovation Foundation, November 2018,
http://www2.itif.org/2018-industrial-robot-adoption.pdf.

13. Some of the highest estimates of factory jobs lost in the West because of trade
with poor countries are those of Adrian Wood in "1990s Trade and Wages Debate." He
suggests that in 2014, there were twelve million fewer manufacturing jobs in the OECD
because of trade with non-OECD countries. That is about 15 per cent of all such jobs,
but two-thirds of the absolute decline from 1985. As I explain in the main text, all the
more detailed country-specific studies come up with significantly lower estimates. But
even in Wood's own model, the estimated job loss declines by more than one-third if
production retained in the West is assumed to enjoy either greater technical efficiency
or higher labour productivity than emerging country factories actually do—let alone
both. For reasons to doubt Wood's estimate, see Sandbu, "In Some Places."

14. The evidence is reviewed by Elhanan Helpman, "Globalisation and Wage Inequality," *Journal of the British Academy* 5 (July 2017): 125–62, https://doi.org /10.5871/jba/005.125. See also Philipp Heimberger, "Does Economic Globalisation Affect Income Inequality? A Meta-analysis" (Vienna Institute for International Economic Studies Working Paper 165, October 2019), https://wiiw.ac.at/does-economic -globalisation-affect-income-inequality-a-meta-analysis-p-5044.html. This metastudy summarises 123 peer-reviewed articles on globalisation's effect on income inequality. It finds a small positive relationship—smaller with trade integration than with financial globalisation—in both poor and rich countries, which suggests that any inequality effect of trade integration is similar to that caused by technological advances pushing up the need for skilled labour.

15. Arvind Subramanian and Martin Kessler, "The Hyperglobalization of Trade and Its Future" (Peterson Institute for International Economics Working Paper 13-6, Washington, DC, July 2013), https://piie.com/publications/working-papers /hyperglobalization-trade-and-its-future. See also Martin Sandbu, "Hyperglobalisa-tion and Its Critics," *Financial Times*, 30 January 2019, https://www.ft.com/content /f0b37e0e-23cf-11e9-8ce6-5db4543da632.

16. Even Wood's model, which is so pessimistic about the impact on rich-country industrial employment, estimates that the number of *skilled* factory jobs has increased because of trade with poorer countries.

17. This overall conclusion is borne out by the empirical evidence as recently surveyed by Jonathan Portes, "The Economics of Migration," *Contexts* 18, no. 2 (May 2019): 12–17, https://doi.org/10.1177/1536504219854712. Moreover, a thorough typology of a range of methodologies used to estimate the wage effects of immigration has established that the most error-prone methods are those that have produced the biggest estimates of negative wage effects for lower-paid native workers (and indeed positive wage effects for higher-paid ones), suggesting that the state-of-the-art empiri-cal models tend to find small or no effects. See Christian Dustmann, Uta Schönberg, and Jan Stuhler, "The Impact of Immigration: Why Do Studies Reach Such Different Results?," *Journal of Economic Perspectives* 30, no. 4 (Fall 2016): 31–56, https://doi .org/10.1257/jep.30.4.31.

18. Martin Sandbu, "Fool's Gold from the Populists," *Financial Times*, 20 June 2016, https://www.ft.com/content/8a29bcbc-36cd-11e6-9a05-82a9b15a8ee7. The quote is from Jonathan Portes, "Immigration and Wages: Getting the Numbers Right," National Institute for Economic and Social Research blog, 11 June 2016, https://www.niesr.ac .uk/blog/immigration-and-wages-getting-numbers-right.

19. Karen Helene Ulltveit-Moe, Andreas Moxnes, Bernt Bratsberg, and Oddbjørn Raaum, "Opening the Floodgates: Industry and Occupation Adjustments to Labor Immigration" (Centre for Economic Policy Research Discussion Paper 13670, London, April 2019), https://cepr.org/active/publications/discussion_papers/dp.php?dpno =13670.

20. In a survey of the empirical research, Sari Pekkala Kerr and William Kerr con-clude, "A number of studies evaluate impacts of immigration, often concluding that the

total economic impact on the host country is relatively small. . . . It is clear that recent immigrants to Northern Europe are likely on average to use more social benefits than natives, especially in the case of refugees. . . . But strong conclusions on other dimensions are not forthcoming. Studies find conflicting evidence on whether immigrants increase or reduce social benefit usage with duration of stay. The estimated net fiscal impact of migrants also varies substantially across studies, but the overall magnitudes relative to the GDP remain modest. . . . The more credible analyses typically find small fiscal effects." Kerr and Kerr, "Economic Impacts of Immigration: A Survey," *Finnish Economic Papers* 24, no. 1 (Spring 2011): 20, 23, http://taloustieteellinenyhdistys.fi /images/stories/fep/fep12011/fep12011_kerr_and_kerr.pdf.

21. Florence Jaumotte, Ksenia Koloskova, and Sweta C. Saxena, "Impact of Migration on Income Levels in Advanced Economies," International Monetary Fund, Spillover Notes 8, October 2016, https://www.imf.org/en/Publications/Spillover-Notes /Issues/2016/12/31/Impact-of-Migration-on-Income-Levels-in-Advanced-Economies -44343.

22. Giovanni Peri and Francisco Requena-Silvente, "Do Immigrants Create Exports? Evidence from Spain," VoxEU, 26 January 2010, https://voxeu.org/article /do-immigrants-create-exports-new-evidence-spain; Christopher Parsons and Pierre-Louis Vézina, "Migrant Networks Boost Trade: Evidence from the Vietnamese Boat People," VoxEU, 15 August 2018, https://voxeu.org/article/migrant-networks -boost-trade; Gianmarco Ottaviano, Giovanni Peri, and Greg Wright, "Immigration, Trade and Productivity in Services," VoxEU, 17 June 2015, https://voxeu.org /article/immigration-trade-and-productivity-services; Konrad Burchardi, Thomas Chaney, and Tarek Hassan, "The Effect of Migration on Foreign Direct Investment," VoxEU, 12 November 2016, https://voxeu.org/article/effect-migration-foreign-direct -investment.

23. There is one more criticism made of migration, although often hypocritically. This is that migration hurts the migrants' *home* countries by draining them of labour and skills. Those most cynically appealing to fears of immigration can hardly be credited with genuine concern for the places immigrants come from. But in any case, the evidence here, too, is that sending countries on the whole benefit from the financial and skill transfers generated by emigration to richer countries. See Michael A. Clemens, "Economics and Emigration: Trillion-Dollar Bills on the Sidewalk?," *Journal of Economic Perspectives* 25, no. 3 (Summer 2011): 83–106, https://doi.org/10.1257 /jep.25.3.83.

24. Of course, low-paid immigrants are often forced to live in the poorer parts of those thriving places, but this does not change the pattern. Those city districts with the West's highest concentration of immigrants generally display positive attitudes. But the exceptions to the pattern are important. They include immigrants living in a struggling area but treating it as a bedroom community from which they commute into successful cities—like the migrant workers of Tilbury (see chapter 2). And after a period of sustained immigration into a country, it tends to disperse from the leading to the lagging regions. Thus we find that the greatest hostility to immigration is often

observed in communities that have a low share of immigrant residents but where that share has recently increased fast from an even lower level.

25. Martin Sandbu, "The Globalisation Pendulum," *Financial Times*, 1 October 2018, https://www.ft.com/content/673f118a-c243-11e8-8d55-54197280d3f7.

26. Bank for International Settlements, "Locational Banking Statistics," last updated 23 October 2019, https://stats.bis.org/statx/toc/LBS.html.

27. Adam Tooze, *Crashed: How a Decade of Financial Crises Changed the World*, New York: Penguin, 2018, 78.

28. Dani Rodrik, "What Does a True Populism Look Like? It Looks Like the New Deal," *New York Times*, 21 February 2018, https://www.nytimes.com/2018/02/21/opinion/populism-new-deal.html.

29. Rodrik.

30. Rodrik.

31. Martin Sandbu, "Strengthening the Centre," *Financial Times*, 6 July 2016, https://www.ft.com/content/be749274-4377-11e6-9b66-0712b3873ae1.

Chapter 6. Economics, Jobs, and the Art of Car Maintenance

1. Karl Ove Moene and Michael Wallerstein, "The Scandinavian Model and Economic Development," *Development Outreach* 8, no. 1 (February 2006): 18–36, https://www.frisch.uio.no/publikasjoner/pdf/TheScandinavianModelandEconomicDevelopment.pdf.

2. Martin Sandbu, "The Economics of Insecurity," *Big Picture* (podcast), *Financial Times*, 28 August 2018, https://www.ft.com/content/31bfd147-9054-420f-8755-7585b4be1598.

3. Sandbu, "The Economics of Insecurity."

4. United States: 373,290 "cleaners of vehicles and equipment" out of a total employment of 146 million in May 2017, or 2.55 per thousand ("Occupational Employment and Wages," Bureau of Labor Statistics, May 2017, https://www.bls.gov/oes/current/oes537061.htm; "Employment, Hours, and Earnings from the Current Employment Statistics Survey [National]," Bureau of Labor Statistics, accessed 6 December 2019, https://data.bls.gov/timeseries/CES0000000001). Norway: 3,038 "car washers" (NIS code 9122) out of a total employment of 2.7 million in the fourth quarter of 2018, or 1.12 per thousand ("Sysselsetting, registerbasert," Statistics Norway, 12 January 2020, https://www.ssb.no/statbank/sq/10030476; "Arbeidskraftundersøkelsen," Statistics Norway, 24 October 2019, https://www.ssb.no/aku). Total number of motor vehicles: 268 million in the United States ("State Motor-Vehicle Registrations—2016," US Department of Transportation, Federal Highway Administration, November 2017, https://www.fhwa.dot.gov/policyinformation/statistics/2016/mv1.cfm); 3.75 million in Norway (counting cars, buses, trucks, and motorcycles/mopeds: "Kjøretøybestanden i Norge," Vegdirektoratet, 31 December 2017, https://www.vegvesen.no/_attachment/2393528/binary/1274186?fast_title=Kj%C3%B8ret%C3%B8ybestanden+i+Norge+2007+-+2017+Ny.pdf).

5. Sandbu, "The Economics of Insecurity."

6. "Chancellor George Osborne's Summer Budget 2015 Speech," Gov.uk, 8 July 2015, https://www.gov.uk/government/speeches/chancellor-george-osbornes -summer-budget-2015-speech. See also Martin Sandbu, "True Blue Budget with a Strain of Scandinavian DNA," *Financial Times*, 9 July 2015, https://www.ft.com /content/1d7c4728-261c-11e5-bd83-71cb60e8f08c.

7. Sarah O'Connor, "Supermarket Shelf Gamble behind UK Minimum Wage," *Financial Times*, 8 March 2016, https://www.ft.com/content/fff1944a-e51c-11e5-a09b -1f8b0d268c39.

8. Sarah O'Connor, "UK's Low Earners Receive Fastest Pay Rise in 20 Years," *Financial Times*, 26 October 2016, https://www.ft.com/content/987e24d4-9b62-11e6 -b8c6-568a43813464.

9. Resolution Foundation, *Weighing Up the Wage Floor: Employer Responses to the National Living Wage*, policy report, February 2016, https://www.resolutionfoundation .org/app/uploads/2016/02/7218-National-Living-Wage-report-WEB.pdf; Conor D'Arcy, *Low Pay Britain 2018*, Resolution Foundation report, May 2018, https://www .resolutionfoundation.org/app/uploads/2018/05/Low-Pay-Britain-2018.pdf.

10. Rui Costa, Swati Dhingra, and Stephen Machin, "Trade and Deskilling: How the Post-referendum Sterling Depreciation Hurt Workers" (Centre for Economic Performance Research Paper CEPCP551, London School of Economics and Political Science, July 2019), https://cep.lse.ac.uk/_new/publications/abstract.asp?index =6289.

11. Richard Croucher, Marian Rizov, and Thomas Lange, "National Minimum Wages Improve Productivity," LSE Business Review blog, London School of Economics and Political Science, 18 January 2017, https://blogs.lse.ac.uk/businessreview /2017/01/18/national-minimum-wages-improve-productivity/; Marian Rizov, Richard Croucher, and Thomas Lange, "The UK National Minimum Wage's Impact on Productivity," *British Journal of Management* 27, no. 4 (October 2016): 819–35, https://doi .org/10.1111/1467-8551.12171.

12. Martin Sandbu, "Raising the Floor," *Financial Times*, 9 August 2016, https:// www.ft.com/content/d0aa46f4-5d68-11e6-bb77-a121aa8abd95.

13. Emily Breza, Supreet Kaur, and Yogita Shamdasani, "The Morale Effects of Pay Inequality" (NBER Working Paper No. 22491, National Bureau of Economic Research, Cambridge, MA, August 2016), https://www.nber.org/papers/w22491.

14. For evidence on these and many other effects, see Justin Wolfers and Jan Zilinsky, "Higher Wages for Low-Income Workers Lead to Higher Productivity," Realtime Economic Issues Watch blog, 13 January 2015, https://piie.com/blogs/realtime -economic-issues-watch/higher-wages-low-income-workers-lead-higher-productivity ?p=4700.

15. Sarah O'Connor, "London Restaurants Look at Dishing Up Paris Practices," *Financial Times*, 4 March 2017, https://www.ft.com/content/74769eae-fff8-11e6-8d8e -a5e3738f9ae4.

16. Arindrajit Dube, *Impacts of Minimum Wages: Review of the International Evidence*, independent report for the UK government, November 2019, https://www

.gov.uk/government/publications/impacts-of-minimum-wages-review-of-the
-international-evidence.

17. "Labour Force Participation Rate," OECD Data, accessed 6 December 2019,
https://data.oecd.org/emp/labour-force-participation-rate.htm.

18. "Adult Skills," Compare Your Country by OECD, accessed 6 December 2019,
https://www.compareyourcountry.org/adult-skills.

19. "Job-to-Job Transitions by Sex and Age—Annual Averages of Quarterly Transitions, Estimated Probabilities," Eurostat, accessed 6 December 2019, http://appsso
.eurostat.ec.europa.eu/nui/show.do?dataset=lfsi_long_e07; Martin Sandbu, "A Policy
for Centrists Who Care about the Left-Behind," *Financial Times*, 2 November 2017,
https://www.ft.com/content/d9eca590-bf05-11e7-b8a3-38a6e068f464.

20. "Public Spending on Education," OECD Data, accessed 6 December 2019,
https://data.oecd.org/eduresource/public-spending-on-education.htm#indicator
-chart.

21. "Public Expenditure and Participant Stocks on LMP," OECD.Stat, accessed 6
December 2019, https://stats.oecd.org/index.aspx?DataSetCode=LMPEXP#.

Chapter 7. Economic Policies for Empowerment

1. Sendhil Mullainathan and Eldar Shafir, *Scarcity: Why Having Too Little Means
So Much*, New York: Henry Holt, 2013.

2. In the United States, competition between employers is also reduced by noncompete clauses in job contracts, which cover as much as one-fifth of the workforce,
according to Alan Krueger and Eric Posner, "A Proposal for Protecting Low-Income
Workers from Monopsony and Collusion" (Hamilton Project Policy Proposal 2018-
05, February 2018), http://www.hamiltonproject.org/assets/files/protecting_low
_income_workers_from_monopsony_collusion_krueger_posner_pp.pdf.

3. "Mental Health," OECD, accessed 6 December 2019, https://www.oecd.org
/health/health-systems/mental-health.htm.

4. For example, the German Council of Economic Experts reports that in Germany,
a single person faces an effective marginal income tax rate of 100 per cent at monthly
incomes between about €1,200 and €1,500, and exceeding 100 per cent for a single
parent at monthly incomes between about €1,600 and €2,000. See German Council of
Economic Experts, *Dealing with Structural Change: Annual Report 2019/20*, executive
summary, https://www.sachverstaendigenrat-wirtschaft.de/en/annualreport-2019.
The European Commission quantifies these benefit traps for thirty-eight countries in
its tax and benefits database: "Tax and Benefits," Economic and Financial Affairs, European Commission, accessed 6 December 2019, https://europa.eu/economy_finance
/db_indicators/tab/#.

5. Different proposals vary in how they treat children and noncitizen residents, as
well as, of course, the specific amounts and rates. For general treatments, see Philippe
Van Parijs and Yannick Vanderborght, *Basic Income: A Radical Proposal for a Free
Society and a Sane Economy*, Cambridge, MA: Harvard University Press, 2017; and

Guy Standing, *Basic Income: And How We Can Make It Happen*, Harmondsworth, UK: Penguin, 2017.

6. Olli Kangas, Signe Jauhiainen, Miska Simanainen, and Minna Ylikännö, eds., *The Basic Income Experiment 2017–2018 in Finland: Preliminary Results* (Helsinki: Ministry of Social Affairs and Health, 2019), https://julkaisut.valtioneuvosto.fi/bitstream/handle/10024/161361/Report_The%20Basic%20Income%20Experiment%20 20172018%20in%20Finland.pdf.

7. Andrew Leigh found that "a 10 percent increase in the generosity of the EITC [earned income tax credit] is associated with a 5 percent fall in the wages of high school dropouts and a 2 percent fall in the wages of those with only a high school diploma." Leigh, "Who Benefits from the Earned Income Tax Credit? Incidence among Recipients, Coworkers and Firms," *B.E. Journal of Economic Analysis and Policy: Advances in Economic Analysis and Policy* 10, no. 1 (2010): article 45, https://doi.org/10.2202/1935-1682.1994.

8. Jesse Rothstein has shown that employers capture 30 per cent of an increase in a tax credit for single mothers in the United States by paying lower wages to those tax credit recipients—but they gain nearly one and a half times as much because of lower wages for those who do not receive the credit. Rothstein, "The Unintended Consequences of Encouraging Work: Tax Incidence and the EITC" (CEPS Working Paper No. 165, Center for Economic Policy Studies, Princeton University, Princeton, NJ, May 2008), https://www.princeton.edu/ceps/workingpapers/165rothstein.pdf.

9. Paul Gregg, Alex Hurrell, and Matthew Whittaker, *Creditworthy: Assessing the Impact of Tax Credits in the Last Decade and Considering What This Means for Universal Credit*, Resolution Foundation report, June 2012, https://www.resolutionfoundation.org/app/uploads/2014/08/Creditworthy.pdf.

10. Jesse Rothstein, "Is the EITC as Good as an NIT? Conditional Cash Transfers and Tax Incidence," *American Economic Journal: Economic Policy* 2, no. 1 (February 2010): 177–208, https://doi.org/10.1257/pol.2.1.177.

11. Damon Jones and Ioana Marinescu, "The Labor Market Impacts of Universal and Permanent Cash Transfers: Evidence from the Alaska Permanent Fund" (NBER Working Paper No. 24312, National Bureau of Economic Research, Cambridge, MA, February 2018), https://www.nber.org/papers/w24312.pdf. The authors found that the permanent cash payments encouraged a small share of people to work part time instead of full time, but overall employment was unaffected. They attribute this result to the "general equilibrium effect" of more demand for local service-sector or "non-tradeable" jobs.

12. Scott Santens, "What Is There to Learn from Finland's Basic Income Experiment? Did It Succeed or Fail?," Medium, 14 February 2019, https://medium.com/basic-income/what-is-there-to-learn-from-finlands-basic-income-experiment-did-it-succeed-or-fail-54b8e5051f60; see also Kangas et al., *Basic Income Experiment*. For the results of earlier basic income experiments, see Andrew Flowers, "What Would Happen If We Just Gave People Money?," FiveThirtyEight, 25 April 2016, https://fivethirtyeight.com/features/universal-basic-income/.

13. Alfie Stirling and Sarah Arnold, *Nothing Personal*, New Economics Foundation report, 11 March 2019, https://neweconomics.org/2019/03/nothing-personal. See also the discussion in Martin Sandbu, "A Simple Fix to Make UK Taxes Fairer," *Financial Times*, 15 March 2019, https://www.ft.com/content/4d3dec6e-4701-11e9 -b168-96a37d002cd3, where I point out that other tax-free allowances that Stirling and Arnold do not touch on (in particular national insurance) could fund more than a 50 per cent increase in their proposed basic income.

14. OECD, *Basic Income as a Policy Option: Can It Add Up?*, policy brief, May 2017, https://www.oecd.org/employment/emp/Basic-Income-Policy-Option-2017.pdf, further discussed in Martin Sandbu, "Budgeting for Utopia," *Financial Times*, 26 May 2017, https://www.ft.com/content/05cb4bd0-41f2-11e7-82b6-896b95f30f58. The affordability of a meaningful UBI is further discussed in Martin Sandbu, "An Affordable Utopia," *Financial Times*, 7 June 2016, https://www.ft.com/content/2b6f1ca6-2bfd -11e6-bf8d-26294ad519fc.

15. OECD, *Negotiating Our Way Up: Collective Bargaining in a Changing World of Work*, 18 November 2019, https://www.oecd.org/employment/negotiating-our-way -up-1fd2da34-en.htm.

16. Florence Jaumotte and Carolina Osorio Buitron, "Union Power and Inequality," VoxEU, 22 October 2015, https://voxeu.org/article/union-power-and-inequality.

17. Henry Farber, Daniel Herbst, Ilyana Kuziemko, and Suresh Naidu, "Unions and Inequality over the Twentieth Century: New Evidence from Survey Data" (NBER Working Paper 24587, National Bureau of Economic Research, Cambridge, MA, May 2018), https://www.nber.org/papers/w24587.

18. Eurofound, *Innovative Changes in European Companies: Evidence from the European Company Survey*, Third European Company Survey (Luxembourg: Publications Office of the European Union, 2017), summarised by the authors in Stavroula Demetriades and Franz Ferdinand Eiffe, "The Human Factor in Innovation," Eurofound blog, 18 June 2018, https://www.eurofound.europa.eu/publications/blog/the-human -factor-in-innovation.

19. Interview with Karl Ove Moene in Martin Sandbu, "Let Unions Erode at Your Peril," *Financial Times*, 4 July 2018, https://www.ft.com/content/c2ee79c4-7f65-11e8 -bc55-50daf11b720d.

20. I have surveyed some of this evidence in Martin Sandbu, "Employee Empowerment and Business Productivity," *Financial Times*, 20 March 2019, https://www.ft .com/content/2e1684d6-4a49-11e9-8b7f-d49067e0f50d.

21. Richard Baldwin, *The Globotics Upheaval: Globalization, Robotics, and the Future of Work*, Oxford: Oxford University Press, 2019.

22. "About Us," IWGB, accessed 6 December 2019, https://iwgb.org.uk/page /about/about.

23. Historian David Alan Corbin quoted in Gwynn Guildford, "The 100-Year Capitalist Experiment That Keeps Appalachia Poor, Sick, and Stuck on Coal," Quartz, 30 December 2017, https://qz.com/1167671/the-100-year-capitalist-experiment-that -keeps-appalachia-poor-sick-and-stuck-on-coal/.

24. Tim Wu, "Be Afraid of Economic 'Bigness.' Be Very Afraid," *New York Times*, 10 November 2018, https://www.nytimes.com/2018/11/10/opinion/sunday/fascism-economy-monopoly.html.

25. Thomas Philippon, *The Great Reversal: How America Gave Up on Free Markets*, Cambridge, MA: Harvard University Press, 2019.

26. Jason Furman and Peter Orszag, "A Firm-Level Perspective on the Role of Rents in the Rise in Inequality" (presentation at "A Just Society," centennial event in honor of Joseph Stiglitz, Columbia University, 16 October 2015), https://obamawhitehouse.archives.gov/sites/default/files/page/files/20151016_firm_level_perspective_on_role_of_rents_in_inequality.pdf.

27. Philippon, *Great Reversal*.

28. See the various contributions to the OECD round table on market concentration: "Market Concentration," OECD, accessed 6 December 2019, http://www.oecd.org/daf/competition/market-concentration.htm. This is not just a US phenomenon; the German Council of Economic Experts, *Dealing with Structural Change*, for example, has noted the falling dynamism of new business creation in Germany.

29. See note 2.

30. Simon van Dorpe, "The Case against Amazon," Politico.eu, 4 March 2019, https://www.politico.eu/article/amazon-europe-competition-giveth-and-amazon-taketh-away/.

31. Nathan Heller, "Estonia, the Digital Republic," *New Yorker*, 18 and 25 December 2017, https://www.newyorker.com/magazine/2017/12/18/estonia-the-digital-republic.

32. David Mardiste, "Embracing Uber, Estonia Shows Tax Needn't Be an Issue," Reuters, 9 June 2016, https://www.reuters.com/article/us-estonia-uber/embracing-uber-estonia-shows-tax-neednt-be-an-issue-idUSKCN0YV1PS.

33. "Now You Can Pay Your Taxes in One Click," e-Estonia, April 2017, https://e-estonia.com/now-you-can-pay-your-taxes-in-one-click/.

34. See "About Entur," Entur, accessed 6 December 2019, https://www.entur.org/about-entur/.

Chapter 8. Macroeconomic Policy for the Left Behind

1. John Maynard Keynes, *The General Theory of Employment, Interest and Money*, chap. 22.

2. Martin Sandbu, "The Left Behind Have Most to Lose from Timid Macroeconomic Policy," *Financial Times*, 7 January 2019, https://www.ft.com/content/5322ec9a-1008-11e9-acdc-4d9976f1533b. For the United Kingdom, see Cara Pacitti and James Smith, *A Problem Shared? What Can We Learn from Past Recessions about the Impact of the Next across the Income Distribution?*, Resolution Foundation report, 5 August 2019, https://www.resolutionfoundation.org/publications/a-problem-shared/.

3. Stephanie Aaronson, Mary Daly, William Wascher, and David Wilcox, "Okun Revisited: Who Benefits Most from a Strong Economy?" (Finance and Economics

Discussion Series Paper 2019-072, Federal Reserve Board, Washington, DC, 2019), https://www.federalreserve.gov/econres/feds/files/2019072pap.pdf.

4. Hilary Hoynes, Douglas Miller, and Jessamyn Schaller, "Who Suffers during Recessions?," *Journal of Economic Perspectives* 26, no. 3 (Summer 2012): 27–48, https://doi.org/10.1257/jep.26.3.27; Stephanie Aaronson et al. "Okun Revisited." See also Sandbu, "Left Behind."

5. Delphine Strauss, "Can Ex-prisoners Help Fill the UK's Labour Shortage?," *Financial Times*, 11 October 2019, https://www.ft.com/content/5212906c-ebf4-11e9 -a240-3b065ef5fc55.

6. See Thiemo Fetzer, "Did Austerity Cause Brexit?," *American Economic Review* 109, no. 11 (November 2019): 3849–86, https://doi.org/10.1257/aer.20181164.

7. Hannes Schwandt and Till M. von Wachter, "Unlucky Cohorts: Estimating the Long-Term Effects of Entering the Labor Market in a Recession in Large Cross-sectional Data Sets" (NBER Working Paper No. 25141, National Bureau of Economic Research, Cambridge, MA, October 2018), https://www.nber.org/papers/w25141.

8. See Martin Sandbu, "The Hidden Costs of Macroeconomic Moderation," *Financial Times*, 21 November 2018, https://www.ft.com/content/c28f34ba-ecba-11e8-89c8 -d36339d835c0, and the references therein.

9. Philippe Aghion, Antonin Bergeaud, Richard Blundell, and Rachel Griffith, "The Innovation Premium to Soft Skills in Low-Skilled Occupations," VoxEU, 2 January.2020, https://voxeu.org/article/innovation-premium-soft-skills-low-skilled-occupations.

10. Valerie Cerra, Sweta Saxena, and Ugo Panizza, "International Evidence on Recovery from Recessions" (IMF Working Paper 09/183, 2009), https://www.imf .org/en/Publications/WP/Issues/2016/12/31/International-Evidence-on-Recovery -from-Recessions-23234.

11. Narayana Kocherlakota, "Growth Begets Growth: Reflections on Total Factor Productivity," blog post, 21 February 2016, https://sites.google.com/site /kocherlakota009/policy/thoughts-on-policy/2-21-16; Martin Sandbu, "Economies Can Take a Lot More Stimulus without Overheating," *Financial Times*, 23 May 2017, https://www.ft.com/content/7ae0866a-3f04-11e7-9d56-25f963e998b2.

12. Xavier Debrun, "Growth Dividend from Stabilizing Fiscal Policies," *IMFBlog*, 8 April 2015, https://blogs.imf.org/2015/04/08/growth-dividend-from-stabilizing -fiscal-policies/.

13. Martin Sandbu, "The US's Lost Decade," *Financial Times*, 31 October 2018, https://www.ft.com/content/ad6535a6-db6e-11e8-8f50-cbae5495d92b.

14. Bradford DeLong and Lawrence Summers, *Fiscal Policy in a Depressed Economy*, Brookings Papers on Economic Activity, Spring 2012, https://www.brookings .edu/bpea-articles/fiscal-policy-in-a-depressed-economy/; Bradford DeLong, "Spending Cuts to Improve Confidence? No, the Arithmetic Goes the Wrong Way," VoxEU, 6 April 2012, https://voxeu.org/article/spending-cuts-improve-confidence -no-arithmetic-goes-wrong-way.

15. Olivier Blanchard and Daniel Leigh, "Growth Forecast Errors and Fiscal Multipliers" (IMF Working Paper 13/1, 3 January 2013), https://www.imf.org/en

/Publications/WP/Issues/2016/12/31/Growth-Forecast-Errors-and-Fiscal-Multipliers
-40200.

16. Christopher House, Christian Proebsting, and Linda Tesar, "Austerity in the Aftermath of the Great Recession," VoxEU, 11 April 2017, https://voxeu.org/article /austerity-aftermath-great-recession.

17. Olivier Blanchard, "Public Debt and Low Interest Rates" (presidential address, American Economic Association, January 2019), https://www.aeaweb.org/aea /2019conference/program/pdf/14020_paper_etZgfbDr.pdf.

Chapter 9. A Smarter Financial System

1. For a view of why this was, see Martin Sandbu, "Talking 'bout a Revolution," *Financial Times*, 19 April 2013, https://www.ft.com/content/91a3782a-a80f-11e2-b031 -00144feabdc0.

2. See, for example, Carmen Reinhart and Kenneth Rogoff, *This Time Is Different: Eight Centuries of Financial Folly*, Princeton, NJ: Princeton University Press, 2009; Atif Mian and Amir Sufi, *House of Debt: How They (and You) Caused the Great Recession, and How We Can Prevent It from Happening Again*, Chicago: University of Chicago Press, 2015; and Valerie Cerra and Sweta Saxena, "Growth Dynamics: The Myth of Economic Recovery," *American Economic Review* 98, no. 1 (2008): 439–57, https:// doi.org/10.1257/aer.98.1.439.

3. Mian and Sufi, *House of Debt*.

4. Martin Sandbu, *Europe's Orphan: The Future of the Euro and the Politics of Debt*, Princeton, NJ: Princeton University Press, 2015, chap. 3.

5. Lucian Bebchuk and Jesse Fried, *Pay without Performance: The Unfulfilled Promise of Executive Compensation*, Cambridge, MA, Harvard University Press, 2009.

6. Nicholas Shaxson, *The Finance Curse: How Global Finance Is Making Us All Poorer*, London: Bodley Head, 2018. See also Nicholas Shaxson, "The Finance Curse: How the Outsized Power of the City of London Makes Britain Poorer," *Guardian*, 5 October 2018, https://www.theguardian.com/news/2018/oct/05/the-finance-curse -how-the-outsized-power-of-the-city-of-london-makes-britain-poorer.

7. For more on this argument, see Martin Sandbu, "From Left Behind to Poles of Attraction," *Financial Times*, 5 December 2018, https://www.ft.com/content /a6b2850e-f867-11e8-af46-2022a0b02a6c; and Martin Sandbu, "A Familiar Yet Strange Type of Bank," *Financial Times*, 1 March 2018, https://www.ft.com/content/bcb2a0c6 -1d36-11e8-aaca-4574d7dabfb6.

8. This argument draws on Bank for International Settlements research. See Stephen Cecchetti and Enisse Kharroubi, "Why Does Financial Sector Growth Crowd Out Real Economic Growth?" (BIS Working Paper 490, Bank for International Settlements, February 2015), https://www.bis.org/publ/work490.htm; and Claudio Borio, Enisse Kharroubi, Christian Upper, and Fabrizio Zampolli, "Labour Reallocation and Productivity Dynamics: Financial Causes, Real Consequences" (BIS Working Paper 534, Bank for International Settlements, January 2016), https://www.bis.org/publ/work534.htm.

9. Stephen Cecchetti and Kim Schoenholtz, "Financing Intangible Capital," VoxEU, 22 February 2018, https://voxeu.org/article/financing-intangible-capital.

10. Boris Cournède and Oliver Denk, "Finance and Economic Growth in OECD and G20 Countries" (OECD Economics Department Working Paper 1223, Organisation for Economic Co-operation and Development, June 2015), https://doi.org/10.1787/5js04v8z0m38-en. See also Ratna Sahay, Martin Čihák, and Papa N'Diaye, "How Much Finance Is Too Much: Stability, Growth & Emerging Markets," *IMF-Blog*, 4 May 2015, https://blogs.imf.org/2015/05/04/how-much-finance-is-too-much-stability-growth-emerging-markets/.

11. Luigi Zingales, "Does Finance Benefit Society?," *Journal of Finance* 70, no. 4 (2015): 1328, https://faculty.chicagobooth.edu/luigi.zingales/papers/research/Finance.pdf.

12. Raghuram Rajan, *Fault Lines: How Hidden Fractures Still Threaten the World Economy*, Princeton, NJ: Princeton University Press, 2010.

13. Irving Fisher, "The Debt-Deflation Theory of Great Depressions," *Econometrica* 1, no. 4 (1933): 337–57; Richard Koo, "Balance Sheet Recession Is the Reason for 'Secular Stagnation,'" VoxEU, 11 August 2014, https://voxeu.org/article/balance-sheet-recession-reason-secular-stagnation.

14. See Robert Shiller, *Finance and the Good Society*, Princeton, NJ: Princeton University Press, 2012, for more on equity-like financial products to make people's lives less risky.

15. Shiller.

16. There are many other reasons for such a move. One is the inefficient provision of electronic money transfers by private financial institutions, especially across borders. Another is the danger of some initiatives for private global e-money, such as the Libra proposed by Facebook.

17. Michael McLeay, Amar Radia, and Ryland Thomas, "Money Creation in the Modern Economy," Bank of England Quarterly Bulletin, 2014, Q1, https://www.bankofengland.co.uk/quarterly-bulletin/2014/q1/money-creation-in-the-modern-economy.

18. For an analysis of such "limited-purpose banking," see Laurence Kotlikoff, *Jimmy Stewart Is Dead: Ending the World's Ongoing Financial Plague with Limited Purpose Banking*, Hoboken, NJ: John Wiley and Sons, 2010.

19. Sandbu, *Europe's Orphan*.

20. See, for example, John Vickers, "Banking Reform Nine Years On," VoxEU, 18 September 2017, https://voxeu.org/article/banking-reform-nine-years.

21. See Pierre-Richard Agénor, Leonardo Gambacorta, Enisse Kharroubi, and Luiz Awazu Pereira da Silva, "The Effects of Prudential Regulation, Financial Development and Financial Openness on Economic Growth" (BIS Working Papers 752, Bank for International Settlements, 5 October 2018), https://www.bis.org/publ/work752.htm. This research shows that good financial regulations improve growth, but that they do so less when the financial systems are more open. The authors suggest this is because of "greater opportunities to borrow abroad or increased scope for cross-border leakages in regulation."

22. Eric Monnet, "Macroprudential Tools, Capital Controls, and the Trilemma: Insights from the Bretton Woods Era," VoxEU, 13 June 2018, https://voxeu.org/article /macroprudential-tools-capital-controls-and-trilemma.

23. Hélène Rey, "International Channels of Transmission of Monetary Policy and the Mundellian Trilemma" (Mundell-Fleming Lecture, Fifteenth Jacques Polak Annual Research Conference, International Monetary Fund, Washington, DC, 13–14 November 2014), https://www.imf.org/external/np/res/seminars/2014/arc/pdf/Rey.pdf.

24. Martin Sandbu, "Learning to Love Negative Interest Rates," *Financial Times*, 14 November 2019, https://www.ft.com/content/96d7c068-0612-11ea-a984 -fbbacad9e7dd.

25. Martin Sandbu, "Can Further Monetary Stimulus Still Be Effective?," *Financial Times*, 3 October 2019, https://www.ft.com/content/3dbca034-df7f-11e9-9743 -db5a370481bc.

26. Olivier Blanchard and Daniel Leigh, "Growth Forecast Errors and Fiscal Multipliers" (IMF Working Paper 13/1, 3 January 2013), https://www.imf.org/en /Publications/WP/Issues/2016/12/31/Growth-Forecast-Errors-and-Fiscal-Multipliers -40200; Christopher House, Christian Proebsting, and Linda Tesar, "Austerity in the Aftermath of the Great Recession," VoxEU, 11 April 2017, https://voxeu.org/article /austerity-aftermath-great-recession.

27. Sandbu, *Europe's Orphan*.

Chapter 10. A Tax Policy for the Left Behind

1. Loukas Karabarbounis and Brent Neiman, "Labour Shares, Inequality, and the Relative Price of Capital," VoxEU, 25 November 2014, https://voxeu.org/article/labour -shares-inequality-and-relative-price-capital; Valentina Romei, "EU Workers Miss Out on Gains of Economic Recovery," *Financial Times*, 7 May 2019, https://www.ft.com /content/0a245c28-6cc3-11e9-80c7-60ee53e6681d.

2. Martin Sandbu, "The Productivity Pessimists," *Financial Times*, 15 September 2015, https://www.ft.com/content/4b9a52b2-5b8c-11e5-9846-de406ccb37f2.

3. Emmanuel Saez and Gabriel Zucman, *The Triumph of Injustice: How the Rich Dodge Taxes and How to Make Them Pay*, New York: W. W. Norton, 2019; Tax Justice Now website, accessed 9 December 2019, https://taxjusticenow.org/.

4. Martin Sandbu, "'Verteilungskampf,' by Marcel Fratzscher," review, *Financial Times*, 25 July 2016, https://www.ft.com/content/9cded0ee-0afa-11e6-b0f1 -61f222853ff3.

5. Matthew Yglesias, "Taxing the Rich Is Extremely Popular," Vox, 4 February 2019, https://www.vox.com/2019/2/4/18210370/warren-wealth-tax-poll.

6. In the Swiss canton of Zug, the top marginal rate is 0.29 per cent, so that each additional million Swiss francs a Zug resident has in the bank incurs an annual tax bill of about 3,000 francs. It is higher in some other cantons; the heaviest net wealth tax is Geneva's, whose rate tops out at 1 per cent, setting its wealthiest residents back 10,000 francs a year for every additional million of net wealth. Most rates are well below. But the tax starts at a low threshold—as low as the tens of thousands, in some

cantons—and it has to be paid year in, year out. For canton-level public finances, it is significant. (According to Heinz Tännler, Zug's business-embracing finance minister, the wealth tax accounts for one-fifth of Zug's tax revenue from personal taxation. See Martin Sandbu, "The Swiss Town That Taxes Its Wealthy without Scaring Them Away," *Financial Times*, 11 February.2019, https://www.ft.com/content/87ccaf2e-2ddd -11e9-8744-e7016697f225.) Norway is similar to Switzerland in that the net wealth tax starts at moderate levels of net wealth, about €150,000, and charges a modest rate of 0.85 per cent, while Spain has a higher threshold but gets up to a top marginal rate of 2.5 per cent.

7. The Warren plan would have the wealth tax only start at $50 million worth of wealth. But by applying rates of 2–3 per cent and because US wealth inequality is so extreme, it has been projected to raise more than $200 billion a year, about 1 per cent of US national income (the same as Switzerland's wealth tax and more than Norway's or Spain's).

8. See Martin Sandbu, "How Much Could a Net Wealth Tax Bring In?," *Financial Times*, 15 February 2019, https://www.ft.com/content/ecd72d22-305d-11e9-ba00 -0251022932c8. The reasoning is as follows. In the large Western economies, the top 10 per cent hold a bit more than half of all private wealth, and in the United States the share is 77 per cent, according to the *World Inequality Report* (Facundo Alvaredo, Lucas Chancel, Thomas Piketty, Emmanuel Saez, and Gabriel Zucman, "World Inequality Report 2018," World Inequality Lab report, 2017, https://wir2018.wid.world/.) The wealth threshold to be in the top tenth, meanwhile, is strikingly similar across countries: it is about or a little more than twice the average wealth level in the United States, the United Kingdom, France, and Spain. That implies the taxable wealth above the threshold is about one-third of total private wealth in most rich countries, and just over half of total private wealth in the United States. Total private wealth amounts to about six times annual national income (in the United States and Germany it is a bit less, but more unequally distributed). The amount above the tax threshold in this hypothetical example would therefore amount to about twice annual income or a little more. So a 2 per cent annual levy on this base should raise at least 4 per cent of gross domestic product. To give a specific example: economist Roger Farmer has estimated that in the United Kingdom, a 2 per cent annual tax on net wealth above £700,000 would affect 5 per cent of taxpayers and would bring in £72 billion a year, or about 3.5 per cent of national income; see Roger Farmer, "Tax Reform: A Proposal for the Chancellor," Roger Farmer's blog, 12 November 2017, http://www.rogerfarmer.com /rogerfarmerblog/2017/11/12/tax-reform-a-proposal-for-the-chancellor.

9. Gueorgui Kambourov, Fatih Guvenen, Burhanettin Kuruscu, and Daphne Chen, "Efficiency Gains from Wealth Taxation" (Society for Economic Dynamics 2013 Meeting Papers 1112, Stonybrook University, Stonybrook, NY, 2013), https:// econpapers.repec.org/paper/redsed013/1112.htm; "Interview with Fatih Guvenen," Federal Reserve Bank of St. Louis, 15–16 October 2015, https://www.stlouisfed.org /connecting-policy-with-frontier-research/2015/fatih-guvenen-interview.

10. Fatih Guvenen, Gueorgui Kambourov, Burhanettin Kuruscu, Sergio Ocampo-Diaz and Daphne Chen, "Use It or Lose It: Efficiency Gains from Wealth Taxation"

(NBER Working Paper 26284, National Bureau of Economic Research, Cambridge, MA, September 2019), https://www.nber.org/papers/w26284.

11. Martin Sandbu, "Why a Wealth Tax Is Capitalism's Handmaiden," *Financial Times*, 19 September 2019, https://www.ft.com/content/8b1aa05c-dab0-11e9-8f9b -77216ebe1f17.

12. Against these impressions, however, one academic study finds a fairly large sensitivity in reported wealth to changes in the wealth tax in Switzerland: Marius Brülhart, Jonathan Gruber, Matthias Krapf, and Kurt Schmidheiny, "Taxing Wealth: Evidence from Switzerland" (NBER Working Paper 22376, National Bureau of Economic Research, Cambridge, MA, June 2016), https://www.nber.org/papers/w22376. The researchers' key estimate is that a 1 percentage point increase in the tax rate reduces reported wealth by 23 per cent—very large, but note that even with such a drastic response, you could still push rates up to at least 3 per cent and continue to increase tax revenues.

There are, however, reasons to think the real sensitivity is smaller. First, even this study finds that the effect is due not to people moving between cantons but only to changes within cantons over time. If it's not that the wealthy are chased away, the question is how fast wealth stocks can actually be changed in respond to tax reforms. The 23 per cent response to a 1 percentage point tax hike was calculated from much smaller actual variations. You cannot easily consume 23 per cent of a large fortune, as doing so would usually just involve buying alternative valuable (hence taxable) assets. Second, studies in Sweden and Denmark (which both had net wealth taxes until recently) show a much smaller response—less than a 1 per cent reduction in reported wealth—to a 1 percentage point higher tax rate. Third, the Swedish study shows that this is almost entirely down to avoidance—underreporting wealth—rather than changes in savings behaviour. This, in other words, is an effect a state determined to enforce honest reporting can minimise. See "Wealth Taxes (and How to Evade Them)," Chart of the Week, American Economic Association, 27 November 2017, https://www.aeaweb .org/research/charts/sweden-wealth-tax-evasion-reporting; and Katrine Jakobsen, Kristian Jakobsen, Henrik Kleven, and Gabriel Zucman, "Wealth Taxation and Wealth Accumulation: Theory and Evidence from Denmark" (NBER Working Paper 24371, National Bureau of Economic Research, Cambridge, MA, March 2018), https://www .nber.org/papers/w24371.

Indeed, the authors of the Swiss study have themselves pointed out that their estimate reflects peculiarities of the Swiss system—the net wealth tax is subnational, tax enforcement is lax, and wealth is not reported by third parties—which means the sensitivity to a rigorously enforced national net wealth tax is likely to be much smaller. See Marius Brülhart, Jonathan Gruber, Matthias Krapf, and Kurt Schmidheiny, "Wealth Taxation: The Swiss Experience," VoxEU, 23 December 2019, https://voxeu.org/article /wealth-taxation-swiss-experience. Rigorous enforcement is naturally crucial. Disputes over how much ambitious net wealth taxes can be expected to bring in in practice largely turn on whether loopholes will remain and what degree of enforcement can be expected. See Martin Sandbu, "Wealth Tax Redux," *Financial Times* 12 September 2019, https://www.ft.com/content/1eeb369e-d3df-11e9-8367-807ebd53ab77.

13. Thomas Wright and Gabriel Zucman, "The Exorbitant Tax Privilege" (NBER Working Paper 24983, National Bureau of Economic Research, Cambridge, MA, September 2018), https://www.nber.org/papers/w24983.

14. Wright and Zucman, 3.

15. Thomas Tørsløv, Ludvig Wier, and Gabriel Zucman, "The Missing Profits of Nations" (NBER Working Paper 24701, National Bureau of Economic Research, Cambridge, MA, August 2018), https://www.nber.org/papers/w24701.

16. "Effective Tax Rates for Multinational Companies in the EU," Greens/EFA in the European Parliament, 21 January 2019, https://www.greens-efa.eu/en/article/document/effective-tax-rates-for-multination-companies-in-the-eu/.

17. Jane Gravelle, *Tax Havens: International Tax Avoidance and Evasion*, CRS Report R40623, Washington, DC: Congressional Research Service, 2015, https://digitalcommons.ilr.cornell.edu/cgi/viewcontent.cgi?article=2387&context=key_workplace; Gabriel Zucman, "Taxing across Borders: Tracking Personal Wealth and Corporate Profits," *Journal of Economic Perspectives* 28, no. 4 (Fall 2014): 121–48, http://dx.doi.org/10.1257/jep.28.4.121.

18. The US rule used to be that US multinationals could defer tax on overseas earnings indefinitely. In the run-up to the 2017 Trump tax cuts, much was made of the need for a tax holiday to "bring home" this money. In reality, however, this money was only "overseas" in an accounting sense; most of it was invested in US securities already. Nonetheless, such a tax holiday was enacted: "repatriated" profits were granted rates of between 8 per cent and 15.5 per cent rather than the normal 35 per cent corporate tax rate. What the US government could have done instead is just cancel the right to defer, and impose the full domestic tax rate with immediate effect. Choosing to give up between 19.5 per cent and 27 per cent of the overseas profits through a lower tax rate unnecessarily cost US taxpayers hundreds of billions of dollars.

19. Jannick Damgaard, Thomas Elkjaer, and Niels Johannesen, "The Rise of Phantom Investments," *Finance and Development* 56, no. 3 (September 2019), https://www.imf.org/external/pubs/ft/fandd/2019/09/the-rise-of-phantom-FDI-in-tax-havens-damgaard.htm.

20. Tom Bergin, "Special Report: How Starbucks Avoids UK Taxes," Reuters, 15 October 2012, https://www.reuters.com/article/us-britain-starbucks-tax/special-report-how-starbucks-avoids-uk-taxes-idUSBRE89E0EX20121015.

21. "International Taxation," OECD, accessed 9 December 2019, https://www.oecd.org/g20/topics/international-taxation/.

22. Christine Lagarde, "An Overhaul of the International Tax System Can Wait No Longer," *Financial Times*, 10 March 2019, https://www.ft.com/content/9c5a1aa4-3ff2-11e9-9499-290979c9807a.

23. Even these treaties do not limit national governments' ability to tax capital as much as is often thought. In addition to not making matters worse by allowing unnecessary exemptions from taxability, governments can employ other taxes when income taxes are constrained by tax treaties. The European strategy to tax Big Tech provides an illustration: it eschews profits taxes (which could fall afoul of treaty obligations), opting instead for turnover taxes designed to mimic a profit tax.

24. Tørsløv, Wier, and Zucman, "Missing Profits of Nations."

25. William Nordhaus, "Climate Change: The Ultimate Challenge for Economics" (2018 Nobel Prize Lecture, Stockholm University, 8 December 2018), https://www.nobelprize.org/prizes/economic-sciences/2018/nordhaus/lecture/; Martin Sandbu, "Nobel Economics Lessons on Climate Change," *Financial Times*, 12 December 2018, https://www.ft.com/content/30c93916-fd3d-11e8-ac00-57a2a826423e.

26. James Hansen, "Cap and Fade," *New York Times*, 6, December 2009, https://www.nytimes.com/2009/12/07/opinion/07hansen.html.

27. Dominique Bureau, Fanny Henriet, and Katheline Schubert, "Pour le climat: Une taxe juste, pas juste une taxe" (Note du CAE 50, Conseil d'analyse économique, Paris, March 2019), http://www.cae-eco.fr/Pour-le-climat-une-taxe-juste-pas-juste-une-taxe; "Special Report: Setting Out for a New Climate Policy," German Council of Economic Experts, press release, 12 July 2019, https://www.sachverstaendigenrat-wirtschaft.de/fileadmin/dateiablage/gutachten/sg2019/190712_SVR_SG-Setting_out_for_a_new_climate_policy.pdf.

28. John Horowitz, Julie-Anne Cronin, Hannah Hawkins, Laura Konda, and Alex Yuskavage, "Methodology for Analyzing a Carbon Tax" (US Department of the Treasury, Office of Tax Analysis Working Paper 115, January 2017), https://www.treasury.gov/resource-center/tax-policy/tax-analysis/Documents/WP-115.pdf.

29. James Hansen, "Environment and Development Challenges: The Imperative of a Carbon Fee and Dividend," in *The Oxford Handbook of the Macroeconomics of Global Warming*, ed. Lucas Bernard and Willi Semmler, chap. 26, 2015, https://csas.earth.columbia.edu/sites/default/files/content/20151110_Hansen.2015.FeAndDividend.OxfordHandbook.pdf.

30. Bureau, Henriet, and Schubert, "Pour le climat," note 26.

Chapter 11. Whose GDP?

1. Anand Menon, "Uniting the United Kingdom," *Foreign Affairs*, 6 July 2016, https://www.foreignaffairs.com/articles/united-kingdom/2016-07-06/uniting-the-united-kingdom.

2. Elisa Giannone, "Skilled-Biased Technical Change and Regional Convergence" (2017 Meeting Papers 190, Society for Economic Dynamics, January 2017), https://economicdynamics.org/meetpapers/2017/paper_190.pdf; Richard Florida, "Welcome to the 'Great Divergence,'" CityLab, 14 February 2017, https://www.citylab.com/life/2017/02/welcome-to-the-great-divergence/513548/; Peter Ganong and Daniel Shoag, "Why Has Regional Income Convergence in the U.S. Declined?," *Journal of Urban Economics* 102 (November 2017): 76–90, https://doi.org/10.1016/j.jue.2017.07.002; Timothy Taylor, "Why Has US Regional Convergence Declined?," *Conversable Economist* (blog), 26 January 2018, https://conversableeconomist.blogspot.com/2018/01/why-has-us-regional-convergence-declined.html; Martin Sandbu, "The Economic Problem Tearing Countries Apart," *Financial Times*, 30 November 2018, https://www.ft.com/content/ab2f8a30-f47c-11e8-ae55-df4bf40f9d0d.

3. Giannone, "Skilled-Biased Technical Change"; David Autor, "Work of the Past, Work of the Future," *American Economic Association Papers and Proceedings* 109

(May 2019): 1–32, https://doi.org/10.1257/pandp.20191110; Emily Badger and Quoctrung Bui, "What If Cities Are No Longer the Land of Opportunity for Low-Skilled Workers?," *New York Times*, 11 January 2019, https://www.nytimes.com/2019/01/11/upshot/big-cities-low-skilled-workers-wages.html.

4. Joan Rosés and Nikolaus Wolf, "The Return of Regional Inequality: Europe from 1900 to Today," VoxEU, 14 March 2018, https://voxeu.org/article/return-regional-inequality-europe-1900-today.

5. Andrés Rodríguez-Pose, "The Revenge of the Places That Don't Matter," VoxEU, 6 February 2018, https://voxeu.org/article/revenge-places-dont-matter.

6. Rodríguez-Pose.

7. Sarah O'Connor, "Left Behind: Can Anyone Save the Towns the Economy Forgot?," *Financial Times*, 16 November 2017, https://www.ft.com/blackpool.

8. Edward Glaeser and Joseph Gyourko, "Urban Decline and Durable Housing" (NBER Working Paper No. 8598, National Bureau of Economic Research, Cambridge, MA, November 2001), http://www.nber.org/papers/w8598; Martin Sandbu, "Economic Lessons from a Left-Behind Town," *Financial Times*, 17 November 2017, https://www.ft.com/content/21ecb032-cad8-11e7-aa33-c63fdc9b8c6c.

9. Anne Case and Angus Deaton, *Mortality and Morbidity in the 21st Century*, Brookings Papers on Economic Activity, Spring 2017, https://www.brookings.edu/bpea-articles/mortality-and-morbidity-in-the-21st-century/.

10. Simon Kuper, "Poor, White and No Longer Forgotten," *Financial Times*, 15 December 2016, https://www.ft.com/content/83e71466-c184-11e6-9bca-2b93a6856354.

11. Simona Iammarino, Andrés Rodríguez-Pose, and Michael Storper, "Regional Inequality in Europe: Evidence, Theory and Policy Implications," *Journal of Economic Geography* 19, no. 2 (March 2019): 273–98, https://doi.org/10.1093/jeg/lby021 (summarised at https://voxeu.org/article/regional-inequality-europe).

12. This draws on Martin Sandbu, "Three Strategies for Left-Behind Places," *Financial Times*, 21 January 2019, https://www.ft.com/content/8f89d904-1cd4-11e9-b126-46fc3ad87c65.

13. Chiara Criscuolo, Ralf Martin, Henry Overman, and John Van Reenen, "Some Causal Effects of an Industrial Policy," *American Economic Review* 109, no. 1 (January 2019): 48–85, https://doi.org/10.1257/aer.20160034.

14. Two reports that show this for the United States are Clara Hendrickson, Mark Muro, and William A. Galston, *Countering the Geography of Discontent: Strategies for Left-Behind Places*, Brookings Institution report, November 2018, https://www.brookings.edu/research/countering-the-geography-of-discontent-strategies-for-left-behind-places/; and Timothy J. Bartik, *Helping Manufacturing-Intensive Communities: What Works?*, Center on Budget and Policy Priorities, Policy Futures report, 9 May 2018, https://www.cbpp.org/research/full-employment/helping-manufacturing-intensive-communities-what-works.

15. "The Biggest Tax Cut You've Never Heard Of," *Economist*, 17 November 2018, https://www.economist.com/leaders/2018/11/17/the-biggest-tax-cut-youve-never-heard-of; Sarah O'Connor, "Big Companies Are Pushing Governments Around,"

Financial Times, 13 November 2019, https://www.ft.com/content/d2472b06-e68e -11e8-8a85-04b8afea6ea3. An intriguing proposal to prevent this, outlined in Hendrickson, Muro, and Galston, *Countering the Geography of Discontent*, is to impose a 100 per cent federal tax on any incentives offered to specific companies by local authorities. In Europe, one can see the European Union's state aid rules as serving a similar function: preventing local or national governments, especially poorer ones, from bidding away development resources in the quest for investment.

16. Richard Florida, "The Hypocrisy of Amazon's HQ2 Process," CityLab, 10 May 2018, https://www.citylab.com/equity/2018/05/the-hypocrisy-of-amazons -hq2-process/560072/; Edward Luce, "Beauty Contest to Host New Amazon Base Reveals Ugly Truths," *Financial Times*, 6 June 2018, https://www.ft.com/content /f9f2b3bc-5eaa-11e8-9334-2218e7146b04. In the end, Amazon decided to split its new site between New York and the Washington suburbs, raising suspicions that it had planned this all along and was just trying to extract the maximum amount of local government support; see David Streitfeld, "Was Amazon's Headquarters Contest a Bait-and-Switch? Critics Say Yes," *New York Times*, 6 November 2018, https://www.nytimes.com/2018/11/06/technology/amazon-hq2-long-island-city -virginia.html.

17. See "Support a Non-aggression Pact for Amazon's HQ2," Change.org, accessed 18 December 2019, https://www.change.org/p/elected-officials-and-community-leaders -of-amazon-hq2-finalist-cities-support-a-non-aggression-pact-for-amazon-s-hq2.

18. See also Martin Sandbu, "A Policy for Centrists Who Care about the Left-Behind," *Financial Times*, 2 November 2017, https://www.ft.com/content/d9eca590 -bf05-11e7-b8a3-38a6e068f464.

19. See Matt Clancy, "Rehabilitating the Death of Distance to Revitalize Rural Economies," Matt Clancy's Academic Homepage, blog post, 29 March 2019, http:// matt-clancy.com/rehabilitating-the-death-of-distance-to-revitalize-rural-economies/.

20. See Emily Badger and Quoctrong Bui, "How Connected Is Your Community to Everywhere Else in America?," *New York Times*, 19 September 2018, https://www .nytimes.com/interactive/2018/09/19/upshot/facebook-county-friendships.html, which uses data from Michael Bailey, Rachel Cao, Theresa Kuchler, Johannes Stroebel, and Arlene Wong, "Social Connectedness: Measurement, Determinants, and Effects," *Journal of Economic Perspectives* 32, no. 3 (Summer 2018): 259–80, https://doi.org/10 .1257/jep.32.3.259.

21. OECD, *Productive Regions for Inclusive Societies*, OECD Regional Outlook 2016 (Paris: OECD, 2016), https://doi.org/10.1787/9789264260245-en.

22. Chris Giles, "The Poor Suffer while Britain Avoids Straight-Talking," *Financial Times*, 14 December 2016, https://www.ft.com/content/e2b0ae90-c14c-11e6-81c2 -f57d90f6741a.

23. Pedro Nicolaci da Costa, "There's a Major Hurdle to Employment That Many Americans Don't Even Think About—and It's Holding the Economy Back," Business Insider, 27 January 2018, https://www.businessinsider.com/lack-of-transport-is-a -major-obstacle-to-employment-for-americas-poor-2018-1.

24. Martin Sandbu, "From Left Behind to Poles of Attraction," *Financial Times*, 5 December 2018, https://www.ft.com/content/a6b2850e-f867-11e8-af46 -2022a0b02a6c.

25. Hendrickson, Muro, and Galston, in *Countering the Geography of Discontent*, summarise the academic research as follows: "Small loans to businesses in rural communities today are half the value they were in 2004 (compare this to small loans to businesses in big cities, which have only fallen a quarter) and rural lending levels today are below what they were in 1996. . . . Since the recession, big banks have significantly reduced the number of loans they make to small businesses. Even as the economy has recovered, many larger banks have stopped issuing loans below a $100,000 threshold. This is bad news for small businesses, since the majority of applications for small business loans are for amounts under $100,000. At the same time, the number of small community banks, which have historically served as an important source of credit for small businesses in smaller communities, has declined." They document that the number of US community banks fell by about two-thirds from 1995 to 2015, a decline starting well before the crisis and related to consolidation following regulatory loosening.

26. Andy Bounds, "What the UK's 'Left-Behind' Areas Want after Brexit," *Financial Times*, 16 July 2019, https://www.ft.com/content/89bff8c8-95dd-11e9-9573 -ee5cbb98ed36; Matthew Bevington, Anand Menon, Mike Hawking, and Katie Schmuecker, *Briefing: Post-Brexit Priorities for Low-Income Voters in Deprived Areas*, Joseph Rowntree Foundation, 31 July 2019, https://ukandeu.ac.uk/wp-content/uploads/2019 /07/Post-Brexit-priorities-for-low-income-voters-in-deprived-areas.pdf.

27. "A Septuagenarian Mayor Is Tackling Decline in His Corner of Rural France," *Economist*, 21 November 2019, https://www.economist.com/europe/2019/11/21/a -septuagenarian-mayor-is-tackling-decline-in-his-corner-of-rural-france.

28. Yann Algan, Clément Malgouyres, Claudia Senik, "Territoires, bien-être et politiques publiques," Note du CAE 55, Conseil d'Analyse Economique, Paris, January 2020, www.cae-eco.fr/Territoires-bien-etre-et-politiques-publiques.

29. See Bartik, *Helping Manufacturing-Intensive Communities*; and Martin Sandbu, "How to Bring Along the Left Behind," *Financial Times*, 3 December 2018, https:// www.ft.com/content/81213a30-f6da-11e8-8b7c-6fa24bd5409c.

30. Erica Peterson, "From Coal to Code: A New Path for Laid-Off Miners in Kentucky," National Public Radio, *All Things Considered*, 6 May 2016, https://www.npr.org /sections/alltechconsidered/2016/05/06/477033781/from-coal-to-code-a-new-path-for -laid-off-miners-in-kentucky; Anne Field, "Turning Coal Miners into Coders—and Preventing a Brain Drain," *Forbes*, 30 January 2017, https://www.forbes.com/sites/annefield /2017/01/30/turning-coal-miners-into-coders-and-preventing-a-brain-drain/.

31. Wolfgang Dauth, Sebastian Findeisen, Enrico Moretti, and Jens Südekum, "Matching in Cities" (NBER Working Paper No. 25227, National Bureau of Economic Research, Cambridge, MA, November 2018), https://www.nber.org/papers/w25227.

32. Martin Sandbu, "Do We Still Need Community Banks?," *Financial Times*, 2 March 2018, https://www.ft.com/content/a41b1ab6-1e03-11e8-956a-43db76e69936.

33. Paul Swinney, *Building the Northern Powerhouse: Lessons from the Rhine-Ruhr and Randstad* (London: Centre for Cities, June 2016), https://www.centreforcities

.org/wp-content/uploads/2016/06/16-05-31-Building-the-Northern-Powerhouse -Lessons-from-the-Rhine-Ruhr-and-Randstad.pdf.

34. Noah Smith, "Rural America's Revival Begins on Campus," Bloomberg Opinion, 16 November 2018, https://www.bloomberg.com/opinion/articles/2018-11-16 /rural-america-s-revival-begins-on-campus.

35. See Anna Valero and John Van Reenen, "The Economic Impact of Universities: Evidence from across the Globe" (CEP Discussion Paper No. 1444, Centre for Economic Performance, London School of Economics and Political Science, September 2018), http://eprints.lse.ac.uk/67680/; and Andy Feng and Anna Valero, "Business Benefits of Local Universities: More Skills and Better Management," *Centre Piece* 24, no. 3 (Autumn 2019): 18–21, https://cep.lse.ac.uk/centrepiece/abstract.asp ?index=6502. Tax incentives for research and development have particularly strong effects in lagging regions, according to Peter Egger and Nicole Loumeau, "The Economic Geography of Innovation," VoxEU, 16 January 2019, https://voxeu.org/article /economic-geography-innovation. The presence of research universities and their links with local inventors and research-intensive businesses may be one reason why lagging regions in North America are more innovative (as measured by patent registrations per population) than lagging regions in Europe even when frontier regions in both have become similarly innovative. See Andrés Rodríguez-Pose and Callum Wilkie, "Innovating in Less Developed Regions of Europe and North America," VoxEU, 1 October 2018, https://voxeu.org/article/innovating-less-developed-regions-europe -and-north-america. Other reasons include North America's better ability to employ high-skilled youths.

36. See "The Wrong Tail: Why Britain's 'Long Tail' Is Not the Cause of Its Productivity Problems," Centre for Cities, briefing, 24 May 2018, https://www.centreforcities .org/publication/the-wrong-tail/.

Chapter 12. Globalisation with a Human Face

1. See Dani Rodrik, "Why Do More Open Economies Have Bigger Governments?," *Journal of Political Economy* 106, no. 5 (October 1998): 997–1032, https://doi.org/10 .1086/250038.

2. "05476: Innvandring, utvandring og nettoinnvandring, etter statsborgerskap 2003–2018," Statistics Norway, accessed 18 December 2019, https://www.ssb.no /statbank/table/05476/.

3. "Holdninger til innvandrere og innvandring," Statistics Norway, accessed 18 December 2019, https://www.ssb.no/innvhold.

4. I do not want to give the impression that Norway's experience with high work migration has been an unalloyed bliss. One study in particular shows that higher low-skilled immigration to a local labour market is associated with greater class differences—that is to say, the better paid benefitted more from immigration than the lower paid (which is not to say that the latter did not benefit). See Maria Hoen, Simen Markussen, and Knut Røed, "Immigration and Social Mobility" (IZA Discussion Paper 11904, Institute for the Study of Labor, Bonn, Germany, October 2018), https://www

.iza.org/publications/dp/11904/immigration-and-social-mobility. However, it seems likely that low-skilled immigrant workers are particularly strongly attracted to localities where the technological and domestic policy dynamics described in the first part of this book are already widening class differences the most. After all, that is where the better off enjoy the greater increase in purchasing power and therefore generate the strongest demand for the services immigrant workers provide.

5. A very thorough study of East European immigration into the United Kingdom after free movement under EU rules in 2004 illustrates the multifaceted effects. In areas with particularly high immigration as compared with relatively low-immigration ones, there was some drag on the lowest wages. At the same time, more native workers shift into occupations with higher socioeconomic status. Compared with low-immigration areas, however, a larger share of native workers left work altogether. High-immigration areas also saw relatively higher pressure on housing and public services. See Sascha O. Becker and Thiemo Fetzer, "Has Eastern European Migration Impacted UK-Born Workers?" (CAGE Working Paper No. 376, Center for Competitive Advantage in the Global Economy, Warwick University, June 2018), https://warwick.ac.uk/fac/soc/economics /research/centres/cage/manage/publications/376-2018_becker_fetzer.pdf.

6. Guntram Wolff, "A Tale of Floods and Dams," Bruegel, 19 March 15, https:// bruegel.org/2015/03/a-tale-of-floods-and-dams/. Another difference between Bulgaria and Greece was that the latter's debt was owed by the state—but other eurozone countries ran into Greece-style crises, notably Spain and Ireland, because of private-sector liabilities. In those cases, too, the liabilities were in the form of debt rather than equity or direct investment. I go into this argument in greater detail, and with attention to the difference between deficit and surplus economies, in Martin Sandbu, "How to Tame Unsustainable Capital Flows," *Financial Times*, 11 July 2017, https://www.ft.com /content/d01c5012-6562-11e7-8526-7b38dcaef614.

7. As the economist Hélène Rey has pointed out, macroprudential financial regulation can work as a substitute for cross-border barriers to capital flows in terms of giving authorities control over domestic credit conditions, which they may lose if they simply remove such barriers without any other policy change. See Hélène Rey, "Dilemma Not Trilemma: The Global Financial Cycle and Monetary Policy Independence" (NBER Working Paper No. 21162, National Bureau of Economic Research, Cambridge, MA, issued May 2015, rev. February 2018), https://www.nber.org/papers/w21162.

Chapter 13. Beyond Left and Right

1. In addition, it is not obvious to define the size of the state's share of the economy unambiguously. The amount the public sector spends on services and investment is reasonably well measured, though even there things are complicated by whether provision is contracted out and priced in a market, or provided directly by government agencies. But a large part of government budgets consists of redistribution from one group (wage earners, say) to another (such as pensioners). The magnitude of this is not well captured by the numbers that appear in government accounts, because gross

numbers of tax revenues and transfer payments could reflect small net redistribution when many people both pay taxes and receive benefits. Consider the tax and benefit reform proposed in chapter 7. The only difference between universal basic income and a negative income tax is one of accounting: in a UBI everyone is paid their basic income, and taxes are collected separately; whereas with a NIT, the benefit is calculated together with the tax liability and only the net transfer is carried out (a citizen only receives a transfer if the basic income due is larger than the gross tax owed). The redistribution is identical in the two systems, but a UBI will be accounted for as involving much larger transfers and tax revenues than a NIT. It would make little sense to say that the former would mean a "bigger state" than the latter.

INDEX

Note: Page numbers in *italic* type refer to figures.

Adbusters (magazine), 148
age, voter behaviour linked to, 41–42
Airbnb, 69, 113
Alaska, 119–20, 203
Alternative for Germany, 15, 41, 45, 192
Amazon, 113, 129, 180–81, 197, 267n16
Amazonian rain forest, 223
American Finance Association, 155
antiglobalisation, 21, 72, 222
antisystem proponents, 6–7, 10, 18, 62–63, 192
Asian tiger economies, 6
austerity measures, 43, 45–46, 134, 137, 144–45
Austria, 38
authoritarianism, 7, 14, 26, 42, 49
automation. *See* technology
Autor, David, 77, 78, 71
Autor-Dorn-Hanson methodology, 78, 81

balance-of-payments crises, 218–20
Bank for International Settlements, 64, 155
Bank of Japan, 165
bankruptcy, 159–60
Bartik, Timothy, 203–4
Belgium, 172, 270n6
Berlin Wall, collapse of, 211
Big Data, 224
Blackpool, England, 193–94
Blair, Tony, 117
Blanchard, Olivier, 145
blue-collar aristocracy, 18, 22, 33
Brazil, 223
Bretton Woods era, 162

Brexit: business investment affected by, 102–3; empowerment sought by supporters of, 111; immigration as issue in, 214; income inequality as factor in support of, 31; political shock of, 7, 18; voter support for, 41, 45–46, 192–93
Britain: effect of global financial crisis on, 67–68; import regulations in, 222–23; social order upset in, 7; voter behaviour in, 31. *See also* United Kingdom
Bulgaria, 219–20
business extension services, 205

Canada, 185, 223
capital: financial, 200–201; human, 199–200; physical, 200; taxation of, *170*, 175–83
capital regions, 189, 191–92
carbon tax, 183–87
carbon taxes, 224
car washes, 96–98, 110
Case, Anne, 194
central bank policies, 63, 66–67, 89, 106, 133–34, 138–39, 143–44, 146, 163–66
Centre for Cities, 206–7
centrist politics: liberal order failed by, 229–33; programme of economics of belonging for, 233–39
China: as alternative to Western social order, 6; economic policies of, 6, 241n1; and globalisation, 72–73, 75; income growth in, 20, 21; manufacturing in, 25, 75; as shock to social market economy, 9, 77–78, 81, 249n8

cities: economic growth in, 29–31; income inequalities involving, 190; knowledge workers in, 29–30; role of, in new economies, 29–31; wealth concentration in, 153–54
climate change, 183–84, 223, 237
Clinton, Bill, 117
Clinton, Hillary, 33, 45
coal mining, 126
Cold War, 6
collective bargaining, 52, 54, 56–58, 61, 101, 103, 110, 121–23
communism, collapse of, 211, 231
community banks, 206, 268n25
comparative advantage, 74
competition, market, 5, 30, 112–13, 127–30
Contract with America, 40
corporate taxes, 178–83, 187, 218–19, 264n18
credit cycle, 160–62
credit financing, 155–60
cross-border supply chains, 74–75
cultural values: conflicts of, 15–16; economic factors vs., as driver of voter behaviour, 15–16, 37–49, 230–31; economic grievance expressed in, 48; economic inequality as influence on, 31; nationalism and, 14–15, 38; political significance of, 15–16, 37, 41–42, 47–49; populism and, 15, 38, 42–43; populist vs. elite, 14–15

deaths of despair, 36, 194
Deaton, Angus, 194
debt deflation, 156
debt financing, 155–60
debt restructuring, 159–60, 166
deindustrialisation, 29, 56–62
DeLong, Bradford, 145
demand management, 106, 132–33, 138–44, 146–47, 151, 216–17
Denmark: economic change as trigger for populism in, 42; education policy in, 108; egalitarianism and prosperity in, 99; employment in, 110; job mobility in, 107–8; job training programmes in, 108

digital revolution, market abuse facilitated by, 30, 113, 128–30
Dustmann, Christian, 47

eastern Europe, 191–92
Eatwell, Roger, 38
eBay, 69
economic change, 17–36; causes of, 18, 21; community-level effects of, 9–10, 29–31, 45–47, 49; cultural values elicited by, 48; cultural values vs., as driver of voter behaviour, 15–16, 37–49; gender as factor in, 33–34; government response to, 9, 11–13, 21, 51, 54–70; grievances about, 8, 18, 35–36, 48; harms suffered by the vulnerable in, 9, 35, 61–62, 68, 135, 137–38, 141; illiberalism linked to, 8, 15, 36, 38–49, 39; manufacturing sector and, 22–26; nationalism linked to, 8; populism linked to, 21, 26, 39–44; role of cognitive skills in, 27–29; structural change and, 55–62; usurpation story about, 18, 21–22, 26; Western income stagnation and, 19–21
economic insecurity: community-level effects of, 9–10; illiberal attitudes mobilised by, 48; income inequality linked to, 58–60; policy decisions exacerbating, 61; precarious employment and, 58–61; social contract undermined by, 58–62; in Sweden, 44. See also economic security
economic radicalism: comprehensiveness required of, 236–37; elimination of low-productivity, low-wage business model, 104–5; proposals for contemporary, 13, 15; proposals for regulating financial system, 155–67; Roosevelt's, 11–12, 50–51, 229; universal basic income (UBI)/negative income tax (NIT), 120–21
economic security: job mobility and, 108; social contract for, 9, 52, 54; welfare system's role in, 113–21. See also economic insecurity

economics of belonging: abuse of power
as threat to, 112–13; empowerment
crucial to, 111–13, 116, 121–25; failure of,
9, 17–36; financial regulation crucial
to, 155–67; globalisation's role in,
71–92, 214–28; government role in,
236; low-paid labour as threat to, 97;
macroeconomic policy's effect on,
131–47; manufacturing jobs as basis
of, 61; monopoly power as obstacle
to, 128–30; Norway as example of,
213–15; place/area-related strategies
for, 199–208; political proposals
for, 233–39; postwar, 8–9, 52–54;
rebuilding of, 10, 131–32; tax policy
appropriate to, 171–87; technology as
means to, 97. *See also* social contract
Economist (newspaper), 17, 20, 32
economy. *See* social market economy;
terms beginning with economic
education: challenges for those lacking
in, 27–29; job training programmes,
108–9, 121; Nordic countries' investment in, 108; public spending on,
109; voter behaviour linked to, 41, 46
Eichengreen, Barry, 47
electronic money, 158, 260n16
elephant chart, 18–21, *19*, 75, 77, 241n3
elites: cultural values of, 14–15; economic gains of, at expense of the
people, 8; populist criticisms of, 7,
10, 14–15. *See also* liberalism and
liberal democracy
employment: abuse-of-power potentials in, 112–13, 117; empowerment
related to, 114–15, 117, 119–25;
flexible/temporary, 58–61, 104,
124–25; gender and, 33–34; immigration's effect on, 82–83, 215–16,
224–25; industrial-era model of,
8–9, 54, 114, 122; in manufacturing
as share of total employment, 76, *76*;
matching services for, 205; mobility
in, 31–33, 107, *107*, 114–15, 117, 119–20,
125, 128; motivations for seeking,
119; technology as cause of, 28–29;
trade as cause of, 78, 249n9, 250n16;
training programmes for, 108–9, 204,
205; unemployment as hindrance to,
138; universal basic income's effect
on, 119–20; worker representation as
component of, 123–24
empowerment: economic, 113–21;
employment-related, 114–15, 117,
119–25; the left behind's need for,
111–13; in the market, 126–30
end of belonging: centrist politicians' failures resulting in, 229–33; in economic
sphere, 9, 17–36; inequalities and
obstacles as signs of, 10; psychology
of, 8, 9, 35; in Western social order, 7
Enlightenment, 5
equity financing, 156–60, 219–20
Estonia, 130
European Central Bank, 67, 164
European Economic Area, 213
European Parliament, 38–39, 47, 179
European Union: debt restructuring in,
159; and globalisation, 72–73, 226–27;
political parties and ideology in,
38–40, *39*; trade policy in, 222–24
Euroscepticism, 42
eurozone, 66, 134, 144–46, 152, 159, 166

factories. *See* industry
factory fetishism, 75, 78
Farage, Nigel, 46
fascism, 7, 10–11
Federal Reserve, 143, 200
Feenstra, Robert, 78
Fetzer, Thiemo, 45–48
financialisation, 86, 88–89, 152
financial sector, 148–67; credit cycle
in, 160–62; and credit financing,
155–60; criticisms of, 148–49, 154–55;
cross-border banking links in, 86–87,
87, 89–90, 155, 161–62, 225–26,
260n21, 270n7; economic problems
linked to mismanagement in, 64–67,
90; globalisation in, 85–90, 155,
160–62, 218–20, 225–26; harms
caused by financialisation, 152–54;
instability created by, 149–52, 160–62;
macroeconomic policy supported
by, 163–65; proposals for regulating,
155–67

Financial Times (newspaper), 20
Finland, 107, 109, 110, 120
fiscal space, 144–46
Five Star Movement (Italy), 31, 45, 192
foreigners, job loss blamed on, 22–23, 25–26, 73, 75–78, 82–83
France: and carbon tax, 184–86; corporate taxes in, 180; economic insecurity in, 59, 61; health declines in, 36; illiberal populism in, 38; the left behind in, 72; regional economic decline in, 192; voter behaviour in, 15, 41–42
France Insoumise (France Unbowed), 192
Fratzscher, Marcel, 60, 171
Freedom Party (Austria), 38
French Revolution, 211
Friedman, Milton, 235

Galston, William A., 267n15, 268n25
GDP. *See* gross domestic product
gender, service sector and, 33–34, 243n22
General Motors, 52
geography of economic change: attraction strategy for, 199–208; community ties/social connection, 32–33, 46, 49, 194, 200–202, 216; connectivity strategy for, 197–99; divergent interests in, 232–33; financialisation's effect on, 153, 201; immigration and, 82–85; left behind places, 192–208; mobility issues, 31–33; multinational vs. place-bound companies, 180; policy proposals to address, 195–208, 217–18; psychological responses, 9–10, 32–33, 45–47, 49, 192–94; reversal strategy for, 195–97; winners and losers in, 29–31, 70, 81–85, 126, 189–208, *190*, *191*, 232
Germany: business aided by population density in, 206–7; and carbon tax, 184–85; economic insecurity in, 59–60; employment gains in, 78; employment problems in, 64, 231; income inequality in, 60, 205; manufacturing technology in, 79;

regional economic decline in, 192; response to global financial crisis in, 133–34, 144; voter behaviour in, 15, 41. *See also* Nazi Germany
gig economy, 69, 124–25
Giles, Chris, 199
gilets jaunes (yellow vests), 61, 192, 202
global financial crisis (2008): cross-border banking links and, 87; effectiveness of initial response to, 63–64, 133; effects of, 62–63, 67–68, 134–35, 143–44; enabling conditions for, 64–65, 161; mishandling of, 13, 67–68, 133–47; recovery from, 133–35, 143–44; social contract undermined by, 62–68; voter behaviour influenced by, 37–41, 43; Western origins of, 6
globalisation: benefits of, 75, 212–28; criticisms of, 13, 212; domestic policy in relation to, 90–92; and economics of belonging, 214–28; financial, 85–90, 155, 160–62, 218–20, 225–26; immigration and, 82–85; impact of, 72–73; income growth during, 19–21, *19*, 241n3; job loss linked to, 70; left-behind places and, 207; national policies/regulations compatible with, 222–28; openness as principle underlying, 7, 13–14, 72–73; policies related to, 72–73, 216–21; scapegoating of, 9, 14, 21, 35, 71–92; technology's role in, 72; trade and, 72–82; Western liberal order associated with, 211–12. *See also* antiglobalisation
Goodwin, Matthew, 38
government: domestic policy mistakes of, 9, 14, 21, 51, 54–70; effective responses of, to economic change, 11–13; globalisation policy possibilities available to, 90–92; role of, in economics of belonging, 236; size of, 234, 270n1; social and economic security provided by, 52, 54. *See also* social contract
Grand Rapids, Michigan, 203–4
Great Depression, 64, 67

Greece, debt crisis in, 64, 146, 152, 165–66, 219–20, 270n6
green new deal, 237
Green Party, 179
Greenspan, Alan, 66, 140
Greggs, 115, 119
gross domestic product (GDP), 188–208; constituencies experiencing different effects of, 188–89; regional variations in, 191–92, *191*; unemployment in relation to, *136*
group identification, 46, 49, 112, 194

Hacker, Jacob, 62
Hansen, James, 185
helicopter money, 165
Hendrickson, Clara, 267n15, 268n25
Hirschman, Albert, 115, 121
Hitler, Adolf, 3–4
human capital, 199–200
hyperglobalisation, 80–81

Iceland, 86, 234
illiberalism: cultural values associated with, 14–15; economic change linked to, 8, 15, 36, 38–49; educational deficits linked to, 41, 46; identities of adherents of, 41–42; popular growth of, 4, 7, 18; of Trump, 7. *See also* antisystem proponents; nationalism
immigration: arguments for restricting, 14–15; economic discouragement of, 217; economic downturns coinciding with, 84–85; employment market effects of, 82–83, 215–16, 224–25, 250n17; exposure to, as factor in attitudes toward, 47, 85, 251n24; globalisation and, 82–85; home countries as affected by, 251n23; labour standards compatible with, 224–25; in Norway, 213–14, 269n4; policy restrictions on, 11; populist criticisms of, 85; public finances affected by, 83–84, 216, 250n20; in United Kingdom, 270n5; voter opposition to, 47
income growth, 19–21, *19*, 52, 241n3

income inequality: cultural values influenced by, 31; economic insecurity linked to, 58–60; in Germany, 60; incomes of lower 50 percent, *63*; market power as factor in, 127; Scandinavia as counterexample to, 99–100; postwar decline in, *53*; regional character of, 153; in Sweden, 43–44; tax policy as contributing factor to, 56–57, 169, 171; technology as factor in, 30; trade not a factor in, 79–82; union declines linked to, 56–58, 121; voter behaviour influenced by, 43–44; wages as factor in, 79–80; and wealth concentration, 169; in Western countries, 20
income per capita, of trading partners, *80*
Independent Workers' Union, 125
industry: China's role in, 25, 75; in emerging economies, 75; employment in, as share of total employment, 76, *76*; geographical effects of changes in, 70, 81; income inequality arising from decline of, 56; output of, 23–25, *24*, *25*; skill levels required in, 81, 106, 199–200, 204; social contract linked to, 52, 54, 61; successful policies to reverse declines in, 203–4; technology in, 79; unemployment linked to, 22–27, *22*, 77; urbanization and, 29
Inglehart, Ronald, 42
interest rates, 163–65
International Monetary Fund, 20, 64, 121, 140, 145, 155, 182
in-work tax credits, 117–18
Ireland, 64, 86, 270n6
Italy: banking crisis in, 150; economic insecurity in, 59; populism in, 31; regional economic decline in, 192; voter behaviour in, 41–42

Japan: manufacturing technology in, 79; negative interest rates in, 164–65; public spending in, 234; response to global financial crisis in, 133; Western social order influential on, 6
Jews, blamed for financial problems, 89

job mobility, 31–33, 107, *107*, 114–15, 117,
119–20, 125, 128
jobs. *See* employment
job training programmes, 108–9, 204,
205
Johnson, Boris, 238

Kentucky, 126, 205
Kerr, Sari Pekkala, 250n20
Kerr, William, 250n20
Kessler, Martin, 79–80
Keynes, John Maynard, 131, 133, 140,
142, 147
knowledge economy, 27–29, 70, 207
Korea, 79
Kuper, Simon, 194

laissez-faire economics, 236
Lakner, Christoph, 19
Law and Justice party (Poland), 45
League party (Italy), 192
left behind, the: carbon tax and,
184–86, *187*; dependence of, 9,
111–12, 116; economic grievances
of, 8, 18, 35–36, 48; education of,
27–29; employment solutions for,
105–6; gender roles as issue for,
33–34; in Germany, 60; harms
inflicted on, by financial sector
instability, 151; harms inflicted on,
by poor policy decisions, 56, 61–62,
68, 70, 134–35, 137–38, 141, 143;
health of, 36, 48–49, 112; loss of
economic and psychological security felt by, 9, 35–36, 44, 48, 61–62,
111–12, 116; macroeconomic policy
choices harmful to, 134–35, 137–38;
macroeconomic policy's effect on,
131–47; in the Nordic countries,
105–6; overlooking of situation of,
232; place-based identification of,
31–33, 45–47, 49; place of residence
of, 29–33; populism's attraction
for, 36, 72; recessions' effects on,
135, 137–38, 141; regional instances
of, 192–208; socioeconomic conditions resulting in, 9–10, 17–36; tax
policy for benefit of, 168–87; Trump

support from, 45; unemployment
of, 135, *136*; vulnerability of, 58,
111–13, 135
Le Pen, Marine, 15, 72
Le Pen family, 41, 192
Lewis, Sinclair, *It Can't Happen Here*, 11
liberalism and liberal democracy: cultural values associated with, 14–15;
divergent interests in, 232–33; economic health as essential bulwark
of, 7–8, 10, 12–16; failures of centrist
politicians in, 229–33; globalisation
associated with, 211–12; globalisation criticised from standpoint of, 9,
13; principles of, 5; rejection of, 7,
10, 15–16, 18; restoration of, 229. *See
also* elites; illiberalism
libertarianism, 236
Linke party (Germany), 192
liquidity trap, 163–64
living standards, 19–20, 67
Louis, Edouard, 35; *Who Killed My
Father?* 36

macroeconomic policy, 131–47; economics of belonging dependent on,
132–33, 141–42, 147; failures to use,
56, 90–92, 141, 144, 146–47, 161, 165,
181; financial policy in support of,
163–65; fiscal austerity as, 144–46;
harms inflicted on the vulnerable by,
56, 61–62, 68, 70, 134–35, 137–38,
141, 143; high-pressure, 106, 132–33,
138–44, 146–47, 151, 216–17; for job
creation, 132; overall economic productivity affected by, 138–40; social
contract undermined by mistakes in,
133; symmetric vs. asymmetric, 142
Macron, Emmanuel, 61, 193, 238
macroprudential regulations, 161–62,
260n21, 270n7
"Make America Great Again," 8, 33
"make work pay" schemes, 43, 47, 61
manufacturing. *See* industry
market abuse, 30, 112–13, 126–30
market concentration, 30, 113, 127, 129.
means-tested benefits, 59, 61, 114–16,
119, 235

Menon, Anand, 188
Mercosur, 223
Midland, Texas, 17, 18, 22–23, 28
Milanovic, Branko, 19, 241n1
minimum wages, 103–4
mission banks, 203, 206
mobility, 31–33
Moene, Karl, 99–101
monetary policy, 134, 146
money. *See* electronic money; helicopter money
monopoly power, 13, 30, 126–30
multinational corporations, 178–81, 264n18
Muro, Mark, 267n15, 268n25

National Front (Italy), 45
National Front (France), 38
nationalism, 8, 14–15, 38. *See also* illiberalism; nativism
national living wage, 102–3
nativism, 14, 16, 37, 41, 49, 112. *See also* nationalism
Nazi Germany, 3–4, 11
Nazi Party, 4
negative income tax (NIT). *See* universal basic income (UBI)/negative income tax (NIT)
Netherlands, 172, 206
net wealth taxes, 172–78, 186, 235, 262n7, 262n8, 263n12
New Deal, 11–12, 230
New Economics Foundation, 120
New York Times (newspaper), 17
noncompete clauses, 128
Nordhaus, William, 183, 185
Nordic countries: economy of belonging in, 97, 212; employment and gender in, 34; labour–productivity synergy in, 99–101, 105–10; openness of, 212–13; unions in, 121, 123. *See also individual countries*
Norris, Pippa, 42–43
North American Free Trade Agreement, 72, 223
Norway: China shock in, 249n8; common digital platform in, 130; economy of belonging bolstered by globalisation in, 213–15; education policy in, 108; egalitarianism and prosperity in, 99–101; employment and technology in, 96–97, 101, 105–6, 110; illiberal populism in, 38; immigration in, 213–14, 269n4; net wealth taxes in, 172, 175, 262n6; unionisation and collective bargaining in, 100–103, 110, 121, 123, 225

Obama, Barack, 16, 45, 127
Occupy Wall Street, 148, 154
O'Connor, Sarah, 193
OECD. *See* Organisation for Economic Co-operation and Development
openness, political/economic: challenges to, 7, 212, 216; European Union as example of, 226–27; in financial sector, 85–90, 155; globalisation's role in, 7, 13–14, 72–73; healthy economy's dependence on, 14, 207–8; in immigration, 82–85; national policies/regulations compatible with, 222–28; principles of, 5; rules of, 7; in trade, 73–82
Organisation for Economic Co-operation and Development (OECD), 64, 77, 108, 120, 155, 175, 182, 198
Osborne, George, 102

pensions, 61
Permanent Fund dividend, 119–20, 203
Perot, Ross, 40
Philippon, Thomas, 127
place of residence, as factor in economic success, 29–33
Poland, 45
populism: antiglobalisation linked to, 72; antisystemic principles of, 10; authoritarianism and, 26, 42; and cultural values, 15, 38, 42–43; economic change linked to, 21, 26, 39–44; immigration as issue for, 85; motivations of adherents of, 26, 36, 112
Portes, Jonathan, 250n17
Portugal, 59
posted workers, 225, 238

precarious employment, 58–61, 104, 124–25
precarity, 58, 112, 116–17
privacy regulations, 224
productivity: corporate tax policy harming, 180; equality of, 235; growth in, 20; macroeconomic policy to stimulate, 106, 138–40, 235; in manufacturing, 26; net wealth taxes and, 176–78; in service sector, 26; technology as means to increasing, 97; wages in relation to, 98–105; winners and losers from, 20, 26–27
Progress Party (Norway), 38
property taxes, 173–74

Rajan, Raghuram, 66
Reagan, Ronald, 57, 230
redistribution of wealth, 234–35
refugee crisis (2015–16), 39, 82
regional effects of economic change. See geography of economic change
relocation, for economic opportunity, 31–33
Republican Party (United States), 40, 45
Rey, Hélène, 270n7
Riksbank, 163–64
robots, 79
Rodríguez-Pose, Andrés, 192–93
Rodrik, Dani, 71–72, 90–92, 222
Romer, Paul, 242n8
Roosevelt, Franklin Delano, 3, 11–12, 50–51, 229
Roosevelt, Theodore, 13, 126
Rothschild family, 89

Sanders, Bernie, 173, 175
Sasahara, Akira, 78
Schröder, Gerhard, 231
Second World War, 13, 50
security. See economic security
service sector, 26, 27, 33–34, 68–70, 243n22
Shaxson, Nicholas, 153
small businesses: competitive disadvantage of, 129; loans to, 201, 206, 268n25
Smith, Noah, 207

social contract: based on economic promise, 8, 51–52; egalitarianism as component of, 8, 51, 52; features of successful, 52, 54; policy mistakes contributing to undoing of, 9, 14, 21, 51, 54–70, 133; populist rejection of, 10. See also economics of belonging
Social Democratic Party (Germany), 231
social market economy: challenges to contemporary, 12–13; failures of, 9–10; in Germany, 60; policies and actions leading to creation of, 11–13; postwar accomplishments of, 8–9; principles of, 5; promise of, 8, 9; restoration of, 10; significance of, for political health of the nation, 7–8, 10, 12–16
soft skills, 33–34
Solow, Robert, 55–56
Soros, George, 89
Soviet Union, 6
Spain, 59, 150, 172, 175, 270n6
Springsteen, Bruce, 35
Starbucks, 181
structural change, mismanagement of, 55–62, 67
Subramanian, Arvind, 79–80
subsidies, 196–97
sudden stop, in money flows, 218
Summers, Lawrence, 66, 145
Sweden: economic change as trigger for populism in, 42–44, 47; egalitarianism and prosperity in, 99–100; job mobility in, 107–8; job training programmes in, 109; manufacturing technology in, 79
Sweden Democrat party, 43–45, 47
swing voters, 16
Switzerland: negative interest rates in, 164; net wealth taxes in, 172, 175, 177, 261n6, 263n12

"Take Back Control," 8, 111, 221
TaskRabbit, 124, 128
tax avoidance, 179–81, 218–19
taxe GAFA (French tax), 180
tax policy, 168–87; carbon tax, 183–87; corporate taxes, 178–83, 218–19; harms inflicted on the vulnerable by,

168–69; income inequality arising from, 56–57, 169, 171; loopholes in, 175; net wealth taxes, 172–78; progressive taxes, 171; Trump's, 179, 264n18. *See also* universal basic income (UBI)/negative income tax (NIT)

tax rates, 115, *170*

tax treaties, 182, 227, 264n23

Tea Party movement, 40

technology: digital, 30, 113, 128–30; economics of belonging aided by, 97; globalisation aided by, 72; government's failed response to, 51; inequalities exaggerated by, 30; job creation by, 28–29; job loss caused by, 17–18, 23, 28–29, 35, 50, 56–62, 68–70, 77, 79; in knowledge economy, 28; labour productivity increased by, 97; low-paid labour vs., 97–98; in manufacturing, 79; market abuse facilitated by, 30, 113, 128–30; Norwegian economy's use of, 96–97, 101; wage structures as means of encouraging investment in, 98–104; wealth concentration aided by, 169

Thatcher, Margaret, 57, 230

third-way political/economic approach, 117, 231, 232

Tilbury, England, 17, 18, 22, 32

Tooze, Adam, 87

trade: classical and non-classical types of, 73–75; employment created by, 78, 249n9, 250n16; globalisation and, 72–82; unemployment linked to, 77–78, 249n9, 249n13

Treaty of Detroit, 52, 55

Trump, Donald: ideological supporters of, 15; illiberalism of, 7; and immigration, 82; and manufacturing, 75; masculinity as value of, 33–34; political shock of, 7, 18; tax policy of, 179, 264n18; voter support for, 16, 33, 41, 45, 46, 72, 192–93

trust, 47–48

Uber, 69, 113, 124, 128, 180–81

unemployment: cultural and psychological consequences of, 9, 26, 35;

employment opportunities lessened by periods of, 138; GDP in relation to, *136*; from global financial crisis, 63; globalisation as cause of, 70, 73, 75–78; immigration's role in, 82–83, 215–16; manufacturing-related, 22–27, *22*, 77; of marginalised groups, 135, *136*; recessions' effects on, 135; technology as cause of, 17–18, 23, 28–29, 35, 50, 56–62, 68–70, 77, 79; trade as cause of, 77–78, 249n9, 249n13; usurpation story about, 18, 21–22, 26, 82, 90

unions: alternatives to traditional, 122–25; decline of, 57–58, 60, 69, 121; future of, 234; for gig workers, 125; in the Nordic countries, 100–103, 110, 121, 123; as obstacles to change, 122; social contract role of, 52, 54, 61; wage structures linked to influence of, 52, 54, 57–58, 60, 121; and workplace empowerment, 121–25. *See also* collective bargaining

United Auto Workers, 52

United Kingdom: employment and technology in, 102–3; health declines in, 36, 193–94; immigration in, 270n5; regional economic decline in, 192; response to global financial crisis in, 133–34, 144–45; union busting in, 57. *See also* Britain

United Kingdom Independence Party, 46

United States: corporate taxes in, 178–79, 264n18; employment gains in, 78; employment problems in, 64, 77; health declines in, 36, 194; job training programmes in, 109; lessons of 1930s for, 3–4, 10–12, 229; minimum wage in, 103–4; net wealth taxes in, 262n7; regional economic decline in, 192; relative regional prosperities in, 189, *190*; response to global financial crisis in, 133–34, 144–45; in Roosevelt years, 3, 11; social order upset in, 7; union busting in, 57; voter behaviour in, 15, 16, 41, 45; xenophobia in, 11

universal basic income (UBI)/negative income tax (NIT), 115–16, 118–20, 186, 202–3, 234–35, 271n1
usurpation narratives, 18, 21–22, 26, 82, 90

wages: compression of, 100–103, 105, 121; immigration's effect on, 83, 215, 250n17; investment in technology encouraged by compression of, 98–104; labour productivity in relation to, 98–105; suppression of, 117–18; union declines linked to, 55–56, 57, 121; universal basic income and, 114–16; welfare supplementation of, 117–18
Warren, Elizabeth, 173–75, 262n7
wealth concentration, 30, 153–54, 169, 170, 175–76.
wealth taxes, 172–78
welfare, 52, 54, 113–21, 213
Western social order: accomplishments of, 5; challenges to, 6, 192; economic health as essential bulwark of, 7–8, 10, 12–16; globalisation associated with, 211–12; ideological opposition to, 15–16, 212; pillars of, 5; restoration of, 10, 229; threats from within, 6–7, 238–39; universal values of, 5–6; variations within, 6
West Michigan Medical Device Consortium, 204
West Virginia, 126
Wood, Adrian, 77, 249n13, 250n16
Wordsworth, William, 211
World Bank, 20
World Trade Organisation, 20, 72
Wright, Thomas, 178–79
write-downs, 159–60, 166, 219

xenophobia, 11, 14, 42, 48, 82, 192

Yeats, William Butler, 4

zero-hours contracts, 58, 104
Zingales, Luigi, 155
Zucman, Gabriel, 178–79, 182

A NOTE ON THE TYPE

This book has been composed in Adobe Text and Gotham.
Adobe Text, designed by Robert Slimbach for Adobe,
bridges the gap between fifteenth- and sixteenth-century
calligraphic and eighteenth-century Modern styles.
Gotham, inspired by New York street signs, was designed
by Tobias Frere-Jones for Hoefler & Co.